EUCHARISTIC PRAYERS

EUCHARISTIC PRAYERS

Samuel Wells and Abigail Kocher

WILLIAM B. EERDMANS PUBLISHING COMPANY

GRAND RAPIDS, MICHIGAN

Wm. B. Eerdmans Publishing Co.
2140 Oak Industrial Drive N.E., Grand Rapids, Michigan 49505
www.eerdmans.com

22 21 20 19 18 17 16   1 2 3 4 5 6 7

ISBN 978-0-8028-7261-6

Library of Congress Cataloging-in-Publication Data

Names: Wells, Samuel, 1965–   author.
Title: Eucharistic prayers / Samuel Wells and Abigail Kocher.
Description: Grand Rapids : Eerdmans Publishing Company, 2016.
Identifiers: LCCN 2016019027 | ISBN 9780802872616 (cloth : alk. paper)
Subjects: LCSH: Church year—Prayers and devotions. | Eucharistic prayers.
Classification: LCC BV245 .W39 2016 | DDC 264/.36—dc23
   LC record available at https://lccn.loc.gov/2016019027

For

Craig Kocher
Rebekah Eklund
and
Marcia Owen

Contents

Preface

This book arises out of a desire to renew the church's worship, to empower the people of God, and to see the kingdom come. It pursues these aims by providing a Eucharistic prayer for every Sunday of the three-year Revised Common Lectionary cycle.

The book is grounded in a love of liturgy—not as a dusty study of ritual and tradition, but because worship is the principal way the church enacts its understanding of its relationship to God and practices to live the holy life to which it is called. The blessing of the bread and the cup should be a thrilling, enthralling, and entrancing moment where the congregation finds all the promises of God meeting their yes in Christ. But our sense is that it tends to be a time of diminished concentration, repetition of tired but seldom fully understood words, and alienation of a laity that is resigned to being unworthy to grasp why everything must be said and done in such a stiff and rigid way—a way apparently so far from the intimacy of the Last Supper, the new social relations of the kingdom, or the glory of the heavenly banquet.

Not all these issues are easy to address. But one thing that can be done is to make the Eucharistic prayer, or prayer of great thanksgiving, more vivid, more accessible, less shrouded in Reformation debates, shorter, and more of a piece with the Ministry of the Word that precedes it. That's what this book seeks to do. Our sense is that many clergy and most laypeople share our frustrations with over-familiar words and less-than-energized celebrations; but as far as we are aware, no resource of the kind this book represents exists, and for most clergy the task of creating a new prayer—theologically appropriate, pastorally fitting, and linguistically satisfying—every Sunday is daunting.

These prayers follow the Revised Common Lectionary readings for each of the 156 Sundays, together with major feast days, of the three-year cycle; they draw out of these readings themes that converge with the action and gift of the Eucharist, bringing salvation history to fulfillment in Christ's death and resurrection; and they chart a transition from remembrance and thanksgiving to intercession and hope for the coming kingdom, by shaping the final section of the prayer as a call for God to make the whole world a Eucharist, freeing the oppressed from domination as forgiveness has freed people from sin, and feeding the hungry as bread and cup have nourished the congregation. Our experience in putting these prayers to work in the congregations we've served has been that the Great Thanksgiving has changed from being a low-energy lull in the liturgy to being a focused, fresh, and engaged moment in which people expect to make discoveries and perceive more deeply.

We are grateful to Nancy Ferree-Clark, onetime colleague when we all three served together at Duke University Chapel, who for two or three years insisted that Sam should attempt a project like this. Sam comes from a tradition in which composing one's own Great Thanksgiving prayers is almost unknown, so it took a great deal of persuasion to begin the project. Sam knew there were aspects of North American church culture, and of mainline Protestantism, in which he would always be a beginner; it needed Abby's grounding in local church ministry, and appetite for seeing the poetry in the prose of mainline practice, to make the word of this project become flesh, turning the writing of occasional prayers into an aspiration to cover the whole liturgical year. We are grateful to those many with whom we have shared in ministry as these prayers have taken shape, been introduced into worship, and been refined and amended.

In particular we wish to thank three friends with whom we have each shared in different kinds of ministry, and with whom we have each come more deeply to know our love of God, our desire to see the empowerment of God's people, and our longing for the coming of God's kingdom. Our perception of the presence of Christ in the Eucharist has been enriched deeply by these fellow worshipers' and disciples' perceptions of Christ in common life, scripture, and the stranger. To these three mutual friends we dedicate this book as a prayer that the kingdom come, and that, in the meantime, God's people inhabit the church till it turns into the kingdom.

Introduction

There are three kinds of things to say by way of introduction.

Understanding the Lord's Supper

Some congregations celebrate Holy Communion monthly or quarterly, because it is so special that they fear to lessen the sense of occasion by enjoying it too often. Other congregations celebrate it weekly, because they cannot comprehend coming together as the body of Christ without breaking bread with one another. Others again celebrate even more frequently, even daily, because they cannot, or have no desire to, live without the bread of life.

What all these diverse congregations agree on is that Holy Communion, or Eucharist, or the Lord's Supper is special. It is the way in which, in word and action, the people of God recall God's saving acts in Christ, anticipate their resurrected life with the Trinity, and are renewed as one body to love and serve in the power of the Spirit to God's praise and glory.

At the center of this celebration is the moment when all eyes are focused on a table, sometimes known as an altar, where bread and cup are laid out, and a pastor, or minister, or priest rehearses Christ's fourfold action at the Last Supper of taking, blessing, breaking, and giving. The first, third, and fourth of these, though practiced differently in various traditions, are nonetheless fairly straightforward, once the convention, in place from very early times, that the meal is a token, and not a full dinner, is accepted. The area of most complexity is the second action—the blessing.

The blessing is conveyed through story. As takes place at a Passover meal, the minister at a celebration of the Lord's Supper tells a story. That story is known as the Eucharistic prayer or the prayer of great thanksgiving. It places the events of the Last Supper, Jesus' taking and sharing of the bread and wine, in the context of his own coming death and resurrection and simultaneously in the sweep of salvation history from creation to the end of all things, including Israel and the church.

One point is easily overlooked, because it is in some ways so obvious: the Eucharistic prayer is actually a prayer. It is an enacted prayer. Unlike some prayers, this one is offered with eyes open, which is not the way we generally think about prayer. The eyes are open for two reasons. One is that, while largely addressed to God, the prayer includes dialogue between the pastor and people—dialogue that gives instructions ("lift up your hearts") that lose their immediacy if the pastor and people are not looking at one another. The other reason is that the Great Thanksgiving consists not only of words but also of gesture, symbol, and tangible representation of sacred mystery. Eyes are focused primarily not on the pastor but on the bread and cup, which are bearers of holy signs. With eyes open, the congregation responds to the extravagant invitation to "taste and see that the Lord is good."

This is what the prayer should be: a flame of holy fire kindled in the hearts of all who are gathered, stirring memories and hopes, evoking gratitude and exaltation, taking worshipers to heaven to sing with the angels and to Calvary to face the horror of the cross and to the tomb to experience the wonder of the resurrection and to voice the groaning of creation and the dream of Christ's second coming, finally leaving the congregation lost in wonder, love, and praise.

But often it isn't like that. It can be prosaic and dull, long and dry, spoken without joy and heard without delight, treated by all like lining up for an entry ticket to the more interactive sharing of communion that follows. While everyone knows the words are supposed to be meaningful and this moment in worship is highly significant, the mixture of familiarity and inactivity seems almost inevitably to lead to diminished concentration and low energy. What should be an experience of heaven is too often an interlude when minds wander and hearts are in low gear.

How can participating in the Eucharistic prayer be an experience of hearts set on fire rather than one of minds meandering? This book offers a proposal. Following the three-year cycle of the Revised Common Lectionary, it provides a Eucharistic prayer for each Sunday—thus around 150 prayers in all. (This number allows for the Sundays when the readings in each of the three years are so similar that only one prayer seemed necessary.) In each prayer the readings for the day are allowed to shape the telling of the story. Some parts of the prayer remain the same in every instance; other parts vary according to the themes of the day, the readings, and the season. What difference does this make?

The first difference is that it expands the range of detail that is brought into the telling of the story. The Bible is a broad canvas—but it's made up of a host of detailed narratives, reflections, and injunctions. It's in the interplay of the epic sweep across time and space and the lyric intensity of circumstance and character that the truth invariably surfaces. Because conventional Eucharistic prayers are intended for use in diverse contexts on varied occasions, they tend to have a generic, epic quality that can seem rather abstract and all-purpose. They also concentrate on the more obvious "tops of the mountains"—creation, sometimes the exodus, incarnation, crucifixion, resurrection, sometimes ascension, Pentecost, and Christ's return. Of course these are the key moments in the story; but taking 150 angles on that narrative offers innumerable insights, perspectives, and challenges to what that story is and the way it is told. Instead of simply referring to "the covenant," a variety of prayers can explore the various covenants with Noah, with Abraham, with Moses, and with David, respectively. Instead of referring to "meals Jesus had with his disciples," the breadth of prayers can inhabit the nuances between the feeding of the five thousand, the meal at the house of Simon the Leper, and the meal with Zacchaeus. Instead of referring to Jesus' compassion for the outcast, the range of prayers can touch on the subtle differences between his relationship with the shunned woman with hemorrhages, the feisty Syro-Phoenician woman, and the much-married Samaritan woman at the well. Such details underline that a universal story and sacrament are made flesh in particular people with a specific time and place. The all-purpose nature of many conventional Eucharistic prayers is replaced with intensity and attention as the story is heard ever-new with different characters and perspectives highlighting fresh understanding and appreciation.

The second difference is that, more specifically, it broadens the focus of the prayer from simply being about the death of Jesus. In some congregations the sermon is always about the cross, and, whatever the readings, the message is always about Jesus' sacrificial death and the need to respond in gratitude and faith. But in many congregations, while still centering on what God has done and shown in Christ, the message has more breadth and the Bible is seen as a good deal more than prophecies of the Messiah and their fulfillment. The same might be said of the Eucharistic prayer. The center of the prayer is undoubtedly Jesus' instruction, "Do this in remembrance of me." The Eucharist is fundamentally an act of obedience to this instruction—joyful, thankful, impassioned, hopeful; but obedient, nonetheless. The breaking of the bread is a vivid gesture that evokes the breaking of Christ's body on the cross. And Christ's crucifixion is without question the central moment in Christian devotion and remembrance. But it is not the only thing that Holy Communion is about. The prayers in this book seek to represent the breadth of scripture's witness to what it means to be God's companions: what it costs God, how God had long sought it, how much creation needs to be liberated in order to enter it, how it was enacted in intimacy and betrayal at the Last Supper. The definitive moment in restoring that companionship is the cross; but other moments illustrate and amplify it too.

Because so many of the Reformation traditions were involved in deep controversies about the nature of Christ's saving work, and because these controversies in many cases became focused on different understandings of what was taking place in Holy Communion in general and in the Eucharistic prayer in particular, a great deal of emphasis and scrutiny have surrounded the precise words used when the priest or pastor takes the bread and cup and remembers how Jesus once did likewise. Rather than ingenuous joy at receiving a wondrous gift, many believers came to assume severe judgment about whether a precise understanding of that gift was being described and practiced and understood. Such anxiety inhibits the sense of entering the company of heaven that participating in the Eucharistic prayer should be about. A key feature of heaven is that all the stray and sometimes lamentable features of our own lives, together with all the unaccountable and mysterious details of scripture and of history, reappear in the story as windows of grace and bearers of wisdom. By incorporating some of the stray details of scripture in these prayers, we seek to enact that characteristic of heaven, and so create the experience we are trying to describe. Likewise some of the lamentable features of our lives and of the world appear as causes for intercession in the later part of the prayer, ensuring that our greatest hope and expectation lie side by side with the definitive expression of God's boundless mercy.

The Eucharistic prayers in use in most mainline Protestant churches today still bear the scars of the Reformation controversies over what takes place at the Eucharistic table when the words "This is my body. . . .This is my blood . . ." are said. In the sixteenth century four broad views emerged; all four are alive and well in mainline traditions today.

- The Roman Catholic view, affirmed by the Council of Trent (1545–1563), is that the bread and wine continue to look like bread and wine, but in fact have been changed into Christ's body and blood. Their accidents (physical properties) remain the same but their substance (inner reality) has changed. This view is sometimes known as transubstantiation.
- The view described by Martin Luther (1483–1546), and still generally held in Lutheran churches, is that the bread and wine remain bread and wine, but that when one eats them, one is genuinely receiving Christ. This view is sometimes known as consubstantiation.
- The view outlined by John Calvin (1509–1564), and widely held in Reformed circles, is that Christ cannot be in the bread and wine because Christ remains fully human (as well as being fully divine) and is at the right hand of the Father in heaven and can't be in more than one place at a time. Thus it is the Holy Spirit that is present in the sharing of communion, with its promise to make present to the believer "Christ and his benefits" (that is, the forgiveness of sins and the life everlasting).
- The view outlined by Huldrych Zwingli (1484–1531), and widely held today in Baptist and nondenominational circles, is that communion is a public demonstration of the salvation Christ has already brought—in

other words, that no saving event actually takes place in the sharing of communion. Instead, the Lord's Supper is a reenactment that reminds believers of what they already have.

The United Methodist and Episcopalian (or Anglican) traditions have tended to steer away from endorsing any one of these four strands. Thus in Episcopalian and Methodist circles the words said by the pastor or priest in giving thanks, remembering Jesus, and calling on the Holy Spirit often blend together phrases reflecting all of these traditions. For example, most such prayers include the word "sacrifice"—thus making a gesture toward the Roman Catholic tradition, in which the Mass is taken to be a present-tense re-presentation of the sacrifice of Calvary. Meanwhile, such prayers almost always, when it comes to the calling down of the Holy Spirit on the bread and cup, ask that they "may be for us the body . . ." In the crucial words "for us" lies an endorsement of the Lutheran insistence that, though the bread and wine do not change, the communicant nonetheless, in receiving them, receives Christ. Another word that usually pops up is "promise." This is a gesture toward the Calvinist interpretation, that the bread and wine are not Christ but are a promise from God that the believer will receive the benefits of Christ's saving work. Yet another word found very frequently is "memorial." This is a way of incorporating the Zwinglian view that nothing actually changes in the Eucharist other than the heart and mind of the worshiper who recalls and is moved by Christ's saving passion. (In many congregations grape juice is used instead of wine, not just as a courtesy to those present who are alcohol-dependent, but for the whole congregation. The foregoing account may help to explain why, for those who take the Zwinglian view, using grape juice seems unproblematic, while for those who take the Lutheran view, with its greater dependence on replicating the elements used at the Last Supper, not using wine seems unsatisfactory.)

The prayers in this book are written in an ecumenical spirit that regards each of these four views as bringing genuine enrichment. But what we do not do—and this may be troubling to some—is go out of our way to include words like "sacrifice," "promise," or "memorial" so as to make that ecumenical spirit explicit. These prayers have not been composed to meet criteria from a post-Reformation need to draw in a variety of specific sacramental interpretations. One reason why the customary prayers can be lengthy and cumbersome is that they include sentences that do not enhance the dynamism of word or action but are more about satisfying various theological constituencies. We do not include such sentences. The one tradition of this kind that we do keep is to maintain the words "be for us the body and blood of our Lord Jesus Christ." We are not Roman Catholics: we do not believe the substance of the bread and wine changes while the accidents remain the same; but we do believe that what takes place at the table is an event worthy of reverence and awe—and we regard these time-honored words as the best way to express that.

Perhaps the most significant way in which these prayers depart from those usually offered in mainline worship today is that they draw upon the Eucharistic significance of the whole of scripture, as ordered in the three-year lectionary. The action of the table or altar is amplified and enriched by the whole story of God. What the prayers don't do is put as exclusive an emphasis as is conventional on the death of Jesus as *the* focal theological moment and the principal event commemorated at the communion table. This event is mentioned in every prayer, but is not repeated, described, and highlighted as often as is customary. The structure of the liturgy in most mainline congregations assumes the Passover heritage and sees Jesus as the Lamb of God who becomes the Passover Lamb through whose blood God passes over our sins, as the Angel of the Lord passed over the houses of the Hebrews on the night of the exodus from Egypt. We relish this heritage. But we do not want this one interpretation so to shape the imagination of the liturgy that it obscures the way the Eucharist is a celebration of the whole of God's story.

There is a downside to the proliferation of prayers. In some traditions a limited range of centrally authorized prayers is a practice of unity, echoing the adage, "the family that prays together, stays together." In such traditions the saying of the same prayer or selection of prayers is a way of affirming and guaranteeing a familiarity of habit, a resonance of repeated phrase, a uniformity of doctrine, and a discipline of conformity. These are, on the whole, good things. They were sufficient reasons for each of us to withhold from writing prayers of our own for many years. At the same time we do believe that the assumptions of this book should permeate Eucharistic worship across the ecumenical traditions. Our foundational beliefs are that prayer is more vivid when infused with the scriptural themes of the day, that there is more to Holy Communion than reenacting the Last Supper and/or remembering the cross, and that worship is enriched when the full breadth of scripture, in detail as well as more generally, is made present verbally and thematically in the Eucharistic prayer. This book is put forward to provoke and invite and be used as a template for a richer fare of recognized and denominationally adopted Eucharistic prayers. Written by a Church of England parish priest and a United Methodist pastor, out of thirty years' combined experience of presiding at Holy Communion, in nine different worshiping communities, reflected through study, pedagogy, publication, and practice in liturgical theology, ethics, devotional prayer, and pastoral theology, across two continents and two denominations, this is designed to be a ministry handbook shaped by ecumenical discernment and refined by liturgical practice.

Component Elements of the Eucharistic Prayer

We understand a Eucharistic prayer to have broadly eight parts, as follows:

- an **opening set of responses,** often known by the Latin term *sursum corda*, referring to the phrase "Lift up your hearts"
- a **preface,** which often allows for seasonal variations
- a **song of joy in God's presence,** often known as the *sanctus* (Latin for the words "Holy, Holy, Holy," which are part of Isaiah's experience in the temple, found in Isaiah 6), or sometimes as the *sanctus* and *benedictus* (the latter referring to the words of the crowd on Palm Sunday, "Blessed is the one who comes in the name of the Lord" in Mark 11:9), in which the congregation (or choir) joins the angels' constant hymn of praise to God
- an **invocation of the Holy Spirit,** often called the *epiclesis* after the Greek term for invocation, and calling on God to bless both the congregation (or church more broadly) and the bread and cup

- **Christ's words at the Last Supper,** often called the *anamnesis* after the Greek term for remembering, and widely described as the "words of institution"
- **acclamations,** in which the congregation joins in a brief summary of what Christ has done and will do
- **intercessions,** which anticipate and request the blessings of God's presence and grace to be extended to all the world
- **doxology,** which builds to a climax of praise in expectation of Christ's final coming in glory.

The elements always follow the same order, except in the case of the *epiclesis*, which sometimes precedes the words of institution and acclamations, and sometimes follows them. In this book the *epiclesis* always precedes the words of institution.

The eight elements may be divided into fixed (those parts whose wording does not change) and variable (those parts that alter to reflect the theme, the season, and the readings of the day). Before looking at each element and noting as we do which we regard as fixed and which we judge to be variable, it's worth exploring the distinction between the two.

Good liturgy, like all non-identically repeated activity, is a mixture of what we always do, what we usually do, what we sometimes do, and what we do once (or once a year). For example, some churches use liturgical colors. They perhaps always dress their pastor or priest in a white alb; they usually add on top a green stole or other vestment, which may sometimes be red or gold or purple, say for Pentecost or Christmas or Advent, respectively; but once a year, on Good Friday, they may have no color—or perhaps not even an alb—at all. Here we see the effectiveness and resonance of always, usually, sometimes, and once. "Always" is empowering: everyone knows what to expect, can remember the words or gestures, doesn't feel foolish or ignorant, and can recall key movements or words at other times and integrate them into faith and life. "Sometimes" or "once" is energizing: the prism of providence is turned to a new angle, and there are discoveries and insights to stimulate reflection and devotion. The problem with "always" is that it can become dull, even mindless; the problems with "sometimes" or "once" are that they can be elitist and exclusionary, can distract from the simplicity of what is being said and done, and can substitute the clever and original for the habitual and good.

While arguing that Eucharistic prayers have tended too much toward the "always," we are not advocating wholesale adoption of the "sometimes." We believe it's a mistake to offer sameness in places where variety would be uplifting, and variety in places where "always" has a lot to be said for it. Here we set out in more detail what we believe should be always, and where variation would be enhancing.

The fixed elements provide the backbone of the prayer. Knowing they aren't going to change gives the members of the congregation confidence to get used to the rhythm of listening out for the variations and relaxing into the fixed parts. They don't need anything in their hands: they can simply focus their attention on the table, on the mystery of presence and the glory of transformation. The Eucharistic prayer ceases to be a formula or rote, and instead becomes an adventure and a dance.

This understanding that there was a distinction to be made between the fixed pieces and the variations was crucial to how the Eucharistic rite was practiced in the early church. The expectation that the fixed elements remained the same allowed the gathered community to participate with confidence in knowing their parts while the celebrant took responsibility for the variations. Before the fourth-century Council of Nicea, at the time when no fixed Eucharistic prayer yet existed, the celebrant was largely free, within a basic outline, to phrase the prayer as seemed best to him. This elasticity was possible because there were fixed parts to the formula.[1] For example, in the Eucharistic celebrations of the early church the exchanges between celebrant and congregation that we call the opening sentences were fixed elements. They were not new to the early church but were carried over from the opening dialogue at the Jewish prayers of thanksgiving, with which the early church sought to be in continuity.[2] The fixed elements carry the history of the community of faith that gave birth to the liturgy we have today.

It's time to look at each of the elements in turn.

1. Gregory Dix, *The Shape of the Liturgy* (New York: Continuum, 2005), 6–7.
2. Dix, *The Shape of the Liturgy*, 126–27.

1. The Opening Responses

The opening responses, or in Latin *sursum corda*, are a dialogue between the presiding minister and the congregation. We regard these as a fixed element, as follows:

> The Lord be with you. **And also with you.**
> Lift up your hearts. **We lift them to the Lord.**
> Let us give thanks to the Lord our God. **It is right to give our thanks and praise.**

A dialogue lacks dynamism and immediacy if people are reading their parts out of a book, off a bulletin, or from a screen. This is a dialogue that needs to be exchanged looking into one another's faces. That can only be done if familiar and repeated words are used. The ideal is that people become so familiar with the words of the exchange that they don't need to look at responses at all. For all Christians, especially new disciples and children, learning these responses by heart is part of the formation in the faith that happens through practice within a body of believers over time. Thus it is an act of hospitality to provide the responses so that all present can participate; but those who know the words well should be encouraged not to hold a service book or have their eyes drawn to the screen. There is a more important focal point: the action at the altar.

In the opening sentences, the pastor or priest is announcing to the members of the congregation what the Eucharist is about to embody—that the Lord is with them. Then there is an unambiguous command to get their souls and minds and bodies in shape for what is about to happen—"Lift up your hearts." (How can a person say such a thing without looking at the people being commanded?) These are words of comfort and encouragement, but also challenge and expectation. (Denominational practice varies as to whether the congregation says "We lift them to the Lord" or "We lift them up to the Lord." We have gone with the practice of the majority.) Then there's an exchange that names the two primary modes of everything that is to follow: thanks and praise. In a short exchange of six sentences, the gathered company have named the principal agent—God; the mood of the event-lifted hearts; and the principal business to be conducted—thanks and praise. We are ready to begin. Said with vigor and reverence, it's an energizing focus and often a change of mood from whatever has preceded it. It would be dissipated if the words were to change every week or season.

2. The Preface

After the opening responses comes the preface. Here is the preface for our prayer for Christmas Eve:

> Almighty God, you shape your very life
>> to create and restore and enjoy us forever.
> We gather around your altar like those who thronged
>>> your Son's manger,
>> longing for you to reassemble men and women,
>>> kings and working people, Jews and Gentiles, heaven and earth
>>>> at the place where our humanity and your divinity meet.
> You had too much love to keep it to yourself;
>> and though we took up arms against you and one another,
>>> you disarmed us in coming into our midst as a defenseless baby.
> As his arms were tied in swaddling clothes,
>> so later his hands were nailed to the cross;
>>> yet you made his birth the foretaste of our redemption
>>>> and his death the gateway to resurrection life.
> You give us such joy and peace in your company
>> that our hearts join the angels in the Christmas sky
>>> and around your eternal throne,
>>>> singing the hymn of your unending praise.

One decision made at the outset was not to try to cover every option provided by the Revised Common Lectionary—or provide alternative prayers for where the lectionary has variations. The lectionary provides one gospel, one further New Testament reading, and two Old Testament lessons and psalms for each Sunday in ordinary time. (There is only one Old Testament lesson and one psalm during Advent, Christmas, Epiphany, Lent, and Easter.) We decided to assume that congregations would be using the first-listed ("continuous") Old Testament reading rather than the second-listed ("themed" or "alternate") reading on each Sunday. We appreciate that this may not always be the case, but we felt an attempt to incorporate all the options would result in failure. For some days such as Christmas Day, Easter, and Ascension Day, the themes are so consistent that only one prayer for all three years is considered necessary. The same is true for the Sunday before Lent (where the theme is the Transfiguration), the Sunday after Easter (where the story of Thomas always figures), and the Fourth Sunday of Easter (where the readings all address the Good Shepherd). On closer inspection there are a number of prayers that would be suitable for any ordinary Sunday, and there are some general use prayers in the final chapter. We have also provided in the final chapter some prayers for occasions that sit loosely to the liturgical year but nonetheless have a place in many congregations' hearts.

The preface is the part of the prayer where variation is most customary. Many traditions provide alternative prefaces for seasons of the liturgical year such as Advent or Easter. While in our prayers we have explored the scriptural themes of the day quite widely, we have generally kept to the following structure for the preface:

- an opening that joins the holiness of God with the joy of thanksgiving
- a phrase or sentence that begins a narrative of salvation history
- a continuation of the narrative through law and/or prophets
- a sentence that brings the narrative up to the coming of Christ, and includes reference to Christ's death and resurrection
- a joining clause that introduces a link into the *sanctus*.

We understand the role of the preface to be that of setting the broad canvas in relation to which the ministry of Jesus in general—and his passion, death, and resurrection in particular—may be seen, understood, and appreciated. The freedom provided by having a different prayer each week is that it's not essential to be comprehensive. On the contrary, it's important to keep a lightness of touch and allusiveness and brevity. What matters is that Jesus isn't seen in isolation, but as part of God's constant purpose and longing to be our companion, to bring us into relationship and restore that relationship at any cost. The Bible tells that story in 600,000 words: it's absurd to try to arrive at a definitive rendering in three or four sentences. What the preface is doing is capturing the wonder and scope of that story as witnessed in the readings for the day.

Before prayers became more systematized, the early church created an abundance of beautiful expressions that came to be used in the preface. In Egypt, an early Eucharistic prayer from the fourth century began thus:

It is meet and right to praise, to hymn, to glorify Thee,
O uncreated Father of the Only-begotten Jesus Christ. . . .
We praise Thee, O Father invisible, giver of immortality.
Thou art the source of life, the source of light,
   the source of all grace and truth,
O lover of men, O lover of the poor,
   who art reconciled to all and drawest all things to Thyself
   by the advent of Thy beloved Son.[3]

A Syrian version of the prayer opened in these words:

Worthy of praise from every mouth and
   confession from every tongue and of
   worship and exaltation from every creature
   is the adorable and glorious name of Thy glorious Trinity,
   who didst create the world by Thy grace
   and its inhabitants by Thy mercy and
   didst save mankind by Thy compassion and
   give great grace unto mortals.[4]

3. Dix, *The Shape of the Liturgy*, 163.
4. Dix, *The Shape of the Liturgy*, 178.

This version was in use by the church in Rome:

We render thanks unto Thee, O God, through Thy Beloved Servant
    Jesus Christ,
Whom in the last times Thou didst send
    to be a Savior and Redeemer and the Angel of Thy counsel;
Who is Thy Word inseparable from Thee;
    through Whom Thou madest all things and
    in Whom Thou wast well-pleased.[5]

In writing our own prayers, we have taken counsel from the early church's sense of creativity and poetry in the preface.

The first thing for the preface to affirm is that the opening responses were right—this is indeed an occasion of gratitude and praise, a moment for hearts to lift in joy. There could be nothing more wonderful than to come into the presence of God and realize anew the mystery of grace. From the very outset the language seeks to dispel any sense of routine or disengaged ritual. But at the same time it directs attention to a specific reason for thanksgiving—and this is the opportunity provided by picking up themes from the readings assigned to the day. Immediately the congregation gets a sense of recognition that the subject of the day's readings, and perhaps also of the sermon, is no outlying issue in the story of salvation but is integral to God's purposes in ways perhaps not previously appreciated. The inference can quickly be made that this congregation may also be integral to God's purposes in ways hitherto not fully understood.

For a very brief account of how Jesus fulfills God's eternal purposes, the point of departure is likely to be creation. Creation is especially suitable for a role in the preface, because it concerns the way God's love is made tangible, just as it was to be in Jesus and as in a different way it is in the sacrament of Holy Communion. It's important that the language does not narrow down the range of theological interpretation. For example, in some understandings the sin of Adam created such disharmony in creation that

5. Dix, *The Shape of the Liturgy*, 157.

only the coming of the second Adam could restore humankind's relation-ship with God. In other accounts, God's will never to be, except to be with us in Christ, meant that the coming of the fully human, fully divine Jesus was inevitable and intended whether or not there had been a sin in the Garden of Eden. Language about creation shouldn't take sides in this kind of venerable debate.

Creation is not the only place to start. The other likely candidate is Abraham. The Eucharist emerges out of the practice of Jewish meals—ones that Jesus shared, and ones that continue to this day. It is important that the prayer recognizes that. The call of Abraham is like a second beginning to the book of Genesis. God says to Abraham that through him all nations will find a blessing—a promise that Christians believe is finally realized in Jesus and the Holy Spirit.

Inherent in any reference to Abraham in a Eucharistic prayer is the question of how God today regards the Jews and how God's eternal cove-nant with them plays out once salvation, after Pentecost, has been taken to the ends of the earth. This ambivalence, together with lament that Jews and Christians are not sharing at God's table together, is an appropriate mood for the prayer, but a difficult one to render with brevity and while preserving the overall tone of the preface in thanksgiving and delight. The Jewish prayer of thanksgiving, said after a meal, begins with the gratitude and joy that we have sought to reflect in this volume:

> Blessed be Thou, O Lord our God, eternal King, who bringest forth bread
>   from the earth . . .
> Blessed art Thou, O Lord our God, who createst the fruit of the vine . . .
> Blessed art Thou, O Lord our God, eternal King,
>   who feedest the whole world with Thy goodness, with grace,
>   with lovingkindness and with tender mercy.
> Thou givest food to all flesh, for Thy lovingkindess endureth forever.
> Through Thy great goodness food hath never failed us:
> O may it not fail us for ever, for Thy great Name's sake.[6]

6. Dix, *The Shape of the Liturgy*, 53.

When Jesus "gave thanks" at the Last Supper, he was offering the prayer that he had come to know by heart as a Jewish child. It's likely the words weren't recorded because they were embedded in a practicing community gathered around so many meals that Jesus had shared with his disciples. Such a gathering was always a time of giving thanks to God.

The central event in the Old Testament, and the template onto which the early church perceived Jesus' death and resurrection, is the exodus. From the beginning Christians have identified Egyptian slavery with human immersion in sin, the Red Sea with the depths of Jesus' death, and the emergence from the water and drowning of the Egyptian pursuers with Jesus' resurrection and our liberation in him. This has a special link with the Lord's Supper because of the deep resemblances of parts of the liturgy to a Passover meal. Most Eucharistic prayers will therefore include some reference to Moses or the exodus. That reference may be more explicitly to the law or covenant made on Mount Sinai. This is particularly significant because Jesus at the Last Supper refers to the new covenant made with his blood. The temple, in which the ark of the covenant, containing the law, was housed, became the visible witness to the presence of God with Israel just as for many Christians the sacrament of Holy Communion is a visible sign of God's constancy to them.

Three further motifs recur frequently in the part of the preface that concerns the Old Testament. The prophets called people back to the principles of the law. They name both Israel's waywardness from the covenant and God's relentless attempts to restore relationship. The kings represent an ambivalent tradition that in some ways strove to imitate God's abiding governance over Israel and in other ways risked displacing it. Finally, the exile names the wilderness season in Israel's history when it seemed all was irretrievably lost and yet Israel found itself understanding God in a whole new way. Thus the preface brings the readings of the day into conversation with the story of creation, call, covenant, prophets, kings, and exile. Not all of these elements are featured every time, but all of the prefaces in this book assume a narrative in which these are the key landmarks.

In most of the prayers this part of the story paves the way for the introduction of Jesus. If Jesus appears at the very beginning, his ministry has no context, and it begs the question of why we read the Old Testament. What shaping the preface around the readings makes possible is a large and illuminating variety of ways into understanding the context for Christ's coming. What it rules out is an assumption that Jesus' coming (or his death) is the only thing the Bible or the Eucharist is about. Jesus' incarnation, ministry, death, and resurrection are the definitive and central actions of God, but they are true to the character of the God encountered in the rest of scripture. This way of rendering the preface makes such a conviction explicit.

One ambiguity in Christian theology that these prayers preserve is whether Jesus came because of human sin or whether, even if there had been no Fall, there would still have been an incarnation, because coming among us was God's purpose from the very beginning. This ambiguity surfaces in the ways the prayers talk about sin, specifically in relationship to the Jews. These prayers assume that all have sinned and fallen short of the glory of God; in other words, the Jews are not to blame any more than the rest of humankind, and we all stand in need of redemption. By lifting up the whole of salvation history, with specific reference to the Old Testament readings of the day, these prayers celebrate God's covenant with the chosen people and trust that that special relationship holds honor and promise for all the world. Once that foundation is established, it is then possible to acknowledge the expressions of God's disappointment in the faithlessness of humankind, both before Christ's coming and after, both among Jews and in the church. And it becomes appropriate to name sin, in times both past and present, as that which God alone is able to overcome.

The prayers exhibit a considered caution when using the term "Israel" to refer to God's own people. The Old Testament records salvation history with frequent use of the name Israel to refer to God's chosen ones and, in particular, associates the patriarch Jacob with the name Israel because he was given that name by God as a sign of blessing. The name Israel today is primarily associated in the public imagination with a nation-state created in 1948 and at the focus of controversy ever since. The use of the name Israel in scripture comes with a different set of meanings: it refers to a people who were called by God to be a holy nation and a royal priesthood—a rather different calling from the way nations are generally understood today. Because a Eucharistic prayer is not the appropriate place to explore such distinctions, we have, with very few exceptions, chosen to avoid the term "Israel" when talking about the people of God.

The preface comes to a climax as it issues in the *sanctus*. The point here is that prayer is joining the worship of God by the saints and angels that is going on all the time. The feeling is like that of being excited and happy and stumbling into a room where there is already a party going on where people are even more excited and happy than you are. There is no definitive description of the personnel gathered around the throne of glory. Some refer to angels and archangels, some add cherubim and seraphim, others add saints, and others again refer more generally to "all the company of heaven." A variety of expression embraces these traditions and offers the opportunity, when the readings suggest it, to inflect the description to pick up anything that might be pertinent, such as an appearance of Gabriel or a mention of seraphim in relation to the ark of the covenant. The whole effect should be one of crescendo that reverberates gratitude at God's mercy and wonder at God's grace, focused in awe at the coming of Christ, cascading into praise of the Trinity and delight at the company discovered to be already in the thick of that praise.

3. The Song of Joy in God's Presence

Then there is the song of joy in God's presence, usually known by its Latin name, the *sanctus*.

> Holy, holy, holy Lord, God of power and might.
> Heaven and earth are full of your glory.
> Hosanna in the highest.
> Blessed is he who comes in the name of the Lord.
> Hosanna in the highest.

We see this as a fixed element as far as the words go, but the way it is sung or said may vary. The two quotations that make up the *sanctus* and *ben-*

edictus mark the continuity and discontinuity of Old and New Testaments. On the one hand the continuity: both are about the temple, for Isaiah's vision takes place in the temple and Jesus is heading toward the temple on Palm Sunday. The temple was understood as the definitive place where God's presence was known and God's glory was revealed. The Eucharist—and in particular the *epiclesis* and *anamnesis* that are about to be enacted—is about God's presence and God's glory. Both quotations end with the words, "Hosanna in the highest." Hosanna means "Save now." Here lies the contrast between the eternal glory of God and the existential urgency of God's people's need for salvation. The Eucharist is about both. The threefold "Holy, Holy, Holy" can easily be taken as an anticipation of the thrice-holy Trinity of Father, Son, and Holy Spirit. On the other hand, the juxtaposition of *sanctus* and *benedictus* highlights the discontinuity of the two Testaments. Isaiah's God is ethereal and distant; the Jesus of Palm Sunday is close, on a smelly donkey, in the thick of the crowd, profoundly "with" us. On the one hand is the word, on the other is the word made flesh.

Our counsel at this point of the prayer to those presiding over communion and preparing worship is to take either of two options. One is the path of variety. In order not to lose the focus of the congregation, it's best to delegate that variety to members of a choir or music group, who can render, briefly, either the familiar words in a different setting or mode, or similar words that speak of God's wonder and presence in the language of awe and intimacy. The alternative is simply to stick to a repertoire of two or three response settings that the members of the congregation know and with which they are comfortable. Some congregations will be more comfortable speaking these words; others will enjoy singing them. Each has advantages and disadvantages. Singing helps newcomers and young children to learn the words; it also lodges thanksgiving in the heart and mind in a way that it is remembered, hummed, and echoed in memory beyond the worship service. The disadvantage of singing is that it can interrupt the sense of corporate mystery and attention. Speaking the words, on the other hand, maintains the same mode of worship and may offer something toward keeping the congregation focused in a spirit of reverence and godly fear. The disadvantage of speaking the words is that the response can become rote recitation. Some words, like the *benedictus*, were always and only a song, and reducing them to spoken sentences turns joining the chorus of angels into plodding through prose.

4. The Invocation of the Holy Spirit

After the *sanctus* comes the invocation of the Holy Spirit, known usually by its Greek name, the *epiclesis*. We regard the location of the *epiclesis* as a fixture but its words as variable. Here is the *epiclesis* in our prayer for Easter Day:

> Joy and gladness are our song, redeeming God,
>> for in your conquest of death we see the destiny of every hope in you.
> Come among us in the power of your Holy Spirit,
>> that your children may be blessed with power and grace,
>>> and that this bread and cup may become for us
>>>> the body and blood of your Son Jesus Christ.

This is the most complex part of the prayer in relation to its history. It was only in the twentieth century that the invocation of the Holy Spirit started to be included in Western Eucharistic prayers. The *epiclesis* and the *anamnesis* balance one another: the *anamnesis* recalls what God did, once, in Jesus; the *epiclesis* asks God, through the Holy Spirit, to bring that saving action to fruition today. Thus does the Last Supper become the Lord's Supper. There are two questions that surround the *epiclesis* in the liturgies of the last fifty years or so. One is, does one pray for the Holy Spirit to come down upon the elements or upon the worshipers, and, if both, at the same moment or at different moments? The other is, does one pray for the Holy Spirit to come down before remembering the events of the Last Supper, or afterwards?

It is easy to see how this can become a debate between a more Catholic notion of the Eucharist, which stresses the activity of the Holy Spirit today, and a more Protestant view, which emphasizes the action of Jesus once and for all two thousand years ago. In this portrayal of the debate, putting the *epiclesis* first tends to the more Catholic view, asking God to act today in the light of what God has previously done. In historic Protestant texts—notably the 1662 Book of Common Prayer, so influential in Anglicanism and Methodism—the *anamnesis* constitutes the whole business of the prayer and there is no *epiclesis* at all. In this light one can see how to ask for the coming down of the Holy Spirit on the elements of bread and wine before the words of institution, and on the congregation afterwards, constitutes a classic ecumenical compromise. One benefit of doing this is to link the prayer for the Spirit to come upon the congregation with a more general prayer for the upbuilding of the church and the advancement of the kingdom, which often characterizes the third part of Eucharistic prayers. Traditions that authorize several prayers tend to offer alternatives that put the *epiclesis* in different places to suit different understandings and emphases.

The prayers in this book all take the same shape. They place the *epiclesis* immediately after the *sanctus*. The prayer for the congregation immediately precedes the prayer for the elements, which leads straight into the remembrance of the Last Supper. This is for four reasons, three practical and one theological. The first practical reason is in keeping with the principle already cited, that altering the sequence of the prayer is, like altering the words of institution, an unnecessary and unhelpful variation, likely to confuse the worshiper without enriching the worship. It has no discernible devotional value. We have chosen one pattern and simply stuck to it, so the worshiper can get used to a reliable shape and enjoy the fresh words within a familiar structure. The second practical reason is that we have reserved the final part of the prayer for intercession—as a place where, as in the preface, the readings can significantly shape the words over three or four sentences. If the *epiclesis* were to be transferred to this point, or divided between this point and an earlier moment, the room for maneuver at this moment in the prayer would be reduced. The third practical reason is simply one of brevity. If the invocation of the Holy Spirit happens once—over the congregation and elements—rather than twice, the number of words involved is generally fewer, while the depth of the sentiment is unchanged.

The theological reason for combining the invocation of the Holy Spirit over both congregation and elements lies in an understanding of what Holy

Communion is. We see a Eucharist as a whole event, from gathering and greeting, through confession of sin and celebration of forgiveness, to hearing the scripture spoken and preached, on to declaring faith, interceding, being reconciled with one another and offering gifts, to praying over the gifts, breaking bread, sharing food, being blessed, and being sent out. A meal is not simply the consumption of food; it is about conversation, hospitality, kindness, consideration, care, generosity, celebration, enjoyment, gentleness, presence, sharing. Likewise the Eucharist is not simply the blessing and consuming of the bread and cup; it is the whole sweep from gathering to being dismissed. Thus the invocation is not simply focused on the elements; it is sought for the people too. To put these two moments together is to say that the blessing of bread and cup is the focal moment within a much longer prayer—a prayer that includes and requires all the other parts of the service just named.

This does have implications for extended communion. In some traditions it is normal practice to save some of the consecrated elements and take them, straightaway or at a later date, to the home of persons whose circumstances make them unable to join the community celebration. The understanding of the Eucharist offered above suits a swift extension of the sharing to a housebound would-be participant. But it does not sit quite so easily with the notion of the elements retaining indefinitely a holy quality that might be shared at an indefinite later date with a wholly or largely separate community. The holiness of communion, in our understanding as expressed in these prayers, resides in the process of preparing for and receiving the elements in this setting—rather than precisely in the elements themselves.

5. Christ's Words at the Last Supper

The center of the Eucharistic prayer comes in the recitation of Christ's words at the Last Supper, the "words of institution," known in Greek as the *anamnesis*. We have chosen in this book to regard this as fixed—that is, to leave it unchanged, as an "always," using the following words:

who, at supper with his disciples, took bread, gave you thanks,
　　broke the bread, and gave it to them, saying,
　　　"Take, eat: this is my body which is given for you;
　　　　do this in remembrance of me."
After supper he took the cup.
Again he gave you thanks, and gave it to his disciples, saying,
　　"Drink this, all of you: this is my blood of the new covenant,
　　　which is shed for you and for many for the forgiveness of sins.
　　Do this, as often as you drink it, in remembrance of me."

It's ideal if the members of the congregation can participate in the prayer unencumbered by a service sheet or book and undistracted by a screen or other prompt. The pastor or priest will inevitably have to refer to a sheet with the prayer on it, but for this central moment it is more than desirable that all, presiding minister included, have their eyes focused on the bread and the cup. The only way to ensure that is to make the words of institution invariable, so there can be no concern of getting them "wrong." Just as at Christmas all eyes are on the crib, which focuses the mystery of the incarnation on how God almighty can be present in the fragile form of this tiny baby, so in the Eucharist all eyes are on the elements, which focus the gift of communion on how God can be made present through this humble, tangible meal. Any diverting of the gaze or fumbling with a sheet of paper diminishes a precious, shared, holy moment—for many, the center of their week; for some, the center of their life. Of course there's a difference between the account of the Last Supper in 1 Corinthians 11 and that in the Gospels of Matthew, Mark, and Luke, and there are interesting divergences between the Gospels themselves. But there's also a theater of celebrating Holy Communion, in a good sense, and the best way to capture that drama is to use the same words of institution each time.

6. The Acclamations

The acclamations follow the words of institution. We regard these as fixed, as follows:

> Great is the mystery of faith.
> **Christ has died; Christ is risen; Christ will come again.**

The acclamations were common in Eastern Orthodox liturgies and started to be introduced into Western Catholic and Protestant worship in recent decades. In traditions where the variety of standard, authorized Eucharistic prayers has been limited, the acclamations have sometimes been seen as an appropriate place for variation. For example, sometimes the members of the congregation say, "Christ has died. Christ is risen. Christ will come again." Other times they say, "Dying you destroyed our death. Rising you restored our life. Lord Jesus, come in glory." Or again, "When we eat this bread and drink this cup we proclaim your death, Lord Jesus, until you come in glory."

For several reasons, we view the acclamations as one part it is best not to vary. The congregation has just experienced a vital, precious, and thrilling moment. It's unnecessary and uselessly distracting to introduce a dimension that leaves worshipers scurrying around to find or recall the right words to say. It's not that one of the above sets of words (or similar) is better than another. The point is to choose one and stick to it. The traditions from which we both come are most familiar with "Christ has died. Christ is risen. Christ will come again." So that's the one we've gone with throughout this book. It says all that needs to be said. It's easily remembered. And, through its simple repetition, it provides admirable clarity and comprehensiveness; it is one of the many ways worship forms the character of a congregation. It doesn't need to be sung: its simplicity is conveyed most directly when said as one body. The tension between the second, present, acclamation and the third, future, one is thrilling and captures exactly the mood of the prayer as a whole: we remember; we enact; we anticipate.

7. The Intercessions

Conventional discourse about the Eucharistic prayer speaks of three sections—the first, running from the *sursum corda* to the end of the *benedictus*, the second, running from the *epiclesis* (as we locate it in this volume) and *anamnesis* to the end of the acclamations, and the third running from there to the final great Amen. Here we discuss the last of these sections.

The final parts of the prayer are the intercessions, doxology, and great Amen. We regard these as variable elements of the prayer. Here are the intercessions in our prayer for Christmas 1, Year B:

> Consoling God, as Mary and Joseph offered a sacrifice in your temple,
>> bring comfort to all who feel today like they are being sacrificed
>>> by the cruel, the merciless, or the fanatical.
>
> As Simeon foresaw your Son would be a sign that would be opposed,
>> bless any who face hostility, anger, and violence.
>
> As the holy family realized a sword would pierce their own soul,
>> speak tenderly to those whose soul knows despair, loss, or betrayal.
>
> Make your church strong, fill your children with wisdom,
>> and set your favor upon all who turn to you.

In the earliest Eucharistic prayers there was no third part of this kind: there was simply a short preface and an *anamnesis*. As the prayer developed, there was enough elasticity to it that the church in Egypt and Syria and Jerusalem began to add in particular intercessions in distinct ways that suited the local context. Such intercessions often included the living and the dead, the congregation gathered, and leaders of the empire and the church. For example, an early Eucharistic prayer in the Jerusalem church (c. AD 348) includes these intercessions:

> Over this sacrifice, we entreat God for the common peace of the churches;
>> for the good ordering of the world;
>> for the emperors; for the army and the allies;
>> for them that are sick;

for them that are afflicted, and in a word,
for all that are in need of help.[7]

As a result, quite diverse practices of including intercessions within the Eucharistic prayer developed. In contemporary Roman Catholic prayers there is usually a very specific form of intercession in this third section, praying for the church, with the pope and the local bishop mentioned by name, and for the kingdom in general, and sometimes particular, terms. By contrast, in contemporary mainline prayers this third section, if not fused with the congregational half of the *epiclesis*, tends to be given to rather general forms of intercession for church and kingdom ("heal the sick, end injustice, let the oppressed walk free . . .").

What we want to affirm in these Catholic and Protestant traditions is the desire to express how we would wish the world (and not just the heart and soul of the worshiper) to change as a result of this celebration of the Eucharist. Among other things, the Eucharist is a portrayal of rightly ordered life. Food finds its purpose in becoming the gift of communion. Money is healed of its negative associations by being offered as the fruits of daily labor. Humanity is fulfilled in gathering around the table just as it will one day gather around the throne, to worship and enjoy God forever. The intercession that follows the words of institution and acclamations is a prayer that the world be rightly ordered in keeping with the kingdom displayed in the passion of Christ. It is highly appropriate that this kingdom be articulated in prayer at this moment of the Lord's Supper. And it is likewise important that church and kingdom often, if not always, feature in this part of the prayer, for "church" names the principal way in and through which God works in the world today, and "kingdom" names all that God will bring to fruition in spite of the shortcomings of the church.

The prayers in this book steer a course between the Catholic pattern, which we find too specific, and the mainline Protestant, which we regard as too general. The Eucharistic prayer should be resonant, captivating, poetic, absorbing. To name individual living people, however lofty, is dis-

---

7. Dix, *The Shape of the Liturgy*, 192–93.

tracting and intrusive; that's what the intercessions in the main body of the service are for. By contrast, falling back on generalities risks platitude and invites abstract piety. What the prayers in this book aim to do is to plead the coming kingdom from a host of perspectives and angles. They read a wide range of scriptural texts as offering windows on how God works and what God has in store. Often, too, those same texts provide a structure for prayer: the Beatitudes of Matthew 5:1–12 suggest nine kinds of reversal; the portrayal of the last judgment in Matthew 25:31–46 offers six acts of mercy through which we might meet Jesus; the temptation narratives in Matthew and Luke incline us to see the issues of discipleship through three lenses; Jesus' words in the synagogue in Nazareth in Luke 4 give us five social locations through which to understand oppression. None of these are exhaustive, and following them precisely would make the prayer too long; but they become the framework for a prayer that expresses their spirit.

And this is the point where we have found writing these prayers a transformative and devotional practice: for the promises of God come alive when one sees anew how word and table, scripture and sacrament converge to embody and proclaim God's inestimable grace in Jesus, God's coming kingdom in the power of the Spirit. We trust that those who use these prayers will share the discoveries we have made in writing them—the hidden connections, the interlinking insights, the echoes of hitherto unconnected stories, the manifestation of what had only been imagined.

8. The Doxology

In this same prayer from the early Jerusalem church the doxology, which looks to God as the final purpose and consummation of all things, concludes as follows:

> until that day when heaven and earth become a temple of your praise
> and your resurrection engulfs all you have made,
> ever one God, Father, Son and Holy Spirit. Amen.

At the end of each prayer we have drawn together two traditions that are both important but are not always practiced in the same prayer. The first and most widespread is that of doxology—that is, a crescendo of praise to God the Holy Trinity, Father, Son, and Holy Spirit. This makes an uncomplicated but important point that God is before all things, and God remains beyond all things, and all human endeavor and prayer is but a tiny shadow on the face of the glory of God, and thus that our worship is fundamentally praise. The second and also widely practiced tradition is to end with an anticipation of God's final renewal of heaven and earth—variously understood as the second coming of Christ, the end of time, the healing of the nations, the last judgment, and the vindication of the oppressed. In these prayers we see the eschatological expectation of God's final renewal as the fulfillment of the prayers of intercession, which themselves name symptoms of all that falls short of the glory of God; and we see the doxological praise of the Trinity as issuing from the completion of the work begun in creation and epitomized in Jesus. In this way there are three high points in the prayer: the climax of salvation history in Jesus, celebrated in the *sanctus*; the presence of Jesus now, appreciated in the acclamations; and the final taking up of all things into God's presence, enjoyed in the great final Amen.

Sources and Criteria

In writing these prayers we have borne in mind three trinities that have acted both as sources of inspiration and as checklists to ensure that each of the prayers has kept its shape.

One trinity is St. Paul's abiding virtues of faith, hope, and love. We regard these as theological terms for the more worldly "past," "future," and "present" respectively. "Faith" names trust in what God has done in the past, both specifically in Abraham, Moses, and the prophets, and in Jesus, the Holy Spirit, and the church, but also more generally in ways largely unrecorded. "Hope" names trust in what God will do in the future, again specifically in healing the earth, vindicating the oppressed, and reconciling the hostile, but more generally in filling the earth with glory as the waters cover the sea. "Love" names the life made possible by that faith and hope—life in the light of the forgiveness of sins and in anticipation of everlasting resurrection, life delivered from being finally rejected or obliterated, life free from fear and devoted to enjoying and imitating the companionship of God. Thus these prayers seek a balance between faith, hope, and love—what God has done, will do, and is doing. The use of the scripture texts for each day isn't a way of simply rehearsing less familiar stories or reiterating recondite passages for greater scriptural comprehension; it's about treating scripture as a lens through which to see God. And this is a God who was, and is, and is to come.

Another trinity is found in the Platonic universals of beauty, truth, and goodness. Psalm 96 enjoins us to worship the Lord in the beauty of holiness. We want our prayers to be beautiful, but not in such a way that they have an aesthetic appeal detached from their purpose as articulating the church's longing to be united with God in this holy meal. At the very least there should be no jarring anachronisms, clumsy juxtapositions, or unwarranted repetitions. At most there may be a memorable phrase, a helpful perspective, a salutary insight. But all emphasis is on heightening the congregation's awareness of the wonder of being in communion with God, made possible by the saving action of Christ, made present in the power of the Spirit. If we have sought to evoke delight, or at least a satisfied purr, it is less with a poetic turn of phrase than with associations seldom made or allusions carefully crafted. This is a way of saying that the aspiration toward beauty must be tempered by the quest for truth. Truth is a quest, rather than an assertion. Words can only say and do so much. No historic formula says all that can or must be said, and turning prayer into a formula is exactly what Jesus criticized the Pharisees for doing. These prayers seek to be beauty in the quest for truth. And they aspire to issue in goodness. That doesn't make them utilitarian; but they are not ends in themselves. The Eucharist, as the invocation of the Holy Spirit on the congregation makes clear, seeks to make us better people—to help us live lives of evident and profound holiness, in a society tangibly redeemed and restored. Our prayers are designed to be beauty, seeking truth, issuing in goodness.

And the most obvious and fundamental trinity is the Holy Trinity of

Father, Son, and Holy Spirit. In very simple terms, it's possible to think of the three conventional parts of the prayer as marking the work primarily of the Father (in salvation history recorded in the preface), of the Son (in the remembrance of the Last Supper), and of the Holy Spirit (in the coming of the kingdom). This would be oversimplified, for orthodox Trinitarian doctrine asserts that all three persons of the Trinity are at work through the actions of any one of the persons. But it illustrates constructive ways in which, when writing each prayer, we have borne in mind the work of all three members of the Trinity at every stage, and remained mindful of those events with which each is particularly associated. The Lord's Supper is not just remembrance of the saving work of Jesus. It's an invitation to the congregation to be engulfed in the communion of saints as it is swathed with the glory of what the Father has imagined, the Son embodied, and the Spirit fulfilled. Every prayer should celebrate all three aspects of this joyous drama.

How to Use This Book

The aim of this book is to provide a prayer of great thanksgiving for every Sunday of the year, and for weekdays when many congregations gather to share Holy Communion, such as Christmas Eve, Christmas Day, Ash Wednesday, Maundy Thursday, and Ascension Day. To do this we have written around 150 prayers, following the three-year Revised Common Lectionary Cycle.

Each prayer is set out in such a way that it can be read by the celebrant at the altar or communion table. There should be no need to touch or hold the book during worship. The intention is that the presiding minister will want to keep his or her hands free to hold or touch the bread and cup, and perhaps to stretch out his or her arms to embody and focus the prayers of the whole congregation. So the book is designed so as to stay open when placed directly on an altar or communion table or on a miniature lectern that rests on such a table in order to prop up the book and make it easier to read. If necessary a photocopy can be taken of the relevant prayer and placed on the altar table or miniature lectern.

The language of the prayers seeks to render the cadences of the scripture and adopt the poetic imagery and rhythm of resonant liturgy. The Eucharistic liturgy is like poetry; thus, the celebrant may need to sit with each prayer for a while to become familiar with its flow and make its delivery his or her own, determining where to pause and where to place emphasis.

The Revised Common Lectionary is based on the 1969 Roman Catholic Lectionary. It was modified for ecumenical use, and since its publication in 1992 it has been adopted by a broad swathe of Protestant denominations. In general terms it follows Matthew in Year A, Mark in Year B, and Luke in Year C, interspersing John across the three years, especially in Year B. It provides an additional New Testament reading for each Sunday. For the seasons of the year—Advent, Christmas, Epiphany, Lent, and Easter—it provides a single Old Testament lesson for each Sunday. For the rest of the year (the "ordinary" Sundays) there are two Old Testament readings, the first of which follows a continuous thread through an Old Testament book, the second of which ties the Old Testament reading more closely to the theme of the two New Testament readings. The prayers in this book assume the "continuous" Old Testament readings and do not attempt to incorporate the "themed" readings.

On several occasions—Christmas Eve, Christmas Day, Epiphany, Ash Wednesday, the Sunday before Lent, Maundy Thursday, Easter Day, the second Sunday of Easter, the fourth Sunday of Easter, Ascension, Pentecost, and All Saints—we have judged that the readings for the three years are so similar that we have provided only one prayer, rather than three. We have not offered a prayer for the week of October 30–November 5, assuming congregations will celebrate that Sunday as All Saints. We have not provided a prayer for Good Friday, since most churches that distribute communion on that day do so from the reserved sacrament, it not being deemed appropriate actually to celebrate communion.

There are some occasions that sit inside a congregation's heart but don't sit easily in a lectionary: Mother's Day is an example. We have offered prayers for such occasions in a chapter at the end. In that chapter there are also additional prayers that may be suitable for any occasion and can be used, for example, when Easter is so early or so late that a Sunday appears, either after Epiphany or immediately after Pentecost, that we do not cover in our regular chapters.

When the prayers speak of God as Trinity, they adopt non-gender-specific language. The Trinity is beyond gender. At one time to use the pronoun "he" for God was seen in church and society as unproblematic. In recent decades it has become clearer to many that this was tied to a hegemony of men in church and society that was a human aberration rather than a divine expectation. To use "he" when "he" is not necessary only affirms that aberration. Hence, while the prayers frequently talk of the first person of the Trinity as Father, they avoid using the pronoun "he" to describe the Father, since the Father does not have a biological gender. Elsewhere the prayers use a range of descriptions and ways of addressing the first person of the Trinity, as evoked from scripture. By contrast, when the prayers speak of the action of Christ, they do use the term "he." Christ is fully human as well as fully divine, and his humanity is gendered as male, although that gender designates no special dignity to maleness. When the prayers refer to the Holy Spirit, they again steer away from assigning gender, because the Spirit, while a divine person, has no human gender.

The prayers invoke the term "Lord" often, because it is the conventional translation of the Hebrew name *Yahweh* and the Greek title *Kyrios*, which are inextricable from the identity of the God of Jesus Christ. To avoid confusion, in these prayers the term "Lord" always refers to the second person of the Trinity, Jesus Christ. Likewise the prayers frequently use the language of kingdom, because, while we understand that it can have unhelpful patriarchal and territorial resonances, we nonetheless find it much the most evocative scriptural term for all that God promises, Christ embodies, and the church anticipates.

We have sought to balance the familiar and the new. The opening responses, *sanctus* and *benedictus*, words of institution, and acclamations are the same in each prayer. The preface, invocation of the Spirit, intercession, and doxology vary throughout, reflecting the scriptures of the day and the themes of the season.

We believe there remains an important place for prayers that are time-honored and well known. We seek not to replace conventional liturgies but to enrich them. We hope that those using these prayers in presiding and sharing at communion will find a renewal in doing so as deep as the joy we have found in writing them.

1. Advent

Advent 1, Year A

The Lord be with you. **And also with you.**
Lift up your hearts. **We lift them to the Lord.**
Let us give thanks to the Lord our God. **It is right to give our thanks and praise.**

Covenant God, in the beginning you called your creation good
  and flooded it with beauty and bounty, with goodness and grace.
In the days of Noah you drowned your creation
  to wash away sin and draw your own sons and daughters to yourself.
Through your covenant with Israel your promises flowed to all nations,
  and in Jesus Christ you drew us out of our waywardness
    into the relentless flood of your mercy.
His death was the drowning of our sin;
  his resurrection and ascension bless all nations
    to stream toward you in glory.
And so we praise you with angels and archangels
  and all the company of heaven as we join their unending hymn.

Holy, holy, holy Lord, God of power and might.
Heaven and earth are full of your glory.
Hosanna in the highest.
Blessed is he who comes in the name of the Lord.
Hosanna in the highest.

Peacemaking God, in Christ you made an ending
  of the life of spears and swords,
    and came to us with plowshares and pruning hooks,
      the tools of planting and cultivating, that we might be fed.
In him you showed us how to study war no more,
  how to lay down our swords and shields,
    and how to feast with the prince of peace.
As you came to us to be our very food and drink,
  send your Holy Spirit upon this bread and cup

and make them be for us the body and blood of your Son Jesus Christ;
who, at supper with his disciples, took bread, gave you thanks,
 broke the bread, and gave it to them, saying,
  "Take, eat: this is my body which is given for you;
   do this in remembrance of me."
After supper he took the cup.
Again he gave you thanks, and gave it to his disciples, saying,
 "Drink this, all of you: this is my blood of the new covenant,
  which is shed for you and for many for the forgiveness of sins.
 Do this, as often as you drink it, in remembrance of me."

Great is the mystery of faith.
Christ has died; Christ is risen; Christ will come again.

God of prophets and promises, as you turn swords into plowshares,
 take our sin and reshape us for salvation.
Take our foolishness and bend us toward faith.
Take our hostility and refashion us for heaven in the crucible of your love.
Stir your church with wakening hope,
 that soon and very soon we are going to see our king.
Quicken our spirits with trust in that day
 when we who have been blessed with such hope
  will gather around your throne with saints of every age,
   in praise and thanksgiving to you,
    one God, Father, Son, and Holy Spirit. **Amen.**

Advent 1, Year B

The Lord be with you. **And also with you.**
Lift up your hearts. **We lift them to the Lord.**
Let us give thanks to the Lord our God. **It is right to give our thanks and praise.**

Eye has not seen, nor ear heard, nor tongue told
    of a glory like yours, Lord God,
        for you are the potter, and we the clay,
            and you fashioned us in your image.
Though the pot was broken in your hands
    in the exile of your people and the rejection of your Son,
        you made an even more wondrous vessel
            out of agony and estrangement.
In Jesus you glorify your chosen people
    and inaugurate your church to be his body in the world.
In his death the pot was broken once and for all,
    but in his resurrection you refashioned a new pot from the same clay
        to feed your people forever.
And so we gladly thank you,
    joining with the company of angels and archangels
        and all the host of heaven in their unending hymn.

Holy, holy, holy Lord, God of power and might.
Heaven and earth are full of your glory.
Hosanna in the highest.
Blessed is he who comes in the name of the Lord.
Hosanna in the highest.

Ever-present God, your prophets longed
    that you would tear the heavens and come down;
        and in your Son Jesus Christ you have come down
            and filled the earth with the splendor of your dwelling among us.
In him you were present to friend and stranger,

the intrigued and the suspicious, the betrayer and the bereft.
Come down now in the power of your Holy Spirit upon this bread and cup
and make them be for us the body and blood of your Son Jesus Christ;
who, at supper with his disciples, took bread, gave you thanks,
broke the bread, and gave it to them, saying,
"Take, eat: this is my body which is given for you;
do this in remembrance of me."
After supper he took the cup.
Again he gave you thanks, and gave it to his disciples, saying,
"Drink this, all of you: this is my blood of the new covenant,
which is shed for you and for many for the forgiveness of sins.
Do this, as often as you drink it, in remembrance of me."

Great is the mystery of faith.
Christ has died; Christ is risen; Christ will come again.

Word of life, though heaven and earth will pass away,
your words will never pass away.
As you feed us with this living bread,
strengthen those who wonder if they can survive this day;
restore any who are downtrodden and heavy-laden;
visit all who are forsaken and alone.
Open the window of your heaven
that your church may glimpse the hope of your glory
and your world may be transfigured by the light of your truth,
until that day when heaven finally comes to earth,
when your Son returns on the clouds
and your Spirit infuses your creation with resurrecting grace,
and you are all in all, one God, now and forever. **Amen.**

Advent 1, Year C

The Lord be with you. **And also with you.**
Lift up your hearts. **We lift them to the Lord.**
Let us give thanks to the Lord our God. **It is right to give our thanks and praise.**

Blessed are you, God of David, for your faithfulness is steadfast
    and your mercy has been from of old.
You draw your people to you with your promise of salvation,
    and every promise you make, in your goodness, you fulfill.
From the house of David you raised up your Messiah
    to restore Judah and to herald that your deliverance was near.
In your Son's righteousness we find our life:
    for his righteousness was more than enough for your people
      who had waited so long for justice,
        who had yearned so long for redemption,
          who had trusted so long in your grace.
Truly in his righteousness is fulfilled
    every hope of salvation in every generation.
By his death we can stand justified before you;
    and through his resurrection we can share your holy life forever.
And so with angels and archangels, we praise your name,
    joining the company of heaven in their unending hymn.

Holy, holy, holy Lord, God of power and might.
Heaven and earth are full of your glory.
Hosanna in the highest.
Blessed is he who comes in the name of the Lord.
Hosanna in the highest.

God of glory, for whose coming we wait,
    make this meal we share a sign that our redemption draws near.
Send your Holy Spirit upon your church:
    strengthen our hearts in all holiness

that we may be heralds of your kingdom.
By your same Spirit, sanctify this bread and this cup,
    that they may be for us the body and blood of your Son,
        Jesus Christ our Lord;
who, at supper with his disciples, took bread, gave you thanks,
    broke the bread, and gave it to them, saying,
        "Take, eat: this is my body which is given for you;
            do this in remembrance of me."
After supper he took the cup.
Again he gave you thanks, and gave it to his disciples, saying,
    "Drink this, all of you: this is my blood of the new covenant,
        which is shed for you and for many for the forgiveness of sins.
    Do this, as often as you drink it, in remembrance of me."

Great is the mystery of faith.
Christ has died; Christ is risen; Christ will come again.

God of power, you have promised to make your way to us:
    come quickly to those who wait for you.
Raise up every head that is bent low in sin.
Lift up every heart that is bowed down in shame.
Uphold every soul that is made heavy by oppression.
Inspire every weary throat to sing of the day
    when justice and mercy meet.
Bring us through all that is passing away
    to the life that shall never pass away,
        when every eye shall be lifted up to gaze upon your Son
            in everlasting glory with all your saints,
                and when the redemption for which we have longed
                    shall forever be ours, in the company of your Son
                        and the power of your Spirit, holy Father, blessed Trinity. **Amen.**

Advent 2, Year A

The Lord be with you. **And also with you.**
Lift up your hearts. **We lift them to the Lord.**
Let us give thanks to the Lord our God. **It is right to give our thanks and praise.**

Holy are you, God of Jesse,
   for the branch of our salvation is rooted in you.
To Abraham you promised to raise up a people bound to you in love,
   and through the household of David
     you brought life greater than our imagining
       in a child of grace, Jesus our Lord.
Though we deny your love for ourselves and
   seek to limit the reach of your mercy to others,
     you beckon us to repentance,
       open our eyes to new life,
         and embrace us to join your family of faith.
In your Son's death we see the depth of our sin;
   yet in his resurrection we see the extent of your grace.
You bless us beyond reckoning, for you welcome us
   into the company of prophets and apostles and saints
     on earth and in heaven, with whom forever we sing your praise.

Holy, holy, holy Lord, God of power and might.
Heaven and earth are full of your glory.
Hosanna in the highest.
Blessed is he who comes in the name of the Lord.
Hosanna in the highest.

Anointing God, your Spirit rested upon your Son
   with wisdom and understanding, counsel and might, knowledge and fear.
In Christ you have anointed your future out of our past,
   your kingdom out of our plans, and your salvation out of our poverty.
As your Spirit rested upon him, send down that same anointing Spirit

upon us and upon these gifts of bread and wine
    that they may be for us the body and blood of our Lord;
who, at supper with his disciples, took bread, gave you thanks,
    broke the bread, and gave it to them, saying,
        "Take, eat: this is my body which is given for you;
            do this in remembrance of me."
After supper he took the cup.
Again he gave you thanks, and gave it to his disciples, saying,
    "Drink this, all of you: this is my blood of the new covenant,
        which is shed for you and for many for the forgiveness of sins.
    Do this, as often as you drink it, in remembrance of me."

Great is the mystery of faith.
Christ has died; Christ is risen; Christ will come again.

Astonishing God, your prophet Isaiah envisioned a day
    when the wolf and lamb would lie down together,
 and the leopard with the kid, and a little child would lead them.
Astonish us anew by your gentle ways of peace.
Shape your church to live from faith, not fear.
Make your future present through the lives of those
    who show us how to love our enemies.
Hasten the day when the earth will be full of the knowledge of you,
    and your fullness will be all in all,
        and all creation from the depths of the sea
            to the heights of the mountains
                will know the peace to which your Son shall lead.
Awaken that dawn when we are surrounded with everlasting praise to you,
    Father, Son, and Holy Spirit. **Amen.**

Advent 2, Year B

The Lord be with you. **And also with you.**
Lift up your hearts. **We lift them to the Lord.**
Let us give thanks to the Lord our God. **It is right to give our thanks and praise.**

Constant God, with you a thousand years are like one day.
We thank and praise you
   because you have not been slow about your promise,
     but have patiently waited that all might come to repentance.
In John the Baptist you sent a herald
   who embodied the prophecies of your chosen people
     and announced the coming of your Son Jesus Christ.
Through baptism you offer us the forgiveness of sins,
   and after the water of cleansing you clothe us anew in your Spirit.
You invite us into the heritage of your prophets
   and the destiny of your saints.
In your Son's death you lay down your life for us,
   and in raising him from the tomb you inaugurate
     your eternal kingdom of peace.
And so we join angels and archangels and the company of heaven,
   singing forever of your glory.

Holy, holy, holy Lord, God of power and might.
Heaven and earth are full of your glory.
Hosanna in the highest.
Blessed is he who comes in the name of the Lord.
Hosanna in the highest.

Holy God, you call your people
   to wait for and hasten the day of your coming.
We long to open wide the gates and spread apart the everlasting doors
   that you, our king of glory, may enter among us,
     and we may say, "Here is our God."

Fulfill our hopes and send now your gracious Spirit on your people
and on these gifts of bread and wine, that they may be for us
the body and blood of our Lord Jesus Christ;
who, at supper with his disciples, took bread, gave you thanks,
broke the bread, and gave it to them, saying,
"Take, eat: this is my body which is given for you;
do this in remembrance of me."
After supper he took the cup.
Again he gave you thanks, and gave it to his disciples, saying,
"Drink this, all of you: this is my blood of the new covenant,
which is shed for you and for many for the forgiveness of sins.
Do this, as often as you drink it, in remembrance of me."

Great is the mystery of faith.
Christ has died; Christ is risen; Christ will come again.

Gentle God, you feed your flock like a shepherd
and gather your lambs in your arms.
Speak tenderly to all who linger
under the shadow of exile, imprisonment, exclusion, or rejection.
Give your children the joy of knowing that they have served their term,
that their penalty is paid, that they shall receive back from your hand
double for all that they have ached to lose.
Where your people are isolated on a mountain top,
cry to them that their mountain will be laid low;
where they are in the valley of despair,
whisper to them that they shall be exalted.
God of our weary years, God of our silent tears,
hasten the coming of our new day begun,
when we shall see the wonder of your tender face,
when the grass never withers and the flower never fades
because you are all in all, Father, Son, and Holy Spirit. **Amen.**

Advent 2, Year C

The Lord be with you. **And also with you.**
Lift up your hearts. **We lift them to the Lord.**
Let us give thanks to the Lord our God. **It is right to give our thanks and praise.**

Blessed be your name, Lord God of time and eternity,
    for you have come to your people and set them free.
You have spoken through the mouth of holy prophets
    and remembered your covenant of old.
You have prepared the way of our salvation by raising up a mighty Savior
    from the house of your servant David.
Your Son Jesus took upon himself on the cross the cost of our sin,
    and through him you revealed the fullness of your promise of mercy.
In his resurrection you gave us knowledge of salvation
    by the forgiveness of our sins
      that we might serve you without fear
        in holiness and righteousness all our days.
And so with angels and archangels and all the company of heaven,
    we join the unending hymn.

Holy, holy, holy Lord, God of power and might.
Heaven and earth are full of your glory.
Hosanna in the highest.
Blessed is he who comes in the name of the Lord.
Hosanna in the highest.

God of the future and the past, you promised that all flesh shall see your salvation:
    show us the salvation you bring through the flesh and blood of your only Son.
As your prophets heralded his saving glory,
    sanctify your church for his promised coming.
Send your Holy Spirit upon this bread and cup
    that they may be for us the body and blood of Christ our Lord;
who, at supper with his disciples, took bread, gave you thanks,

broke the bread, and gave it to them, saying,
  "Take, eat: this is my body which is given for you;
    do this in remembrance of me."
After supper he took the cup.
Again he gave you thanks, and gave it to his disciples, saying,
  "Drink this, all of you: this is my blood of the new covenant,
    which is shed for you and for many for the forgiveness of sins.
  Do this, as often as you drink it, in remembrance of me."

Great is the mystery of faith.
Christ has died; Christ is risen; Christ will come again.

Refining Spirit, you burn away all that does not endure your presence.
Reveal your mercy in the very crucible of your love.
Protect your sons and daughters who are facing a crucible
  of trial or temptation or testing,
    and amid the suffering of your children reveal your eternal grace.
Refine and strengthen the hope of your church
  through every adversity and every danger.
Set the hearts of your people on fire
  to seek your justice and share your mercy;
    until your dawn from on high breaks upon us,
      and on the day of your coming we stand clothed
        in the righteousness of the Son, in the presence of the Father,
          by the refining power of the Holy Spirit,
            one God, now and forever. **Amen.**

Advent 3, Year A

The Lord be with you. **And also with you.**
Lift up your hearts. **We lift them to the Lord.**
Let us give thanks to the Lord our God. **It is right to give our thanks and praise.**

Blessed are you, Lord God of time and eternity,
   for you have opened the eyes of the blind
     and unstopped the ears of the deaf;
       you have made the lame leap like a deer
         and the tongue of the speechless sing for joy.
You made this world as a playground of delights,
   and you called a people to be your companions forever.
In Jesus you showed us who you are,
   who we are, how far we have strayed from you,
     and how to become your companions again.
In his death you opened a path for our redemption,
   and in his resurrection you brought us
     the joy of forgiveness and everlasting life.
And so our souls magnify you, with angels and archangels
   and all the company of heaven, singing the hymn of your unending praise.

Holy, holy, holy Lord, God of power and might.
Heaven and earth are full of your glory.
Hosanna in the highest.
Blessed is he who comes in the name of the Lord.
Hosanna in the highest.

God of blessing, in Jesus you fill the hungry with good things.
You bestow mercy from generation to generation.
You show us the cost and glory of your salvation
   in the breaking and pouring and sharing of bread and wine.
Send down your Holy Spirit, that your people may be sanctified by your grace,
   and these gifts of bread and wine may be for us

the body and blood of your Son Jesus Christ;
who, at supper with his disciples, took bread, gave you thanks,
   broke the bread, and gave it to them, saying,
      "Take, eat: this is my body which is given for you;
         do this in remembrance of me."
After supper he took the cup.
Again he gave you thanks, and gave it to his disciples, saying,
   "Drink this, all of you: this is my blood of the new covenant,
      which is shed for you and for many for the forgiveness of sins.
   Do this, as often as you drink it, in remembrance of me."

Great is the mystery of faith.
Christ has died; Christ is risen; Christ will come again.

Delivering God, we call on you to fulfill your Advent promise.
May waters break forth in the wilderness, and streams in the desert;
   make a highway on which no traveler, not even fools, shall go astray.
Bring home those who are in exile;
   fill their hearts with singing and shower their heads with everlasting joy.
Unite your church, clothe us with the fruits of your Spirit,
   and fill us with the hope of Advent,
      the substance of things hoped for and the knowledge of things unseen,
         until all bow before your throne and worship in your glory,
            ever one God, Father, Son, and Holy Spirit. **Amen.**

Advent 3, Year B

The Lord be with you. **And also with you.**
Lift up your hearts. **We lift them to the Lord.**
Let us give thanks to the Lord our God. **It is right to give our thanks and praise.**

It is indeed right to give you thanks and praise, Lord God,
  for you have clothed us with the garments of salvation,
    and covered us with the robe of righteousness.
In baptism you forgive our sins,
  part the waters of our liberation,
    and bring us to the safe shore of everlasting life.
In faithfulness you keep our spirit and soul and body
  sound and blameless until the coming of your Son Jesus Christ.
In his death you dismantle the power of death,
  and in his resurrection you raise up the joy of everlasting life.
And so we greatly rejoice and exult with our whole being
  in the sanctified company of angels and archangels of heaven,
    joining the unending hymn.

Holy, holy, holy Lord, God of power and might.
Heaven and earth are full of your glory.
Hosanna in the highest.
Blessed is he who comes in the name of the Lord.
Hosanna in the highest.

Abiding God, you made an everlasting covenant with your people,
  and when that covenant was jeopardized you sent your Son Jesus.
In bread and wine he reenacted your Passover promises,
  and became the Lamb of God that takes away our sin.
Send now your Holy Spirit on us that we may hold fast to what is good
  and live in the freedom of being your children.
Send your Spirit upon this bread and this cup, that they may be for us
  the body and blood of your Son, Jesus Christ our Lord;

who, at supper with his disciples, took bread, gave you thanks,
  broke the bread, and gave it to them, saying,
    "Take, eat: this is my body which is given for you;
      do this in remembrance of me."
After supper he took the cup.
Again he gave you thanks, and gave it to his disciples, saying,
  "Drink this, all of you: this is my blood of the new covenant,
    which is shed for you and for many for the forgiveness of sins.
  Do this, as often as you drink it, in remembrance of me."

Great is the mystery of faith.
Christ has died; Christ is risen; Christ will come again.

God of justice, send your Spirit upon your people in their wilderness.
Bring good news to the oppressed
  and all who live with the chains of debt.
Bind up the brokenhearted and any who languish
  in the slavery of another's scheming or the exile of their own folly.
Proclaim liberty to the captives and those who live under the shadow of fear
  at home, at work, or in their neighborhood.
Announce release to the prisoners and to all who are incarcerated
  by their own body or the travails of their own mind.
Usher in the year of your favor
  and deliver your people from sin and guilt and addiction and shame.
Provide for those who mourn that they may have a garland instead of ashes,
  and the oil of gladness instead of mourning.
Show us your face, everlasting God,
  Father, Son, and Holy Spirit. **Amen.**

Advent 3, Year C

The Lord be with you. **And also with you.**
Lift up your hearts. **We lift them to the Lord.**
Let us give thanks to the Lord our God. **It is right to give our thanks and praise.**

Surely it is you, Lord God, who saves us,
   for you are our stronghold and our sure defense,
     and you shall be our Savior forever.
From bondage and then from exile you brought your people home;
   you gave Zion a song, filled Jerusalem with joy,
     and renewed your children in praise.
When your creation was captive to sin, you sent your Son to restore your people:
   upon the cross he bore the sin of the world,
     and through his resurrection you have become our salvation.
In your love and by your Spirit, you have opened the wells of salvation
   to flow through all the earth with the water of rejoicing.
And so we give you thanks with the saints of every age
   and exalt you in the company of heaven as we join their unending hymn.

Holy, holy, holy Lord, God of power and might.
Heaven and earth are full of your glory.
Hosanna in the highest.
Blessed is he who comes in the name of the Lord.
Hosanna in the highest.

Gathering God, as grain is collected from the fields,
   in your Son you draw us to yourself; and as that grain is drawn together,
     in this holy meal you make us one.
Send your Holy Spirit upon your church
   to make us your harvest of righteousness.
Sanctify this bread and cup that they may be for us
   the body and blood of Christ our Lord;
who, at supper with his disciples, took bread, gave you thanks,

broke the bread, and gave it to them, saying,
  "Take, eat: this is my body which is given for you;
    do this in remembrance of me."
After supper he took the cup.
Again he gave you thanks, and gave it to his disciples, saying,
  "Drink this, all of you: this is my blood of the new covenant,
    which is shed for you and for many for the forgiveness of sins.
  Do this, as often as you drink it, in remembrance of me."

Great is the mystery of faith.
Christ has died; Christ is risen; Christ will come again.

Holy One of Israel, you are the great one in our midst.
Come and dwell among those who long to know you amid toil and strife.
Where your loved ones have been exiled by judgments against them,
  remove every fear from their hearts and give them hope.
Where your sons and daughters face the threat of enemies,
  show them how best to love their persecutors.
Where oppression has turned your children into outcasts,
  gather them in your arms and carry them home.
Bring us to that day when shame turns to praise
  and all creation resounds with rejoicing in your midst,
    Holy One, eternal Trinity, Father, Son, and Holy Spirit. **Amen.**

Advent 4, Year A

The Lord be with you. **And also with you.**
Lift up your hearts. **We lift them to the Lord.**
Let us give thanks to the Lord our God. **It is right to give our thanks and praise.**

Bountiful God, we give our thanks to you,
 for you brought into being your glorious creation
  and crafted human life in your image.
Your prophets promised that a virgin would conceive a son,
 the One in whom your truth would live, God with us.
Through the voice of Mary, your Holy Spirit rejoiced
 in the wonder of the child eternally begotten of the Father.
Through the lips of Joseph
 you spoke the long-awaited name Emmanuel.
A sword pierced their hearts when your Son Jesus
 was crucified at the hands of sinners,
  but in his resurrection you make a new family
   of the redeemed, the restored, and the renewed.
And so with angels and archangels and all the company of earth and heaven,
 we lift our voices in joyful celebration as we join the unending hymn.

Holy, holy, holy Lord, God of power and might.
Heaven and earth are full of your glory.
Hosanna in the highest.
Blessed is he who comes in the name of the Lord.
Hosanna in the highest.

Living God, as your Son was nourished by Mary's body,
 feed and nourish us, your body,
  with this holy meal, your very self,
   that we may grow into fullness of life,
    dwelling in you as your Spirit breathes through us.
Send your Holy Spirit on us now that we may be

your one, holy, catholic, and apostolic body,
  to nourish the life of your world.
Send your Spirit upon this bread and this cup, that they may be for us
  the body and blood of your Son, Jesus Christ our Lord;
who, at supper with his disciples, took bread, gave you thanks,
  broke the bread, and gave it to them, saying,
    "Take, eat: this is my body which is given for you;
      do this in remembrance of me."
After supper he took the cup.
Again he gave you thanks, and gave it to his disciples, saying,
  "Drink this, all of you: this is my blood of the new covenant,
    which is shed for you and for many for the forgiveness of sins.
  Do this, as often as you drink it, in remembrance of me."

Great is the mystery of faith.
Christ has died; Christ is risen; Christ will come again.

Fearless God, who came in a dream to Joseph,
  dream through us anew today.
Speak into our places of fear.
Transcend and transform all that keeps us from living your dream.
Cast out our sin and enter in; be born in us today.
Dream into life in this very place a church renewed
  by the leading of your Spirit.
Dream through our hands and feet your kingdom,
  where the hungry are filled with good things,
    the lowly lifted up, and the oppressed set free,
      until that day when the life of heaven and earth shall be made one,
      and all your children gather in glory around you,
        everlasting God, Father, Son, and Holy Spirit. **Amen.**

Advent 4, Year B

The Lord be with you. **And also with you.**
Lift up your hearts. **We lift them to the Lord.**
Let us give thanks to the Lord our God. **It is right to give our thanks and praise.**

Life-giving and breath-taking God, we delight to give you thanks and praise,
    because nothing is impossible with you.
You were with Abraham in the promise of a people
    and with Jacob in the promise of a land
        and with David in the promise of a house to dwell in.
As Israel had been your place to abide,
    so the blessed Virgin Mary became the temple
        in which the Holy Spirit made your Son Jesus Christ flesh among us.
Just as Elizabeth brought forth the wonders of your mercy,
    so we look to you to bring out of the barrenness of our lives
        the wondrous fruits of your grace.
As our sin took your Son to the cross,
    yet from the tomb you raised him in the glory of resurrection.
And so with Gabriel and all the angels
    and the whole company of earth and heaven,
        we magnify your name.

Holy, holy, holy Lord, God of power and might.
Heaven and earth are full of your glory.
Hosanna in the highest.
Blessed is he who comes in the name of the Lord.
Hosanna in the highest.

Holy God, you dwelt in ark and temple,
    and in the fullness of time you became incarnate
        in the presence of Jesus Christ among us.
In him you promise to come among us whenever two or three are gathered
    and to be made known in the breaking of the bread.

Send down your Holy Spirit that your church may be dependent on you
   like your Son's tiny body in Mary's womb.
Send that same Spirit upon this bread and this cup,
   that they may be for us the body and blood of your Son,
      Jesus Christ our Lord;
who, at supper with his disciples, took bread, gave you thanks,
   broke the bread, and gave it to them, saying,
      "Take, eat: this is my body which is given for you;
         do this in remembrance of me."
After supper he took the cup.
Again he gave you thanks, and gave it to his disciples, saying,
   "Drink this, all of you: this is my blood of the new covenant,
      which is shed for you and for many for the forgiveness of sins.
   Do this, as often as you drink it, in remembrance of me."

Great is the mystery of faith.
Christ has died; Christ is risen; Christ will come again.

Glorious God, look with favor on the lowliness of your servants;
   show mercy on those who fear you.
Where your children have grown proud,
   scatter them in the imagination of their hearts;
      where your people are hungry, fill them with good things.
Where the powerful are bent on oppression,
   bring them down from their thrones;
      where the rich have no mercy, send them empty away.
For in Christ, you, the mighty, came down from your seat
   and became humble, that in him the meek might inherit the earth.
Reshape your people in the image of Mary,
   that we may bring forth the fruit of the Spirit in love and joy and peace,
      until that day when sorrow and tears are no more,
         and you are all in all, ever one God, Father, Son, and Holy Spirit. **Amen.**

Advent 4, Year C

The Lord be with you. **And also with you.**
Lift up your hearts. **We lift them to the Lord.**
Let us give thanks to the Lord our God. **It is right to give our thanks and praise.**

It is a good and joyful thing to give our thanks to you, Lord God of hosts,
    O ancient of days, for from of old you have called forth life.
You brought into being every detail of creation
    and gave birth to your covenant people.
When the time drew near,
    you called upon Bethlehem to bear the hope you promised,
        and summoned Mary to bear your holy child.
By your grace the child grew to be the one to bear
    not only our sins but the sins of the world.
In his dying and rising you gave birth to everlasting life for all your children.
And so with your people on earth and all the company of heaven
    we sing your praise and join the unending hymn.

Holy, holy, holy Lord, God of power and might.
Heaven and earth are full of your glory.
Hosanna in the highest.
Blessed is he who comes in the name of the Lord.
Hosanna in the highest.

God of Mary, whose womb bore the sacred fruit of our salvation,
    bring forth from this fruit of the vine your cup of blessing.
As we remember around this table your Son's saving passion poured out for us,
    send your Holy Spirit upon your church
        to make us bearers of your Christ, your mercy, and your hope.
Sanctify this bread and cup that they may be for us
    the body and blood of Jesus our Lord;
who, at supper with his disciples, took bread, gave you thanks,
    broke the bread, and gave it to them, saying,

"Take, eat: this is my body which is given for you;
   do this in remembrance of me."
After supper he took the cup.
Again he gave you thanks, and gave it to his disciples, saying,
   "Drink this, all of you: this is my blood of the new covenant,
      which is shed for you and for many for the forgiveness of sins.
   Do this, as often as you drink it, in remembrance of me."

Great is the mystery of faith.
Christ has died; Christ is risen; Christ will come again.

God of holy expectation, let your face shine upon us
   and your dawn break upon us that we may be saved.
Make your church expectant in faith as we labor for what we cannot yet see.
Come and dwell with your people
   who yearn to be restored, to be forgiven, to belong.
Let the warmth of your face shine upon those who seek the peace long promised
   for Bethlehem, for Jerusalem, and for all your waiting world.
Bring us, with the saints who have looked for your coming,
   to the day when we and all your children shall celebrate and leap for joy
      in your holy presence, one God, Father, Son, and Holy Spirit. **Amen.**

2. Christmas

Christmas Eve

The Lord be with you. **And also with you.**
Lift up your hearts. **We lift them to the Lord.**
Let us give thanks to the Lord our God. **It is right to give our thanks and praise.**

Almighty God, you shape your very life
   to create and restore and enjoy us forever.
We gather around your altar like those who thronged your Son's manger,
   longing for you to reassemble men and women,
      kings and working people, Jews and Gentiles, heaven and earth
         at the place where our humanity and your divinity meet.
You had too much love to keep it to yourself;
   and though we took up arms against you and one another,
      you disarmed us in coming into our midst as a defenseless baby.
As his arms were tied in swaddling clothes,
   so later his hands were nailed to the cross;
      yet you made his birth the foretaste of our redemption
         and his death the gateway to resurrection life.
You give us such joy and peace in your company
   that our hearts join the angels in the Christmas sky
      and around your eternal throne,
         singing the hymn of your unending praise.

Holy, holy, holy Lord, God of power and might.
Heaven and earth are full of your glory.
Hosanna in the highest.
Blessed is he who comes in the name of the Lord.
Hosanna in the highest.

God of new birth, as you laid your Son in Mary's arms,
  you place these gifts of bread and wine in our hands.
Sanctify your church to be as fragile and tender and true
   as the infant Savior.

Send down your Holy Spirit,
that this bread of wheat gathered from the fields
and this cup of grapes gathered from the vineyards
may be for us the body and blood of your Son Jesus Christ;
who, at supper with his disciples, took bread, gave you thanks,
broke the bread, and gave it to them, saying,
"Take, eat: this is my body which is given for you;
do this in remembrance of me."
After supper he took the cup.
Again he gave you thanks, and gave it to his disciples, saying,
"Drink this, all of you: this is my blood of the new covenant,
which is shed for you and for many for the forgiveness of sins.
Do this, as often as you drink it, in remembrance of me."

Great is the mystery of faith.
Christ has died; Christ is risen; Christ will come again.

God who exalts the humble and humbles the exalted,
as you drew the magi to the place of your epiphany,
call us to yourself, and bring your creation to its consummation.
Lift your whole church, living and departed, to the vision of your glory,
once made flesh in a humble family,
now exalted and reigning with justice and mercy.
In this banquet restore us in your image,
surround us with your company,
and prepare us for your freedom, after the pattern of your Son,
through whom and with whom and in whom,
in the unity of the Holy Spirit, all honor and glory are yours,
now and forever. **Amen.**

Christmas Day

The Lord be with you. **And also with you.**
Lift up your hearts. **We lift them to the Lord.**
Let us give thanks to the Lord our God. **It is right to give our thanks and praise.**

Holy are you, embracing God,
   for through your Word all things came into being,
     and without you not one thing was made.
As your Word spoke through your covenant,
   you created a people bound to you.
Through promise and pardon, slavery and exile,
   you showed that what had come into being through you was life.
Your prophets promised that life as a light for all people,
   and spoke of a day of comfort and redemption
     when ruins and waste places would break forth into song.
When that day came, and the Word became flesh,
   your angels sang for joy and put a new song into our hearts.
And even when we rejected your Son,
   you brought forth from his death a resurrection of everlasting glory.
You welcome us as your forgiven people, uniting heaven and earth
   and joining our voices with angels and archangels,
     in the unending hymn.

Holy, holy, holy Lord, God of power and might.
Heaven and earth are full of your glory.
Hosanna in the highest.
Blessed is he who comes in the name of the Lord.
Hosanna in the highest.

Life-giving God, as your Word became flesh and lived among us,
   come among us now in the fullness of your grace and truth.
Make us holy as you are holy, that your Word may become flesh anew today.
Send your Holy Spirit upon this bread and wine

and make them be for us the body and blood of Jesus;
who, at supper with his disciples, took bread, gave you thanks,
   broke the bread, and gave it to them, saying,
      "Take, eat: this is my body which is given for you;
         do this in remembrance of me."
After supper he took the cup.
Again he gave you thanks, and gave it to his disciples, saying,
   "Drink this, all of you: this is my blood of the new covenant,
      which is shed for you and for many for the forgiveness of sins.
   Do this, as often as you drink it, in remembrance of me."

Great is the mystery of faith.
Christ has died; Christ is risen; Christ will come again.

God of glory, make your church a sign of new-born hope in your kingdom.
Be born in us today.
Where your children are faced with ruin, show them redemption.
Where sorrow endures, bring your holy comfort.
Where division excludes, give your grace.
Where bondage confines, sing your new song.
Restore our hope in you, until the day
   when all that you have brought into being finds its everlasting destiny
      in the glory of your only Son,
         when nothing in heaven or on earth falls outside your redeeming purpose,
            and when all things shall be full of grace and truth in you,
               one God, Father, Son, and Holy Spirit. **Amen.**

Christmas 1, Year A

The Lord be with you. **And also with you.**
Lift up your hearts. **We lift them to the Lord.**
Let us give thanks to the Lord our God. **It is right to give our thanks and praise.**

Steadfast God, you alone are worthy of praise and thanksgiving.
You created all there is
   and welcomed us to share in every detail with you;
      your persevering hold on all you have created never relents.
Through Rachel and Joseph you shaped your people
   to be a blessing to the nations,
      in times of joy but also in sorrow and suffering.
When the torment of slavery seemed unbreakable,
   your imagination unlocked unyielding shackles.
When exile seemed endless, your mercies never failed.
And when your Son came to be born in the midst of all you created,
   you did not spare him human sorrow and suffering, even the cross.
He knew exile while still an infant.
As he and his parents escaped to safety
   when so many other children went to death,
      years later in Jerusalem he went to death
         that all your children might live with you in resurrection glory.
And so we give you thanks, praising you with angels and archangels,
   as we join their unending hymn.

Holy, holy, holy Lord, God of power and might.
Heaven and earth are full of your glory.
Hosanna in the highest.
Blessed is he who comes in the name of the Lord.
Hosanna in the highest.

God of mercy, the Lamb who takes away the sins of the world,
   pour your grace upon us through your very lifeblood in this holy meal.

Send your Holy Spirit upon us to make us merciful as you are merciful.
By the blood of the Lamb, sign our names in your book of life.
Send your Holy Spirit upon this breaking bread and this sharing cup
   that they may be for us the body and the blood of Christ;
who, at supper with his disciples, took bread, gave you thanks,
   broke the bread, and gave it to them, saying,
     "Take, eat: this is my body which is given for you;
       do this in remembrance of me."
After supper he took the cup.
Again he gave you thanks, and gave it to his disciples, saying,
   "Drink this, all of you: this is my blood of the new covenant,
     which is shed for you and for many for the forgiveness of sins.
   Do this, as often as you drink it, in remembrance of me."

Great is the mystery of faith.
Christ has died; Christ is risen; Christ will come again.

God of all consolation, pierce the heart of your church
   with the same cries that pierce your heart.
Where suppressed years of history have left blood crying from the ground,
   make us people who seek the truth.
Where the innocent die as bystanders, make us people who remember.
Where families fleeing for safety seek refuge in unfamiliar lands,
   make us people of welcome.
Where parents weep over the death of a child,
   make us people of tenacious love.
Meet our tears with your holy comfort
   and turn our sorrow into wisdom for others to share,
     until that day when we gather around the throne of the Lamb
       in endless praise to you, living God, Father, Son, and Holy Spirit. **Amen.**

Christmas 1, Year B

The Lord be with you. **And also with you.**
Lift up your hearts. **We lift them to the Lord.**
Let us give thanks to the Lord our God. **It is right to give our thanks and praise.**

We lift our hearts to give you thanks and praise, Lord God,
   because you made your whole creation a temple of your glory
      and invited us into it to enjoy you forever.
When you called Israel out of Egypt, you made yourself known
   through your covenant in a tabernacle of your presence.
In Solomon you allowed your people to meet you
   in a temple built by human hands.
Finally, in Simeon you showed us what it means to wait faithfully
   to see your salvation in your incarnate Son,
     in whom your own heart was pierced
       that we might be made one with you.
In your Son's death the temple of his body was destroyed,
   but in three days you raised him
     to be the place of our dwelling with you forever.
And so with angels and archangels and the whole host of heaven,
   we join in the eternal song of your glory.

Holy, holy, holy Lord, God of power and might.
Heaven and earth are full of your glory.
Hosanna in the highest.
Blessed is he who comes in the name of the Lord.
Hosanna in the highest.

God of peace and light,
   you have prepared a table before us in the presence of all peoples,
     and you have made it a gift of revelation and glory.
Your servant Anna waited for you with fasting and prayer night and day.
Visit your people that the secrets of our hearts may be laid bare

and the secret of your heart be revealed;
   and make your people holy as you are holy.
Send your Holy Spirit on this bread and this wine,
   that they may be for us the body and blood of our Lord Jesus Christ;
who, at supper with his disciples, took bread, gave you thanks,
   broke the bread, and gave it to them, saying,
      "Take, eat: this is my body which is given for you;
         do this in remembrance of me."
After supper he took the cup.
Again he gave you thanks, and gave it to his disciples, saying,
   "Drink this, all of you: this is my blood of the new covenant,
      which is shed for you and for many for the forgiveness of sins.
   Do this, as often as you drink it, in remembrance of me."

Great is the mystery of faith.
Christ has died; Christ is risen; Christ will come again.

Consoling God, as Mary and Joseph offered a sacrifice in your temple,
   bring comfort to all who feel today like they are being sacrificed
      by the cruel, the merciless, or the fanatical.
As Simeon foresaw that your Son would be a sign that would be opposed,
   bless any who face hostility, anger, and violence.
As the holy family realized that a sword would pierce their own soul,
   speak tenderly to those whose soul knows despair, loss, or betrayal.
Make your church strong, fill your children with wisdom,
   and set your favor upon all who turn to you;
      until that day when heaven and earth become a temple of your praise
         and your resurrection engulfs all you have made,
            ever one God, Father, Son, and Holy Spirit. **Amen.**

Christmas 1, Year C

The Lord be with you. **And also with you.**
Lift up your hearts. **We lift them to the Lord.**
Let us give thanks to the Lord our God. **It is right to give our thanks and praise.**

God of grace and truth, we lift our hearts to you in thanks and praise,
   because before all things began you shaped your life to be with us in Christ.
In the sacred temple of Jerusalem you gave your people
   a way to be close to you, and an invitation
     to be restored in relationship with one another and with you.
In Jesus you came into that temple and became the very place of encounter
   between yourself and your people.
When his parents did not know how to find their son and yours,
   they discovered his purpose was to be the person and place
     through whom all people would find their destiny in you.
In Christ's death and resurrection you show us
   the cost of our being utterly lost
     and the glory of your finding us and bringing us home forever.
And so with glad and joyful hearts we join the company of heaven
   in the song of your never-ending glory.

Holy, holy, holy Lord, God of power and might.
Heaven and earth are full of your glory.
Hosanna in the highest.
Blessed is he who comes in the name of the Lord.
Hosanna in the highest.

Generous God, your Son Jesus Christ became the sacrifice
   that restored our covenant with you,
     and his resurrection unveiled for us the wonder of everlasting life.
Send down your Holy Spirit upon those who gather in your name.
Let your Son's peace rule in our hearts
   and his word and wisdom dwell in us richly.

Sanctify this bread and cup that they may be for us
   the body and blood of your Son;
who, at supper with his disciples, took bread, gave you thanks,
   broke the bread, and gave it to them, saying,
      "Take, eat: this is my body which is given for you;
         do this in remembrance of me."
After supper he took the cup.
Again he gave you thanks, and gave it to his disciples, saying,
   "Drink this, all of you: this is my blood of the new covenant,
      which is shed for you and for many for the forgiveness of sins.
   Do this, as often as you drink it, in remembrance of me."

Great is the mystery of faith.
Christ has died; Christ is risen; Christ will come again.

Astonishing God, your servant Mary
   treasured your wondrous deeds in her heart.
Be close to any who wander in search of a loved one,
   a purpose in life, or a place to call home.
Surround your faithful with good teachers
   and give your church good questions to ask.
Walk with those for whom resentment or regret about the past
   inhibits flourishing life in the present:
      by the power of your Spirit, let your truth set us free.
Open our eyes to the joy of your love and the wisdom of your grace
   in the eyes of a child,
      until together with all your sons and daughters in your eternal kingdom
         we behold you face to face, one God, Father, Son, and Holy Spirit. **Amen.**

3. Epiphany

The Epiphany

The Lord be with you. **And also with you.**
Lift up your hearts. **We lift them to the Lord.**
Let us give thanks to the Lord our God. **It is right to give our thanks and praise.**

Revealing God, you send the light of a star,
  and in that light we see
    the truth of who you are and the truth of who we are.
Like the magi you call us to worship you,
  but like the magi we mistake
    where you truly belong and where we truly belong.
Yet in revelation you direct us to yourself
  and in incarnation you meet us in yourself.
You become what we are that we might become what you are.
And so you draw us to the company where your angels gather
  around your eternal throne, singing their hymn of unending praise.

Holy, holy, holy Lord, God of power and might.
Heaven and earth are full of your glory.
Hosanna in the highest.
Blessed is he who comes in the name of the Lord.
Hosanna in the highest.

God of wonder, as the magi brought gifts of gold, frankincense, and myrrh,
  so we bring these gifts of bread and wine.
In those gifts we see your grief at the way
  we crucified your Son, the holy one among us,
    but also the wonder of how you raised him to be our king in glory forever.
Send down your Holy Spirit, that we may discover
  what it means to be of you and in you,
    and that this bread of honest toil and this wine of joyous celebration
      may be for us the body and blood of your Son Jesus Christ;
who, at supper with his disciples, took bread, gave you thanks,

broke the bread, and gave it to them, saying,
   "Take, eat: this is my body which is given for you;
      do this in remembrance of me."
After supper he took the cup.
Again he gave you thanks, and gave it to his disciples, saying,
   "Drink this, all of you: this is my blood of the new covenant,
      which is shed for you and for many for the forgiveness of sins.
   Do this, as often as you drink it, in remembrance of me."

Great is the mystery of faith.
Christ has died; Christ is risen; Christ will come again.

God of wisdom, as the magi brought gold,
   bring your whole church, living and departed, to the vision of your glory.
As the magi brought frankincense,
   infuse all who seek you with the beauty of your holiness.
As the magi brought myrrh, embrace all who suffer
   until the time comes when you flood the whole creation
      with justice and mercy.
In this banquet restore us in your image,
   surround us with your company,
      and prepare us for your freedom;
         that we may come to resemble your Son,
            through whom, and with whom, and in whom,
               in the unity of the Holy Spirit,
                  all honor and glory are yours, now and forever. **Amen.**

Baptism of the Lord

The Lord be with you. **And also with you.**
Lift up your hearts. **We lift them to the Lord.**
Let us give thanks to the Lord our God. **It is right to give our thanks and praise.**

God of hope, in your Holy Spirit
　you hovered over the face of the waters in creation,
　　and in your pillar of fire you led your people to liberation across the Red Sea.
Through the waters you brought your people
　into the life and land of promise.
In your Son's baptism at the Jordan
　we see your creative and liberating purpose at work
　　amid our human flaws and failures,
　　　and we hear anew with hope the promise of your voice.
In our own baptism you number us among your saints,
　created and redeemed for your glory.
Through baptism you bury us in death with Christ
　yet raise us to new life with him forever.
And so we gladly thank you, with saints and angels and archangels,
　and all the company of heaven, singing the hymn of your unending praise.

Holy, holy, holy Lord, God of power and might.
Heaven and earth are full of your glory.
Hosanna in the highest.
Blessed is he who comes in the name of the Lord.
Hosanna in the highest.

Blessing God, who sent down your Holy Spirit like a dove upon your Beloved,
　send your Spirit among us now to sanctify us by your grace.
By the power of that same Spirit, make these gifts of bread and wine be for us
　the body and blood of your Son Jesus Christ;
who, at supper with his disciples, took bread, gave you thanks,
　broke the bread, and gave it to them, saying,

"Take, eat: this is my body which is given for you;
   do this in remembrance of me."
After supper he took the cup.
Again he gave you thanks, and gave it to his disciples, saying,
   "Drink this, all of you: this is my blood of the new covenant,
      which is shed for you and for many for the forgiveness of sins.
   Do this, as often as you drink it, in remembrance of me."

Great is the mystery of faith.
Christ has died; Christ is risen; Christ will come again.

Father of glory, you have opened your heaven and come among us.
Be close to those who ache for your liberating power in the midst of travails
   and seek your open heaven.
Visit all who need the healing, forgiving, peacemaking, and restoring touch
   of your Spirit and look for your kingdom to come.
Bless all who long to be called beloved,
   by sibling or parent or spouse or friend or child,
      and any who are searching for the love that only you can bring,
         until all stand in your presence, and sing your name,
            and are enfolded in your embrace,
               Father, Son, and Holy Spirit, ever one God. **Amen.**

Epiphany 2, Year A

The Lord be with you. **And also with you.**
Lift up your hearts. **We lift them to the Lord.**
Let us give thanks to the Lord our God. **It is right to give our thanks and praise.**

Blessed are you, Holy One on high,
　　for you have made all things in your sacred womb,
　　　　and you have named and called forth all things
　　　　　　according to your eternal purpose.
Praise upon praise is yours, for you created such goodness,
　　and it was too light a thing that you should stop there,
　　　　so you shaped your life through making a covenant with your people.
When that covenant foundered, it was too light a thing
　　for you to raise up only the tribes of Jacob
　　　　and restore only the survivors of your chosen people,
　　　　and so you gave your Son to be a light to all nations.
As your Son lived our life and died our death, you showed
　　it was too light a thing that your glory should be kept in heaven,
　　　　and so in Jesus' resurrection and ascension
　　　　　　you made your glory known to the ends of the earth.
And so with angels and archangels and the resounding company of saints
　　we join in the unending hymn.

Holy, holy, holy Lord, God of power and might.
Heaven and earth are full of your glory.
Hosanna in the highest.
Blessed is he who comes in the name of the Lord.
Hosanna in the highest.

Summoning God, you beckoned the first disciples
　　to come and see your anointed Son,
　　　　and through him you anointed each new follower with purpose and power.
Bless us as we come to be with you at this feast today.

Send your Holy Spirit and anoint us to be the body of our living Lord,
   beckoning others to come and see the wonders of your love.
Send down your Spirit upon this breaking bread and this sharing cup
   that they may be for us the body and blood of your Son Jesus Christ;
who, at supper with his disciples, took bread, gave you thanks,
   broke the bread, and gave it to them, saying,
      "Take, eat: this is my body which is given for you;
         do this in remembrance of me."
After supper he took the cup.
Again he gave you thanks, and gave it to his disciples, saying,
   "Drink this, all of you: this is my blood of the new covenant,
      which is shed for you and for many for the forgiveness of sins.
   Do this, as often as you drink it, in remembrance of me."

Great is the mystery of faith.
Christ has died; Christ is risen; Christ will come again.

Inviting God, who calls all creation to one perfect end,
   give your people grace to receive
      the invitation you offer each of us this very day.
When you ask us to take holy risks, deepen our faith.
When you call us to be faithful in small things, give us perseverance.
When you invite us to do beautiful things in the life of your kingdom,
   inspire our imagination.
When you call us to forgiveness, lead us by the way of the cross,
   until you bring every good work you have begun to its completion
      and you gather heaven and earth
         into a kingdom that shall have no end;
            where you reign for evermore as one God,
               Father, Son, and Holy Spirit, now and forever. **Amen.**

Epiphany 2, Year B

The Lord be with you. **And also with you.**
Lift up your hearts. **We lift them to the Lord.**
Let us give thanks to the Lord our God. **It is right to give our thanks and praise.**

Summoning God, we thank and praise you
  because over and over again you call your people
    to hear your voice and entrust our lives to you.
You make a temple of encounter in our bodies
  and a tent of meeting in the body of your Son.
You sing to us through the Law and the Prophets,
  and when we close our ears, you speak through a little child.
Should we find the voice or the timing or the place of your vocation
  too strange to understand, you bid us simply to come and see.
And so with heaven open and angels and archangels
  ascending and descending around your throne,
    we join the song of your eternal glory.

Holy, holy, holy Lord, God of power and might.
Heaven and earth are full of your glory.
Hosanna in the highest.
Blessed is he who comes in the name of the Lord.
Hosanna in the highest.

Holy God, in baptism you have made our bodies parts of your Son's body.
In his death we have died with him, and in his resurrection
  you have given us the freedom of the glory of your children.
Take the brokenness of our flesh,
  and through the power of your Spirit
    make your church a temple of your living presence
      and a crucible of encounter and reconciliation with you.
Send your Holy Spirit upon this bread and wine that they may be for us
  the body and blood of your Son Jesus Christ;

who, at supper with his disciples, took bread, gave you thanks,
   broke the bread, and gave it to them, saying,
      "Take, eat: this is my body which is given for you;
         do this in remembrance of me."
After supper he took the cup.
Again he gave you thanks, and gave it to his disciples, saying,
   "Drink this, all of you: this is my blood of the new covenant,
      which is shed for you and for many for the forgiveness of sins.
   Do this, as often as you drink it, in remembrance of me."

Great is the mystery of faith.
Christ has died; Christ is risen; Christ will come again.

Merciful God, in Christ you call us
   from our places of belonging and safety
      to the adventure of your kingdom and the wonder of your mission.
Bless all who today have nowhere to lay their head,
   no community in which to belong,
      no good work through which to serve,
         and no future for which to hope.
In the power of your Spirit,
   Andrew found Simon and Philip found Nathanael:
      send companions to any who experience life
         as isolation, defeat, or disgrace.
Make your church a sheepfold where
   the bewildered may enter a home,
      the abandoned may discover a welcome,
         the tired may find rest, and the imprisoned may be set free,
            until the last traces of discord disappear from your creation
               and you are all in all, one God, Father, Son, and Holy Spirit. **Amen.**

Epiphany 2, Year C

The Lord be with you. **And also with you.**
Lift up your hearts. **We lift them to the Lord.**
Let us give thanks to the Lord our God. **It is right to give our thanks and praise.**

Redeeming God, we cannot keep silent,
   because your vindication of your people shines out like the dawn,
     and your salvation like a burning torch.
You renew the nature of creation by the grace of your saving power.
Though your children wander far from your ways,
   you call us a crown of beauty and a royal diadem in your hand.
In the death of your Son we showed you the depth of our estrangement;
   but in his resurrection and ascension and the coming of your Spirit
     you showed us the height and breadth of your love.
And so we thank and praise you with the company of heaven,
   singing the hymn of your boundless glory.

Holy, holy, holy Lord, God of power and might.
Heaven and earth are full of your glory.
Hosanna in the highest.
Blessed is he who comes in the name of the Lord.
Hosanna in the highest.

Gracious God, in your Holy Spirit you empower us
   with gifts of wisdom and knowledge and faith and healing
     and miracles and prophecy and revelation and discernment.
Send that Spirit upon us now,
   that your world may see your divinity through our humanity.
Sanctify this bread of humility and wine of joy
   that they may be for us the body and blood of your Son Jesus Christ;
who, at supper with his disciples, took bread, gave you thanks,
   broke the bread, and gave it to them, saying,
     "Take, eat: this is my body which is given for you;

do this in remembrance of me."
After supper he took the cup.
Again he gave you thanks, and gave it to his disciples, saying,
  "Drink this, all of you: this is my blood of the new covenant,
    which is shed for you and for many for the forgiveness of sins.
  Do this, as often as you drink it, in remembrance of me."

Great is the mystery of faith.
Christ has died; Christ is risen; Christ will come again.

God of justice and mercy, as at Cana the wine was good,
  bless your whole creation.
As at Cana the wine ran short,
  be close to all who know their need of you.
As at Cana the wine ran out,
  succor those living in the midst of death,
    and dying in the midst of life.
As at Cana you saved the best till last,
  flood this earth with the wine of your kingdom,
    that justice may roll down like a river,
      and righteousness like a never-failing stream,
        until we see you face to face, and recognize our diverse faces
          in the face of your Son, through whom, and with whom,
            and in whom, in the unity of the Holy Spirit,
              all honor and glory are yours, now and forever. **Amen.**

Epiphany 3, Year A

The Lord be with you. **And also with you.**
Lift up your hearts. **We lift them to the Lord.**
Let us give thanks to the Lord our God. **It is right to give our thanks and praise.**

Worthy of praise and thanksgiving are you, Lord God,
   for you summoned all things into being,
      and from the beginning you beckoned your creation
         to fullness of life in you.
Through covenant you claimed a people to share your life;
   in slavery you called them to freedom;
      in exile you summoned them to faithfulness;
         in their sin you beckoned them toward your light.
From the first day until now
   you have called creation to share your goodness.
In Christ you came seeking our salvation with your very life,
   bidding us to come and follow.
Our rejection of him led to the horror of the cross,
   but you have drawn us to yourself forever
      through the glory of his resurrection.
And so with your people on earth and with the company of heaven,
   we join the unending hymn.

Holy, holy, holy Lord, God of power and might.
Heaven and earth are full of your glory.
Hosanna in the highest.
Blessed is he who comes in the name of the Lord.
Hosanna in the highest.

Sustaining God, in you many become one.
You gathered fishermen from their nets to become apostles;
   just so you take grain from the fields and grapes from the vine
      to make this holy meal.

And now you gather us around this table
   to remember the story of our redemption.
Make us one body.
Sustain us by the grace of the one bread we share
   and one cup of blessing which we bless.
Send your Spirit upon this bread and wine that it may be for us
   the body and blood of Christ;
who, at supper with his disciples, took bread, gave you thanks,
   broke the bread, and gave it to them, saying,
      "Take, eat: this is my body which is given for you;
         do this in remembrance of me."
After supper he took the cup.
Again he gave you thanks, and gave it to his disciples, saying,
      "Drink this, all of you: this is my blood of the new covenant,
         which is shed for you and for many for the forgiveness of sins.
      Do this, as often as you drink it, in remembrance of me."

Great is the mystery of faith.
Christ has died; Christ is risen; Christ will come again.

Generous God, in Christ you threw wide the net of your grace,
   calling disciples one by one to be your followers;
      not in their own righteousness,
         but because you would have us be your companions
            and share your glory forever.
Reveal in your church the wideness of your mercy.
Bless those today who wonder if they have strayed too far
   to be found by you or to belong among your people.
Inspire all who struggle to know their purpose in your kingdom
   and long to hear your voice.
Beckon your disciples to come and follow, to work alongside you,
   casting the net of grace, until all are gathered in and one in you,
      ever-seeking and ever-saving God,
         Father, Son, and Holy Spirit, now and forever. **Amen.**

Epiphany 3, Year B

The Lord be with you. **And also with you.**
Lift up your hearts. **We lift them to the Lord.**
Let us give thanks to the Lord our God. **It is right to give our thanks and praise.**

It is with joy that we give you thanks and praise, summoning Lord,
    for you called creation into being; you invited a people to be your own;
        and in your prophets you called your children time after time
            to return to your ways and live.
In Jesus you embodied your call to the whole world to worship you,
    to be your friends, and to eat at this table with you.
Through the Spirit you continue to beckon us
    to become members of your body and channels of your grace.
Even when our sin put your Son on the cross,
    your mercy turned death into resurrection and shame into glory.
And so we enjoy you now and forever,
    with saints and angels and archangels,
        and all the company of heaven, singing the hymn of your unending praise.

Holy, holy, holy Lord, God of power and might.
Heaven and earth are full of your glory.
Hosanna in the highest.
Blessed is he who comes in the name of the Lord.
Hosanna in the highest.

Restoring God, at your Son's birth you called together
    heaven and earth, rich and poor, humans and animals;
    among your Son's disciples you called together
        fishermen, tax collectors, and zealots;
    in his ministry you summoned
        soldiers and widows, criminals and Samaritans;
    at this table now you draw together
        the food of daily endeavor and the cup of celebration.

Send your Holy Spirit among us
  to make us your diverse but holy people.
By the power of your Spirit, make these gifts of bread and wine
  be for us the body and blood of your Son Jesus Christ;
who, at supper with his disciples, took bread, gave you thanks,
  broke the bread, and gave it to them, saying,
    "Take, eat: this is my body which is given for you;
      do this in remembrance of me."
After supper he took the cup.
Again he gave you thanks, and gave it to his disciples, saying,
  "Drink this, all of you: this is my blood of the new covenant,
    which is shed for you and for many for the forgiveness of sins.
    Do this, as often as you drink it, in remembrance of me."

Great is the mystery of faith.
Christ has died; Christ is risen; Christ will come again.

Calling God, you find us where we are
  and summon us to follow you.
As you sent your disciples to fish in the waters of the world,
  renew your people in their vocations and ministries;
    sanctify your children to share your good news
      and discover your kingdom near and far;
        mend the nets of those who labor long and in vain,
          that all who look to you in faith may find from you
            fitting work to do:
              until that day when you gather your whole creation
                into one great net of grace,
                  and shower your universe with the wonder of your glory,
                    ever one God, Father, Son, and Holy Spirit. **Amen.**

Epiphany 3, Year C

The Lord be with you. **And also with you.**
Lift up your hearts. **We lift them to the Lord.**
Let us give thanks to the Lord our God. **It is right to give our thanks and praise.**

To worship you, Lord God, is our joy and our strength.
As the heavens tell your glory and the firmament proclaims your handiwork,
   we open our hearts in thanksgiving to pour forth your praise.
Your prophets foretold a day when your Anointed One would bring
   good news to the poor, release to the captives,
     and recovery of sight to the blind.
In Christ you proclaimed the year of your favor
   and fulfilled the promise of your glory.
In his death he faced your world's impulse to remain in the prison of sin,
   but by raising him from death
     you opened the gates of life eternal and set us free.
And so with the saints in heaven above and on earth below,
   we praise your name and join their unending hymn.

Holy, holy, holy Lord, God of power and might.
Heaven and earth are full of your glory.
Hosanna in the highest.
Blessed is he who comes in the name of the Lord.
Hosanna in the highest.

Baptizing God, as you created the body with many members,
   each in need of one another, and from many members make us one,
     transform us around this table to realize our common need for one another.
Sanctify us as we drink of the one Spirit to make us one in you.
Send your Holy Spirit upon this bread and cup that they may be for us
   the body and blood of your Son;
who, at supper with his disciples, took bread, gave you thanks,
   broke the bread, and gave it to them, saying,

"Take, eat: this is my body which is given for you;
   do this in remembrance of me."
After supper he took the cup.
Again he gave you thanks, and gave it to his disciples, saying,
  "Drink this, all of you: this is my blood of the new covenant,
     which is shed for you and for many for the forgiveness of sins.
  Do this, as often as you drink it, in remembrance of me."

Great is the mystery of faith.
Christ has died; Christ is risen; Christ will come again.

Wondrous God,
  whose ways are more to be desired than gold, even much fine gold,
     hasten the day when those ways shall be known in all the earth.
Fix your promise in the hearts of your children who suffer,
  that as members of your body they may never suffer alone.
Let loose your praise from the lips of those who rejoice,
  that in your body they may never rejoice alone.
Make the simplest among us the wisest in you.
Revive the souls that wait on you
  and restore the hearts that rest in you, until eternity dawns
     and the voice of thanksgiving is heard through all the earth,
        giving glory to you, our living God, Father, Son, and Holy Spirit. **Amen.**

Epiphany 4, Year A

The Lord be with you. **And also with you.**
Lift up your hearts. **We lift them to the Lord.**
Let us give thanks to the Lord our God. **It is right to give our thanks and praise.**

Blessed are you, Lord God, for you have been everything you call us to be.
You have been pure in heart,
   for you called Israel to be your people in whom all would find a blessing.
You have been merciful,
   for in your tender mercy you made the dawn from on high
     to break upon your people,
       to guide us in the ways of peace.
You have been a peacemaker,
   for in Jesus you broke down the dividing wall of hostility.
And so we gladly thank you, with angels and archangels
   and all the company of heaven, singing the hymn of your unending praise.

Holy, holy, holy Lord, God of power and might.
Heaven and earth are full of your glory.
Hosanna in the highest.
Blessed is he who comes in the name of the Lord.
Hosanna in the highest.

God our companion, in Jesus you comfort those who mourn
   and replenish those who hunger and thirst.
Fill your people now, by the power of your Holy Spirit,
   that your children may be sanctified by your grace,
     and these gifts of bread and wine may be for us
       the body and blood of your Son Jesus Christ;
who, at supper with his disciples, took bread, gave you thanks,
   broke the bread, and gave it to them, saying,
     "Take, eat: this is my body which is given for you;
       do this in remembrance of me."

After supper he took the cup.
Again he gave you thanks, and gave it to his disciples, saying,
  "Drink this, all of you: this is my blood of the new covenant,
    which is shed for you and for many for the forgiveness of sins.
  Do this, as often as you drink it, in remembrance of me."

Great is the mystery of faith.
Christ has died; Christ is risen; Christ will come again.

God of glory, you promise that the meek will inherit the earth,
  and that to the poor in spirit belongs the kingdom of heaven.
Visit now those who are persecuted for your righteousness
  and reviled on account of your name.
Shape your church to reflect the image of those you call blessed,
  and lead all whom you call blessed to find a home in your church,
    that the church may be full of your prophets,
      and your prophets may be full of your grace,
        until all tongues cease and tears are shed no more,
          in the presence and communion of your Holy Trinity,
          Father, Son, and Holy Spirit, ever one God. **Amen.**

Epiphany 4, Year B

The Lord be with you. **And also with you.**
Lift up your hearts. **We lift them to the Lord.**
Let us give thanks to the Lord our God. **It is right to give our thanks and praise.**

God of glory and truth, we praise your holy name with thanksgiving,
    because you sent prophets to inscribe the story of creation,
        to recall the shaping of your covenant with Israel,
            and to hold your people to account for their life in you.
Those same prophets told of a day
    when you would restore your covenant
        and open wide your arms to bring your people home to you.
In Jesus we see those promises fulfilled.
In his death and resurrection we know our sins are forgiven
    and receive the promise of everlasting life with you.
And so with angels and archangels, and the company of heaven,
    we join the everlasting hymn to your praise.

Holy, holy, holy Lord, God of power and might.
Heaven and earth are full of your glory.
Hosanna in the highest.
Blessed is he who comes in the name of the Lord.
Hosanna in the highest.

Gracious God, your Son Jesus ate with friend and stranger,
    with devoted disciple and skeptical scrutinizer,
        with the one who would betray and the one who had denied.
He made food a place of encounter with you.
By the power of your Holy Spirit visit your people
    and sanctify us in the image of your crucified Son.
Through the same Spirit, make these gifts of bread and wine be for us
    the body and blood of your Son Jesus Christ;
who, at supper with his disciples, took bread, gave you thanks,

broke the bread, and gave it to them, saying,
> "Take, eat: this is my body which is given for you;
>> do this in remembrance of me."

After supper he took the cup.
Again he gave you thanks, and gave it to his disciples, saying,
> "Drink this, all of you: this is my blood of the new covenant,
>> which is shed for you and for many for the forgiveness of sins.
> Do this, as often as you drink it, in remembrance of me."

Great is the mystery of faith.
Christ has died; Christ is risen; Christ will come again.

Cleansing God, your Son Jesus taught and healed as one with authority.
Where your children search in vain for someone to trust,
> show them your face.

Where your people long for one to lead or a path to follow,
> send them your pillar of cloud by day and of fire by night.

Where your church is faltering in fear and doubt,
> make yourself known in the ones we regard as the least of these.

Usher in the day when all may taste and see the riches of your grace,
> and your arms of love will all the world embrace,
>> in Jesus Christ through the power of the Holy Spirit
>>> in union with the Father. **Amen.**

Epiphany 4, Year C

The Lord be with you. **And also with you.**
Lift up your hearts. **We lift them to the Lord.**
Let us give thanks to the Lord our God. **It is right to give our thanks and praise.**

God of love, you shaped your purposes
  for your chosen people and your church
    before the foundation of the world;
      and you knew each one of us before you formed us in the womb.
You have given your people tongues to speak your name,
  prophecy to see your works, and faith to see your power;
    but most of all you have given us love to imitate your life.
In that love your Son laid down his life for us on the cross,
  and through that love you raised him to glorious life.
Moved by that love, and inspired by the tongues of angels and archangels,
  we join the heavenly song of everlasting praise.

Holy, holy, holy Lord, God of power and might.
Heaven and earth are full of your glory.
Hosanna in the highest.
Blessed is he who comes in the name of the Lord.
Hosanna in the highest.

Generous God, as you turn the texture of wheat into bread,
  and change the juice of grapes into wine, send down your Holy Spirit,
    that we may be transformed into the likeness of your living Word,
      and that these signs of your creation may be for us
        the gifts of your new creation,
          the body and blood of your Son Jesus Christ;
who, at supper with his disciples, took bread, gave you thanks,
  broke the bread, and gave it to them, saying,
    "Take, eat: this is my body which is given for you;
      do this in remembrance of me."

After supper he took the cup.

Again he gave you thanks, and gave it to his disciples, saying,
　"Drink this, all of you: this is my blood of the new covenant,
　　which is shed for you and for many for the forgiveness of sins.
　Do this, as often as you drink it, in remembrance of me."

Great is the mystery of faith.
Christ has died; Christ is risen; Christ will come again.

Revealing God, you give us prophecies, but they come to an end;
　you give us tongues, but they cease;
　　you give us knowledge, but it is only partial.
Give us in this sacred meal faith to move mountains,
　hope in the power of your transforming kingdom,
　　and love that never comes to an end;
　　　until the day when we look in the mirror
　　　　and see your face in the face of your church—
　　　　　fully known by you and transformed into the image of your Son;
　　　　　through whom, and with whom, and in whom,
　　　　　　in the unity of the Holy Spirit,
　　　　　　　all honor and glory are yours, now and forever. **Amen.**

Epiphany 5, Year A

The Lord be with you. **And also with you.**
Lift up your hearts. **We lift them to the Lord.**
Let us give thanks to the Lord our God. **It is right to give our thanks and praise.**

Empowering God, you established your creation like a watered garden,
   and when your people's hopes lay in ruins you answered their call
      and removed the yoke from among them.
You guided them continually and satisfied their needs in parched places.
In the death and resurrection of Christ
   you repaired the breach between us and you
      and opened the way of peace for all your people.
And so we gladly thank you, with angels and archangels,
   and all the company of heaven, singing the hymn of your unending praise.

Holy, holy, holy Lord, God of power and might.
Heaven and earth are full of your glory.
Hosanna in the highest.
Blessed is he who comes in the name of the Lord.
Hosanna in the highest.

Eye has not seen nor ear heard, beckoning God,
   what you have prepared for those who love you.
In Jesus you are the salt that preserves us with you forever,
   and you are the light that transforms the darkness of death.
On his last evening with the disciples
   your Son took the broken body and spilt blood of the cross
      and turned them into the glory of resurrection.
Come among us now and turn the brokenness of our lives
   and the spiltness of your world into the wonder of your new life.
Take these gifts of bread and wine and make them for us
   the body and blood of your Son Jesus Christ;
who, at supper with his disciples, took bread, gave you thanks,

broke the bread, and gave it to them, saying,
"Take, eat: this is my body which is given for you;
do this in remembrance of me."
After supper he took the cup.
Again he gave you thanks, and gave it to his disciples, saying,
"Drink this, all of you: this is my blood of the new covenant,
which is shed for you and for many for the forgiveness of sins.
Do this, as often as you drink it, in remembrance of me."

Great is the mystery of faith.
Christ has died; Christ is risen; Christ will come again.

Inspiring God, you instill in us the wisdom of your Son's cross,
and you send us the Spirit who searches the depths of your heart
and the depths of ours.
Shape your people in the image of your Son to be repairers of the breach;
send us to be beside those who cry, among any who are afflicted,
alongside all whose foundations lie in ruins.
Bless your church that it may bear the marks of its risen and ascended Lord.
Raise up saints to embody your truth in our midst,
loose the bonds of injustice, undo the thongs of the yoke,
and let the oppressed go free, until the day when you are all in all,
one God, Father, Son, and Holy Spirit. **Amen.**

Epiphany 5, Year B

The Lord be with you. **And also with you.**
Lift up your hearts. **We lift them to the Lord.**
Let us give thanks to the Lord our God. **It is right to give our thanks and praise.**

Ever-living God, we have known and we have heard
   that you are the creator of the ends of the earth
     and your understanding is unsearchable.
You give power to the faint and strength to the powerless;
   when your people grew weary
     you lifted them up in Christ with wings like eagles,
       and when your church falls exhausted
         you send your Holy Spirit so that we may walk and run
           in your strength and not our own.
By the depth of your mercy, you turned the agony of your Son's cross
   into the grace of his resurrection.
And so we gladly thank you, with saints and angels and archangels,
   and all the company of heaven, singing the hymn of your unending praise.

Holy, holy, holy Lord, God of power and might.
Heaven and earth are full of your glory.
Hosanna in the highest.
Blessed is he who comes in the name of the Lord.
Hosanna in the highest.

Everlasting God, in Jesus you enter our house,
   take us by the hand, lift us up, and give us life again.
Enter among us now, in the power of your Holy Spirit,
   that your people may be sanctified,
     and these gifts of bread and wine may be for us
       the body and blood of your Son Jesus Christ;
who, at supper with his disciples, took bread, gave you thanks,
   broke the bread, and gave it to them, saying,

"Take, eat: this is my body which is given for you;
  do this in remembrance of me."
After supper he took the cup.
Again he gave you thanks, and gave it to his disciples, saying,
  "Drink this, all of you: this is my blood of the new covenant,
    which is shed for you and for many for the forgiveness of sins.
  Do this, as often as you drink it, in remembrance of me."

Great is the mystery of faith.
Christ has died; Christ is risen; Christ will come again.

Ever-loving God, everyone is searching for you.
We seek for you in solitude, and we long for you in company;
  we hope for you in distress, and we ache for you in the darkness.
Meet us in our suffering and in our trials;
  cast out the demons that beset our public life
    and dog our personal struggles;
      heal us when we are stricken and hopeless;
        and raise us up when we are faint and weary.
Hasten the day when every enemy becomes a friend in you,
  every hunger is filled in you, and every tear is comforted by you,
    and you are all in all, ever one God,
      Father, Son, and Holy Spirit. **Amen.**

Epiphany 5, Year C

The Lord be with you. **And also with you.**
Lift up your hearts. **We lift them to the Lord.**
Let us give thanks to the Lord our God. **It is right to give our thanks and praise.**

Holy, holy, holy are you, Lord God of hosts,
   for all the earth is full of your glory.
From your heavenly throne
   you touched the lips of your prophet Isaiah to remove his guilt;
      and you sent him to awaken your people.
In the fullness of time you sent your Son,
   proclaiming through his lips your promise of life
      and through his death and resurrection your forgiveness of sins.
At his ascension he sent forth his disciples in your name,
   trusting your good news to the lips of the redeemed.
And so we give our thanks and praise
   in the great company of sinners become saints,
      joining together in their unending hymn.

Holy, holy, holy Lord, God of power and might.
Heaven and earth are full of your glory.
Hosanna in the highest.
Blessed is he who comes in the name of the Lord.
Hosanna in the highest.

Plenteous God, as you transformed fishermen into followers
   and filled empty nets with more than their boat could hold,
      show us your abundance in the joy of this feast.
Sanctify us by your Holy Spirit that we might be faithful followers,
   sent into the world in strength.
By your same Spirit, make this bread and cup be for us
   the body and blood of your Son Jesus Christ;
who, at supper with his disciples, took bread, gave you thanks,

broke the bread, and gave it to them, saying,
"Take, eat: this is my body which is given for you;
do this in remembrance of me."
After supper he took the cup.
Again he gave you thanks, and gave it to his disciples, saying,
"Drink this, all of you: this is my blood of the new covenant,
which is shed for you and for many for the forgiveness of sins.
Do this, as often as you drink it, in remembrance of me."

Great is the mystery of faith.
Christ has died; Christ is risen; Christ will come again.

God of holy presence, in your temple, what is ordinary is made holy.
Before your throne of grace, make your children into prophets of peace
and heralds of mercy.
Bless every man and woman and every boy and girl
with courage to follow where you call,
trusting the depth of your purpose.
Meet with your grace every soul rendered an outcast
by the judgments of others,
and restore the fallen as your faithful followers.
Renew your church to seek you in your dwelling places,
among the poor and the forgotten,
the sick and the imprisoned,
the hungry and the homeless.
Gather all your children into your holy presence
as you draw angels around your throne;
until we enter your eternal temple in fullness of joy
and dwell with you forever,
one God, Father, Son, and Holy Spirit. **Amen.**

Epiphany 6, Year A

The Lord be with you. **And also with you.**
Lift up your hearts. **We lift them to the Lord.**
Let us give thanks to the Lord our God. **It is right to give our thanks and praise.**

Gracious God, you chose life when you established your creation,
   when you called your people, and when you made a covenant with them.
You chose life when you came among us in Jesus to restore that covenant
   and when, after we had chosen death, you raised him in glory.
You chose life when you empowered your disciples through your Holy Spirit
   and when you gave birth to your church
     so that we might give life to the world.
And so we gladly thank you, with angels and archangels
   and all the company of heaven, singing the hymn of your unending praise.

Holy, holy, holy Lord, God of power and might.
Heaven and earth are full of your glory.
Hosanna in the highest.
Blessed is he who comes in the name of the Lord.
Hosanna in the highest.

God of mercy, in your Son's broken body we see how much we mean to you,
   and how much our faithlessness costs you.
Come among us in the power of your Holy Spirit,
   that your people may be transformed by your hospitality
     and sanctified by your grace,
       and these gifts of bread and wine may become for us
         the body and blood of your Son Jesus Christ;
who, at supper with his disciples, took bread, gave you thanks,
   broke the bread, and gave it to them, saying,
     "Take, eat: this is my body which is given for you;
       do this in remembrance of me."
After supper he took the cup.

Again he gave you thanks, and gave it to his disciples, saying,
  "Drink this, all of you: this is my blood of the new covenant,
    which is shed for you and for many for the forgiveness of sins.
  Do this, as often as you drink it, in remembrance of me."

Great is the mystery of faith.
Christ has died; Christ is risen; Christ will come again.

God of glory, you uphold the most vulnerable and hear the cries of the lost.
Through this sacrament unite your divided people,
  living and departed, faithful and unbelieving, merciful and mighty,
    sorrowful and ashamed, able and disabled,
      that you may through resurrection and coming kingdom
        make one body out of so many broken bodies.
Restore your people in the image of your Son,
  that they may be a community of compassion, forgiveness, and hope;
    that your church may be full of your prophets,
      and your prophets may be full of your grace,
        until all tongues cease and tears are shed no more,
          in the presence and communion of your Holy Trinity,
            Father, Son, and Holy Spirit, ever one God. **Amen.**

Epiphany 6, Year B

The Lord be with you. **And also with you.**
Lift up your hearts. **We lift them to the Lord.**
Let us give thanks to the Lord our God. **It is right to give our thanks and praise.**

Healing and redeeming God, it is our honor and our joy
   to give you thanks and praise,
     because you have looked with mercy on us in our fallenness.
In the liberation of your people from slavery
   and the making of the covenant with Moses
     we see your constant purpose to restore us to fullness of life
       and everlasting relationship with you.
You turn outcasts into disciples,
   and in moments of healing you give us a foretaste
     of our calling to be whole and holy in your presence.
In Jesus you show us what it means to be wholly alive and wholly yours.
And so with the whole company of earth and heaven, we glorify your name.

Holy, holy, holy Lord, God of power and might.
Heaven and earth are full of your glory.
Hosanna in the highest.
Blessed is he who comes in the name of the Lord.
Hosanna in the highest.

God of life and breath, you bathe us in the waters of baptism,
   feed us in the fellowship of communion, and renew us through acts of mercy.
In this holy meal you show us the cost of your Son's crucifixion
   and the glory of his resurrection,
     and you empower us to shape our lives after his.
Send down your Holy Spirit that your church may find its very life
   in the healing of your world.
Send that same Spirit upon this bread and this cup,
   that they may be for us the body and blood of your Son, Jesus Christ our Lord;

who, at supper with his disciples, took bread, gave you thanks,
   broke the bread, and gave it to them, saying,
      "Take, eat: this is my body which is given for you;
         do this in remembrance of me."
After supper he took the cup.
Again he gave you thanks, and gave it to his disciples, saying,
   "Drink this, all of you: this is my blood of the new covenant,
      which is shed for you and for many for the forgiveness of sins.
   Do this, as often as you drink it, in remembrance of me."

Great is the mystery of faith.
Christ has died; Christ is risen; Christ will come again.

Humble God, in Christ you became what we are
   that we might become what you are.
You call us to do difficult things in the power of your Spirit,
   and you invite us to do simple things to respond to your grace.
Embolden your people with strength and courage
   to do the difficult things you call them to do;
      but also bless your children with patience and dignity
         when you summon them to do simple things.
Visit all who labor with chronic illness or challenging disability.
Renew your body in the world to embrace those who are excluded
   from freedom or companionship.
Heal your creation, and bring forth the day
   when your abundant life flows like rivers of gold;
      through Jesus Christ, in the power of the Spirit,
         we pray to you, O Father. **Amen.**

Epiphany 6, Year C

The Lord be with you. **And also with you.**
Lift up your hearts. **We lift them to the Lord.**
Let us give thanks to the Lord our God. **It is right to give our thanks and praise.**

It is a good and joyful thing
   always and everywhere to give our thanks to you, God of glory,
     for you formed a people to trust in you,
     to root their life in yours, and to bear fruit without end.
When they were parched by sin and thirsting for righteousness,
   you sent your Son and let them drink of your forgiving mercies.
So you made them like trees planted by streams of water
   whose leaves do not wither.
By the power of your Holy Spirit you raised your Son from death to life,
   the firstfruits of those who have died.
Trusting in your all-sufficient ways, your church is rooted in you
   and continues to bear the fruits of resurrection.
And so with your people on earth and with all the company of heaven,
   we praise your name and join the hymn of glory.

Holy, holy, holy Lord, God of power and might.
Heaven and earth are full of your glory.
Hosanna in the highest.
Blessed is he who comes in the name of the Lord.
Hosanna in the highest.

Replenishing God, you have the power to transform hunger into blessing;
   fill us with faith as we feast around this table.
As your Son blessed the hungry, send your Spirit upon your church.
As we remember his saving passion, show us the fullness of your love.
Sanctify this bread and cup that they may be for us
   the body and blood of your Son;
who, at supper with his disciples, took bread, gave you thanks,

broke the bread, and gave it to them, saying,
"Take, eat: this is my body which is given for you;
do this in remembrance of me."
After supper he took the cup.
Again he gave you thanks, and gave it to his disciples, saying,
"Drink this, all of you: this is my blood of the new covenant,
which is shed for you and for many for the forgiveness of sins.
Do this, as often as you drink it, in remembrance of me."

Great is the mystery of faith.
Christ has died; Christ is risen; Christ will come again.

Patient God, you promise that your kingdom belongs to the poor:
bless your church through the faithful company of those who know poverty.
As you bestow laughter upon those who weep,
comfort your sons and daughters who cry and show them unfailing joy.
As you extend your goodness to all who are excluded on account of your Son,
give courage to those who are persecuted.
And as you promise to uphold all who hunger,
fill your children, body and soul, with the food that truly satisfies.
Bring us to the great day of heavenly reward,
that dawn of unending blessedness which we shall share with all your saints,
rejoicing in your glory, ever-faithful God,
Father, Son, and Holy Spirit. **Amen.**

Epiphany 7, Year A

The Lord be with you. **And also with you.**
Lift up your hearts. **We lift them to the Lord.**
Let us give thanks to the Lord our God. **It is right to give our thanks and praise.**

Most worthy are you of praise, Lord God,
  for your abundance is beyond all we could dream or desire.
Your creation abounds in growing goodness,
  and your heart overflows with manifold mercies.
You shaped a people whose life, like yours,
   welcomed the poor and the stranger;
    whose fields fed the hungry;
     whose vineyards were places where grace could be gleaned.
In Christ you showed us an abundance that reaches
  to the very edges of the field,
   embracing neighbor and enemy with the same perfect love,
    feeding every harvester, every gleaner, and every hungry soul.
And so, with your people on earth and with angels and archangels
  and all the company of heaven, we join their unending hymn.

Holy, holy, holy Lord, God of power and might.
Heaven and earth are full of your glory.
Hosanna in the highest.
Blessed is he who comes in the name of the Lord.
Hosanna in the highest.

Indwelling God, in your Son you have given us to eat and drink
  of your very self in abundance for eternity.
By your Holy Spirit dwelling in us, make us holy as you are holy,
  as we, around your table, remember Christ's death,
   claim his resurrection, and look for his coming in glory.
Send down your Spirit upon this bread and cup that they may be for us
  the body and blood of your Son;

who, at supper with his disciples, took bread, gave you thanks,
   broke the bread, and gave it to them, saying,
      "Take, eat: this is my body which is given for you;
         do this in remembrance of me."
After supper he took the cup.
Again he gave you thanks, and gave it to his disciples, saying,
   "Drink this, all of you: this is my blood of the new covenant,
      which is shed for you and for many for the forgiveness of sins.
   Do this, as often as you drink it, in remembrance of me."

Great is the mystery of faith.
Christ has died; Christ is risen; Christ will come again.

Restoring God, you bear the cost of the love that makes us yours.
Give your children faith to turn the other cheek,
   dignity to walk the second mile,
      and compassion to give the coat from their back.
Give your wisdom to those whose enemies are close at hand
   and all who struggle to embrace one who has hurt them.
Make your church a community where every beggar finds a friend,
   every enemy finds love, and every sinner finds forgiveness;
      until that day when your kingdom comes
         with every abundance, every justice, and every joy,
            ever-living God, Father, Son, and Holy Spirit. **Amen.**

Epiphany 7, Year B

The Lord be with you. **And also with you.**
Lift up your hearts. **We lift them to the Lord.**
Let us give thanks to the Lord our God. **It is right to give our thanks and praise.**

Glorious God, we rejoice to give you thanks and praise.
In Christ you meet the paralysis of your people
   and dismantle the barrier between heaven and earth.
You heal our past through forgiveness,
   and you overcome our limitations through the gift of everlasting life.
You turn us from burdens on others into carriers of one another's burdens.
When your Son's liberating ministry brought him
   to suffering and cruel death,
      you raised him from the dead and showed us the power of your love.
And so we gladly thank you, with all the company of heaven,
   joining their endless song.

Holy, holy, holy Lord, God of power and might.
Heaven and earth are full of your glory.
Hosanna in the highest.
Blessed is he who comes in the name of the Lord.
Hosanna in the highest.

Faithful God, all your promises find their "Yes" in your Son Jesus Christ.
In him you put your seal upon us and anoint us,
   and you give us your Spirit in our hearts
      as a first installment of your coming glory.
Sanctify us, that as we share in your Son's death
   we may also share in his resurrection.
Send down your Spirit upon this bread and cup that they may be for us
   the body and blood of your Son;
who, at supper with his disciples, took bread, gave you thanks,
   broke the bread, and gave it to them, saying,

"Take, eat: this is my body which is given for you;
  do this in remembrance of me."
After supper he took the cup.
Again he gave you thanks, and gave it to his disciples, saying,
  "Drink this, all of you: this is my blood of the new covenant,
    which is shed for you and for many for the forgiveness of sins.
  Do this, as often as you drink it, in remembrance of me."

Great is the mystery of faith.
Christ has died; Christ is risen; Christ will come again.

Redeeming and restoring God, you make a way in the wilderness
  and rivers in the desert.
Bless all who find themselves eager for the new thing you are doing
  that is about to spring forth.
Visit any who are left alone to dwell on their own mistakes,
  and all who feel rejected or neglected while the world passes them by.
Strengthen those who are in a desert of hunger, pain, or despair.
Raise up among your people prophets to speak the truth
  and priests to bring people close to you,
    that as you form your people for yourself
      they may fulfill their purpose to declare your praise;
        until the day when the weary, the burdened, and the transgressor
          unite in the chorus of your grace, and you are all in all,
            one God, Father, Son, and Holy Spirit. **Amen.**

Epiphany 7, Year C

The Lord be with you. **And also with you.**
Lift up your hearts. **We lift them to the Lord.**
Let us give thanks to the Lord our God. **It is right to give our thanks and praise.**

Blessed above all are you, Lord God of creation,
   for in the beginning you formed the earth in magnificent splendor,
     and from humble dust you raised up a man made in your image.
You brought forth your Adam, together with Eve,
   from earthly dust to human life.
From the beginning you sought the very people you had made,
   yearning to share your life with them.
When your people no longer sought you with their whole hearts,
   in the fullness of your love you raised up another man in your image.
Your Christ of heaven came among your people of dust,
   to raise us up out of the dust of sin,
     that in our earthly life we might bear the image of heaven.
And so we join our voices with angels and archangels,
   praising your name and joining their unending hymn.

Holy, holy, holy Lord, God of power and might.
Heaven and earth are full of your glory.
Hosanna in the highest.
Blessed is he who comes in the name of the Lord.
Hosanna in the highest.

Providing God, you look with mercy upon the hungry
   and meet famine with your plenty.
Show us your eternal provision of plenteous grace around this table.
Send your Holy Spirit upon your church,
   and make your people merciful as you are merciful.
Sanctify this bread and cup that they may be for us
   the body and blood of your Son;

who, at supper with his disciples, took bread, gave you thanks,
   broke the bread, and gave it to them, saying,
      "Take, eat: this is my body which is given for you;
         do this in remembrance of me."
After supper he took the cup.
Again he gave you thanks, and gave it to his disciples, saying,
   "Drink this, all of you: this is my blood of the new covenant,
      which is shed for you and for many for the forgiveness of sins.
   Do this, as often as you drink it, in remembrance of me."

Great is the mystery of faith.
Christ has died; Christ is risen; Christ will come again.

Merciful God, by the cross of Christ you transform hatred into love,
   curse into blessing, and evil into good.
Meet your children anew today with the power of your Holy Spirit,
   that wherever there is hatred, they may live love;
      wherever there are enemies, they may do good;
         wherever there are beggars, they may give grace;
            wherever there are persecutors, they may bring blessing.
Make your resurrecting power known
   through the grace you give your people to love in the face of fear
      with forgiveness that passes understanding.
Raise us on the last day with all the saints
   who have made your kingdom their one sure hope
      and your grace their imperishable trust,
         ever-living God, Father, Son, and Holy Spirit, now and forever. **Amen.**

Transfiguration Sunday

The Lord be with you. **And also with you.**
Lift up your hearts. **We lift them to the Lord.**
Let us give thanks to the Lord our God. **It is right to give our thanks and praise.**

Creating and liberating God, you called your people into covenant with you
   and sealed your trust with Moses on the mountain;
      you called your people back to that covenant through your prophets
        and spoke in a still small voice to Elijah on a mountain.
Then, in your Son Jesus, on a mountain you stood between
   the Law and the Prophets
      and revealed the radiance of your gospel.
On Calvary's hill your Son redeemed us by the blood of your new covenant,
   and on the mountain in Galilee he ascended to your right hand on high.
And so we gladly thank you, celebrating your glory
   with angels and archangels, and all the company of heaven,
      dazzled by your face and singing the hymn of your unending praise.

Holy, holy, holy Lord, God of power and might.
Heaven and earth are full of your glory.
Hosanna in the highest.
Blessed is he who comes in the name of the Lord.
Hosanna in the highest.

Dazzling God, you set up your tent and make your dwelling among us.
Abide with us now through the power of your Holy Spirit,
   that your people may become a temple of your presence,
      and these gifts of bread and wine may be for us
        the body and blood of your Son Jesus Christ;
who, at supper with his disciples, took bread, gave you thanks,
   broke the bread, and gave it to them, saying,
      "Take, eat: this is my body which is given for you;
        do this in remembrance of me."

After supper he took the cup.
Again he gave you thanks, and gave it to his disciples, saying,
"Drink this, all of you: this is my blood of the new covenant,
which is shed for you and for many for the forgiveness of sins.
Do this, as often as you drink it, in remembrance of me."

Great is the mystery of faith.
Christ has died; Christ is risen; Christ will come again.

Transfiguring God, it is good for us to be here.
Through this holy sacrament make us your sons and daughters,
and be close to all children who have no one
to share your love and mercy with them.
Make us your beloved, and visit all who have no one to call them beloved.
Give us grace to listen to your voice,
and bring to your heart any who have no one to listen to them.
Surround us with your prophetic company
and take us up into the whirlwind of your glory,
until the day comes when the waters of the Jordan are parted
and the heavens are opened
and the chariots bring us home to you,
ever one God, Father, Son, and Holy Spirit. **Amen.**

4. Lent

Ash Wednesday

The Lord be with you. **And also with you.**
Lift up your hearts. **We lift them to the Lord.**
Let us give thanks to the Lord our God. **It is right to give our thanks and praise.**

Creator God, we lift our hearts to you
   because you made the universe from nothing
      and formed human beings in your image from the dust of the earth.
In Adam you saw your hopes for creation turn to ashes,
   and yet in Abraham and Moses
      you called a people out of wilderness and slavery.
You showed your face to your people in exile,
   and in Christ the new Adam you raised your children
      to new life out of the ashes of sin and death.
And so we gladly praise and thank you,
   with angels and archangels and the company of heaven,
      singing your unending praise.

Holy, holy, holy Lord, God of power and might.
Heaven and earth are full of your glory.
Hosanna in the highest.
Blessed is he who comes in the name of the Lord.
Hosanna in the highest.

Redeemer God, over forty days you flooded the earth,
   over forty years you led your people through the wilderness,
      and over forty days your Spirit led Jesus through the desert.
Bless us through the sustenance of this food and drink
   to profess your Son's death and resurrection.
Send down your Holy Spirit, that we may come
   to resemble and follow our crucified and risen Savior,
      and that this bread and this cup may become for us
         our everlasting banquet,

the body and blood of your Son Jesus Christ;
who, at supper with his disciples, took bread, gave you thanks,
   broke the bread, and gave it to them, saying,
      "Take, eat: this is my body which is given for you;
         do this in remembrance of me."
After supper he took the cup.
Again he gave you thanks, and gave it to his disciples, saying,
   "Drink this, all of you: this is my blood of the new covenant,
      which is shed for you and for many for the forgiveness of sins.
   Do this, as often as you drink it, in remembrance of me."

Great is the mystery of faith.
Christ has died; Christ is risen; Christ will come again.

Sanctifying God, where your children are in the wilderness,
   lead them to your heart.
Where your people are hungry for you,
   give them practices of fasting and scripture reading
      and almsgiving and repentance and prayer.
Where your followers know beatings, imprisonments,
   hardships and calamities,
      visit them with the comforting power of your presence.
Raise up the glory of your resurrection
   from the ashes of our pride and sloth and greed,
      that all your church and the whole creation
         may celebrate the wonders of your love,
            until the day when every eye shall see you
               and every tongue shall praise you, and you are all in all,
                  ever one God, Father, Son, and Holy Spirit. **Amen.**

Lent 1, Year A

The Lord be with you. **And also with you.**
Lift up your hearts. **We lift them to the Lord.**
Let us give thanks to the Lord our God. **It is right to give our thanks and praise.**

Praise and thanks are yours, Lord God,
   because you remain faithful through our unfaith
      and constant amid our failure.
Adam and Eve could see only scarcity,
   but you continue to offer us abundance.
Though sin came into the world and poisoned your good creation,
   you nonetheless called the children of Abraham
      to be your companions,
         and in Jesus you faced the cost of our sin
            and received its poison in your own body,
               transforming death into life.
And so we give you humble thanks
   for your forgiveness and our new life,
      with angels and archangels and the company of heaven,
         singing your unending praise.

Holy, holy, holy Lord, God of power and might.
Heaven and earth are full of your glory.
Hosanna in the highest.
Blessed is he who comes in the name of the Lord.
Hosanna in the highest.

Righteous God, in Jesus you were tempted to make stones into bread—
   but instead in him you make us living stones
      and you make bread become his body.
Send down your Holy Spirit,
   that we may be transformed into your body for the life of your world,
      and this bread and this cup may become for us our strength and stay,

the body and blood of your Son Jesus Christ;
who, at supper with his disciples, took bread, gave you thanks,
   broke the bread, and gave it to them, saying,
      "Take, eat: this is my body which is given for you;
         do this in remembrance of me."
After supper he took the cup.
Again he gave you thanks, and gave it to his disciples, saying,
   "Drink this, all of you: this is my blood of the new covenant,
      which is shed for you and for many for the forgiveness of sins.
   Do this, as often as you drink it, in remembrance of me."

Great is the mystery of faith.
Christ has died; Christ is risen; Christ will come again.

Justifying God, in your patience you see the hunger of your children:
   send upon us your Word
      that in your living bread we may never be hungry again.
In your mercy you know your people's craving for drama and miracle:
   raise up among us witnesses to the triumphs of your grace,
      that we may see you face to face.
In your glory you hear your fragile world's cries for justice:
   shape in us the habits of faithfulness,
      the disciplines of holiness, and the practices of peace,
         that we may find your justice
            as we walk with your Son on the way of the cross,
               until that day when you surprise us in the joy of resurrection,
                  one God, Father, Son, and Holy Spirit,
                     full of grace and truth. **Amen.**

Lent 1, Year B

The Lord be with you. **And also with you.**
Lift up your hearts. **We lift them to the Lord.**
Let us give thanks to the Lord our God. **It is right to give our thanks and praise.**

Blessed are you, God of everlasting covenant,
   for your promises are steadfast and your provision is sure.
Through the forty years of your people's desert wanderings
   you were constant in fire and cloud;
     with manna and mercy you sustained every step.
You made Jesus' temptation of forty days
   a theater of truth where your Word stood strong.
In every age you have shaped your people
   through times of wilderness and wandering, of temptation and trial,
     and brought them into the land of promise and the life of covenant.
And so with all who have walked the wilderness way in every time
   and all who walk it this day, with angels and archangels
     and all the company of heaven, we join the unending hymn.

Holy, holy, holy Lord, God of power and might.
Heaven and earth are full of your glory.
Hosanna in the highest.
Blessed is he who comes in the name of the Lord.
Hosanna in the highest.

Enduring God, as you sustained Jesus in hunger and thirst,
   through this meal strengthen us to keep our Lenten fast.
Send your Holy Spirit upon us as we remember Jesus' saving passion;
   transform our insatiable desires into hunger for the feast of this table.
Send your Holy Spirit upon this bread and wine
   that they may be for us the body and blood of Christ;
who, at supper with his disciples, took bread, gave you thanks,
   broke the bread, and gave it to them, saying,

"Take, eat: this is my body which is given for you;
   do this in remembrance of me."
After supper he took the cup.
Again he gave you thanks, and gave it to his disciples, saying,
   "Drink this, all of you: this is my blood of the new covenant,
      which is shed for you and for many for the forgiveness of sins.
   Do this, as often as you drink it, in remembrance of me."

Great is the mystery of faith.
Christ has died; Christ is risen; Christ will come again.

Forgiving God, in this season of repentance,
   make your mercy sufficient for every need.
Come to your children who are in their own wilderness
   and make their wanderings holy paths of learning your truth.
Strengthen all who face the threshold of temptation or the tumult of trial.
Seek those whose hearts are contrite and meet them with grace.
Come alongside your children who suffer under the sin of another
   and give them power to live as your beloved sons and daughters.
Renew your church from the depths of your heart,
   where justice and mercy meet.
Bring us with all your saints to the day
   when all who watch and pray for your kingdom
      behold your salvation and meet you in your resurrection,
         God most glorious, Father, Son, and Holy Spirit. **Amen.**

Lent 1, Year C

The Lord be with you. **And also with you.**
Lift up your hearts. **We lift them to the Lord.**
Let us give thanks to the Lord our God. **It is right to give our thanks and praise.**

Praise and thanksgiving belong to you, God of every blessing,
   for you shaped all creation
     to grow into your abundant and eternal harvest.
You called a holy people to share life with you,
   and when they were captive in Egypt,
     with a mighty hand and an outstretched arm
       you brought them out of oppression,
         through the temptations of the wilderness,
           into a land flowing with milk and honey.
In time, your Son came among us,
   facing wilderness and temptation and hunger
     to bring us out of bondage to sin
       and to taste and see that you, the Lord, are good.
And so we thank you with angels and archangels
   and all the company of heaven as we join the unending hymn.

Holy, holy, holy Lord, God of power and might.
Heaven and earth are full of your glory.
Hosanna in the highest.
Blessed is he who comes in the name of the Lord.
Hosanna in the highest.

God of mercy, you gave your people manna day by day
   during their time of testing;
     and because no one can live by bread alone,
       you gave Jesus to be our bread from heaven.
Send your Holy Spirit upon your church to live as a sign
   of the way you transform this manna into mercy for all.

With your Spirit, bless this bread and this cup,
   that they may be for us the body and blood of our Lord Jesus Christ;
who, at supper with his disciples, took bread, gave you thanks,
   broke the bread, and gave it to them, saying,
      "Take, eat: this is my body which is given for you;
         do this in remembrance of me."
After supper he took the cup.
Again he gave you thanks, and gave it to his disciples, saying,
   "Drink this, all of you: this is my blood of the new covenant,
      which is shed for you and for many for the forgiveness of sins.
   Do this, as often as you drink it, in remembrance of me."

Great is the mystery of faith.
Christ has died; Christ is risen; Christ will come again.

Faithful God, whose Son did not escape suffering and death
   but accepted and finally overcame them,
      bring your disciples by the way of his cross to the joy of Easter.
Strengthen your church to resist evil of every kind and turn from sin.
With your mighty hand and outstretched arm,
   uphold those enduring trials and any who know their very life is at stake.
Be with your children who are heavy laden,
   and all who labor beneath the misuse of power by another.
Amid temptations to be successful,
   shape your children first to be faithful to your kingdom,
      until the day when in your resurrected glory there is one life,
         one sharing, one holy communion among all saints
            with you to whom all glory belongs forever,
               Father, Son, and Holy Spirit. **Amen.**

Lent 2, Year A

The Lord be with you. **And also with you.**
Lift up your hearts. **We lift them to the Lord.**
Let us give thanks to the Lord our God. **It is right to give our thanks and praise.**

Blessings and thanks belong to you, promising God.
You made the sands of the desert and the stars in the sky,
   and in Abraham you called a people to be a great nation
     in whom all the families of the earth would find a blessing.
In Jesus you raised up a new Abraham
   to be a blessing to all the people.
In his death and resurrection, sin died and eternal life was born.
And so we look forward to the fulfillment of your promise,
   rejoicing with you, with angels and archangels,
     and with all the company of heaven, singing your unending praise.

Holy, holy, holy Lord, God of power and might.
Heaven and earth are full of your glory.
Hosanna in the highest.
Blessed is he who comes in the name of the Lord.
Hosanna in the highest.

Faithful God, in Jesus you fulfilled all righteousness.
In him you turn our duty into joy, and our sorrow into dancing.
You give us new birth through water and the Spirit.
Send down your Holy Spirit now,
   that your people may become a blessing to you and all the world,
     and that the bread of sustenance and the wine of celebration
       may become for us the body and blood of your Son Jesus Christ;
who, at supper with his disciples, took bread, gave you thanks,
   broke the bread, and gave it to them, saying,
     "Take, eat: this is my body which is given for you;
       do this in remembrance of me."

After supper he took the cup.
Again he gave you thanks, and gave it to his disciples, saying,
   "Drink this, all of you: this is my blood of the new covenant,
      which is shed for you and for many for the forgiveness of sins.
   Do this, as often as you drink it, in remembrance of me."

Great is the mystery of faith.
Christ has died; Christ is risen; Christ will come again.

Generous God, you loved the world so much that you gave your only Son;
   look now upon the places where your people are perishing,
      where they are being condemned,
         where they are being born under the shadow
            of disease and destruction and despair.
Infuse your church with Spirit and truth,
   walk with your beloved people the Jews
      as they seek security, companionship, and freedom in your world,
         and fill your saints with the hope of eternal life,
            that all may come to praise your name,
               and every grain of sand and star in the sky
                  be stirred with the wonders of your grace,
                     ever one God, Father, Son, and Holy Spirit,
                        now and forever. **Amen.**

Lent 2, Year B

The Lord be with you. **And also with you.**
Lift up your hearts. **We lift them to the Lord.**
Let us give thanks to the Lord our God. **It is right to give our thanks and praise.**

Glory to you, God of Abraham and Sarah,
  for you uphold every hope of redemption and upon you rests eternity.
In every age you have called your people
  to receive your blessing by faith,
    trusting not their own righteousness
      but the promise that rests forever on your grace.
In Christ you came to bear the weight of our sin,
  carry our offenses, and take up the hope of our salvation;
    and, through your power, the cross he bears across his shoulders
      has become for us the resurrection and the life.
And so with your people on earth and all the company of heaven,
  we join the unending hymn.

Holy, holy, holy Lord, God of power and might.
Heaven and earth are full of your glory.
Hosanna in the highest.
Blessed is he who comes in the name of the Lord.
Hosanna in the highest.

Renewing God, through the cross of Christ
  you redeem our failures by welcoming us to the feast of the forgiven.
As there is nothing we can give you in return for our life,
  send your Holy Spirit to meet us in the grace of this meal;
    and send your Spirit upon this bread and wine
      that they may be for us the body and blood of Christ;
who, at supper with his disciples, took bread, gave you thanks,
  broke the bread, and gave it to them, saying,
    "Take, eat: this is my body which is given for you;

do this in remembrance of me."
After supper he took the cup.
Again he gave you thanks, and gave it to his disciples, saying,
  "Drink this, all of you: this is my blood of the new covenant,
    which is shed for you and for many for the forgiveness of sins.
  Do this, as often as you drink it, in remembrance of me."

Great is the mystery of faith.
Christ has died; Christ is risen; Christ will come again.

Saving God, show your church the path of life.
Give each one of your children courage and wisdom
  to take up their cross and follow you.
Stretch every heart with compassion
  for the heavy burdens their neighbors carry,
    and transform all who are weighed down
      to become carriers of one another's burdens.
Come alongside any who shoulder heavy cares alone
  and give them companions in walking each step.
Take upon yourself the suffering
  of all who bear impossible weights at the demand of another,
    are forced to labor, or given no rest,
      until all that is bowed low in sin or weighed down by struggle
        is lifted up and carried by your grace and transcended in your glory,
          ever reigning God, forever one, Father, Son, and Holy Spirit. **Amen.**

Lent 2, Year C

The Lord be with you. **And also with you.**
Lift up your hearts. **We lift them to the Lord.**
Let us give thanks to the Lord our God. **It is right to give our thanks and praise.**

Maternal God, you long to gather your children
   as a mother hen gathers her brood under her wings.
You have made the descendants of Abraham
   as many as the stars in the sky and the sands in the desert;
     and in your great mercy you have made us, too,
       children of your blessed unbreakable covenant.
In Jesus you came among us in grace and truth;
   in his death we showed the depth of our departure from your ways;
     in his resurrection you demonstrate that nothing is impossible with you.
And so we gather at your table like angels at your throne,
   joining the archangels as they continually sing anthems of heavenly praise.

Holy, holy, holy Lord, God of power and might.
Heaven and earth are full of your glory.
Hosanna in the highest.
Blessed is he who comes in the name of the Lord.
Hosanna in the highest.

God our salvation, you have made us a people for your own possession,
   and we become yours as you become ours
     in the sharing of this meal of bread and cup.
Send down your Holy Spirit,
   that these tokens of earthly sustenance and heavenly joy
     may be for us the body and blood of your Son Jesus Christ;
who, at supper with his disciples, took bread, gave you thanks,
   broke the bread, and gave it to them, saying,
     "Take, eat: this is my body which is given for you;
       do this in remembrance of me."

After supper he took the cup.
Again he gave you thanks, and gave it to his disciples, saying,
  "Drink this, all of you: this is my blood of the new covenant,
    which is shed for you and for many for the forgiveness of sins.
  Do this, as often as you drink it, in remembrance of me."

Great is the mystery of faith.
Christ has died; Christ is risen; Christ will come again.

God our stronghold,
  as we walk this Lenten journey through the wilderness with you,
    make this eternal food enough to feed us
      through times of uncertainty and fear.
Soften in us the impulse of greed, that, as we share the bread of life,
  we may continue to understand the word "enough."
Shape our hearts to long for that day
  when you gather your children to yourself,
    and inspire us to make all who are created in your image
      our companions at this and other tables,
        until the day when all our hungers are satisfied
          and every friendship is fulfilled
            in the company of your Holy Trinity,
              through whom, and with whom, and in whom
                all honor and glory are yours, now and forever. **Amen.**

Lent 3, Year A

The Lord be with you. **And also with you.**
Lift up your hearts. **We lift them to the Lord.**
Let us give thanks to the Lord our God. **It is right to give our thanks and praise.**

Living God, you created all things out of nothing;
  you called a people out of the desert;
    you sent your Son to us
      when we were hard-hearted and far from your grace;
      and you send your Holy Spirit to us today
        despite our foolishness and forgetfulness.
Through your servant Moses you drew water out of the rock,
  and in your Son Jesus you brought living water
    that we might never be thirsty again.
Out of your Son's pierced side on the cross flowed water and blood,
  and in the glory of his resurrection we are baptized
    into wondrous forgiveness and everlasting life with you.
And so we gladly thank you, with angels and archangels
  and all the company of heaven, singing the hymn of your unending praise.

Holy, holy, holy Lord, God of power and might.
Heaven and earth are full of your glory.
Hosanna in the highest.
Blessed is he who comes in the name of the Lord.
Hosanna in the highest.

Overflowing God, in you we discover that all our striving and thirsting
  are truly a striving and thirsting for you,
    and in all our desert wanderings we find that only you can satisfy.
Come among us in the power of your Holy Spirit,
  that your people may taste your living water,
    and that these gifts of bread and wine may become for us
      the body and blood of your Son Jesus Christ;

who, at supper with his disciples, took bread, gave you thanks,
　broke the bread, and gave it to them, saying,
　　"Take, eat: this is my body which is given for you;
　　　do this in remembrance of me."
After supper he took the cup.
Again he gave you thanks, and gave it to his disciples, saying,
　"Drink this, all of you: this is my blood of the new covenant,
　　which is shed for you and for many for the forgiveness of sins.
　Do this, as often as you drink it, in remembrance of me."

Great is the mystery of faith.
Christ has died; Christ is risen; Christ will come again.

Cleansing God, bring the healing power of your living water
　to visit all who labor with disease today.
Pour the refreshment of your living water
　to invigorate all who are weary.
Send the momentum of your living water
　to roll down justice like a never-failing stream.
Make us, your church, a fountain of your living water,
　until the day when hunger and thirst are no more,
　　and we live your life abundant with the communion of saints,
　　　and you are all in all,
　　　　in the presence and companionship of your Holy Trinity,
　　　　Father, Son, and Holy Spirit, ever one God. **Amen.**

Lent 3, Year B

The Lord be with you. **And also with you.**
Lift up your hearts. **We lift them to the Lord.**
Let us give thanks to the Lord our God. **It is right to give our thanks and praise.**

Covenanting God, you made this world and us to be your companions,
    and in Moses you revealed to us
        the spirit of freedom and the freedom of your Spirit.
On Sinai you showed your people
    how to keep their freedom and walk in your Spirit.
You called them to be a priestly kingdom and a holy nation.
In your temple you enshrined your law and made your mercy seat
    the place of your people's reconciliation with you.
Then in Jesus you came among your people
    as the embodiment of your law and the personification of your temple
        and the emblem of your freedom.
His cross is the mercy seat in which you forgive our sin,
    and his resurrection is the new law of life with you forever.
And so we gladly thank you, with angels and archangels,
    and all the company of heaven, singing the hymn of your unending praise.

Holy, holy, holy Lord, God of power and might.
Heaven and earth are full of your glory.
Hosanna in the highest.
Blessed is he who comes in the name of the Lord.
Hosanna in the highest.

Righteous God, your Son said,
    "Destroy this temple and in three days I will raise it up."
Here we gather before you to lament the agony of that destruction
    and to celebrate the glory of that raising up.
Come into the temple of this your body,
    that your people may become a temple of your presence,

and that these gifts of bread and wine may be for us
  the body and blood of your Son Jesus Christ;
who, at supper with his disciples, took bread, gave you thanks,
  broke the bread, and gave it to them, saying,
    "Take, eat: this is my body which is given for you;
      do this in remembrance of me."
After supper he took the cup.
Again he gave you thanks, and gave it to his disciples, saying,
  "Drink this, all of you: this is my blood of the new covenant,
    which is shed for you and for many for the forgiveness of sins.
  Do this, as often as you drink it, in remembrance of me."

Great is the mystery of faith.
Christ has died; Christ is risen; Christ will come again.

Merciful Father, in your commandments we see
  the simplicity and the sacrifice of our life with you and your life with us.
Make us holy as you are holy; raise up saints from this community,
  and make us quick to recognize the saints we encounter elsewhere.
Fill our hearts with prophetic zeal for your house, for your holiness,
  for your kingdom, and for your grace.
Take out of your church the idolatries that grieve you,
  and fill your church with the transparency of heart that honors you,
    until the day when all sin is transformed by your grace,
      all scarcity suffused with your abundance,
        and all disorder healed by your mercy,
          and you are all in all, Father, Son, and Holy Spirit. **Amen.**

Lent 3, Year C

The Lord be with you. **And also with you.**
Lift up your hearts. **We lift them to the Lord.**
Let us give thanks to the Lord our God. **It is right to give our thanks and praise.**

It is right, and a good and joyful thing,
   to give our thanks to you, Holy One on high,
      for you shaped all living beings and every wonder of creation
         to bear fruit that glorifies you.
In the soil of covenant you planted a life with your chosen people
   and nourished a family to bless all the earth.
When through human faithlessness that life was grieved and barren,
   you sent your Son to be the soil of our redemption.
Through his resurrection you brought us out of the deadness of sin
   into the fullness of your fruit-bearing, fruit-sharing life.
And so we rejoice with angels and archangels
   and all the company of heaven as we join the unending hymn.

Holy, holy, holy Lord, God of power and might.
Heaven and earth are full of your glory.
Hosanna in the highest.
Blessed is he who comes in the name of the Lord.
Hosanna in the highest.

God who summons everyone who thirsts to come and drink,
   make all who drink from this cup thirst for the wine of your kingdom.
As we remember through this fruit of the vine your Son's saving passion,
   send your Holy Spirit to lead us into life.
By your same Spirit, bless this bread and cup that they may be for us
   the body and blood of our Lord Jesus Christ;
who, at supper with his disciples, took bread, gave you thanks,
   broke the bread, and gave it to them, saying,
      "Take, eat: this is my body which is given for you;

do this in remembrance of me."
After supper he took the cup.
Again he gave you thanks, and gave it to his disciples, saying,
   "Drink this, all of you: this is my blood of the new covenant,
      which is shed for you and for many for the forgiveness of sins.
   Do this, as often as you drink it, in remembrance of me."

Great is the mystery of faith.
Christ has died; Christ is risen; Christ will come again.

God of all flourishing, through the fast of Lent
   nourish in your church a life that is wholly fruitful.
Give patience to all who abide through long seasons of barrenness
   and long for new life.
Tend and care for any who hunger for mercy and thirst for forgiveness.
Bless your children when they seek restored relationships
   in church and community in a spirit of humble confession.
Shape your people to hunger and thirst for the day
   when there is one shared flourishing for all,
      one feasting with you in glory,
         when with the saints, apostles, and martyrs
            your creation shall be, at last, wholly fruitful in you,
               one God, Father, Son, and Holy Spirit. **Amen.**

Lent 4, Year A

The Lord be with you. **And also with you.**
Lift up your hearts. **We lift them to the Lord.**
Let us give thanks to the Lord our God. **It is right to give our thanks and praise.**

Praise upon praise belongs to you, God of David,
   for through the length of days your goodness faileth never.
You created a world of verdant pastures
   and streams of living water where we should nothing lack.
Out of the house of Jesse
   you named a shepherd son to be your people's king.
With rod and staff you walked with your children
   through the shadow of slavery and the valley of exile
     and every kind of evil.
When your sheep strayed in sin, you sent your own Son
   to be our shepherd king and to restore our souls.
He came to lay each one of us across his shoulders
   and bring us home to you.
He set a table in the face of his enemies
   and laid down his life that you might take it up again in glory.
And because you promise goodness and mercy to follow us all our days,
   we give our thanks with all who dwell in your house forever,
     with angels and archangels and all the company of heaven
       as we join the unending hymn.

Holy, holy, holy Lord, God of power and might.
Heaven and earth are full of your glory.
Hosanna in the highest.
Blessed is he who comes in the name of the Lord.
Hosanna in the highest.

Anointing God, Samuel poured oil on the head of David,
   and your Spirit came mightily upon him.

Send your Holy Spirit upon your church to make us faithful disciples
   and, with your same Spirit, anoint these gifts of bread and wine
      that they may be for us the body and blood of our Lord Jesus Christ;
who, at supper with his disciples, took bread, gave you thanks,
   broke the bread, and gave it to them, saying,
      "Take, eat: this is my body which is given for you;
         do this in remembrance of me."
After supper he took the cup.
Again he gave you thanks, and gave it to his disciples, saying,
   "Drink this, all of you: this is my blood of the new covenant,
      which is shed for you and for many for the forgiveness of sins.
   Do this, as often as you drink it, in remembrance of me."

Great is the mystery of faith.
Christ has died; Christ is risen; Christ will come again.

Searching God, you alone give your followers eyes of faith.
Teach your church to see as you see,
   and set its sights on your kingdom.
In the face of evil, lift the burden of fear.
In the shadow of death, give comfort.
In the company of enemies, spread your welcome table
   until that day when every cup runneth over
      and your children look upon one everlasting banquet,
         and all are made one around your heavenly feast,
            as faith shall at last be made sight;
               through your Son, Jesus Christ our Lord,
                  in the power of the Holy Spirit, with all honor and glory,
                     one God, now and forever. **Amen.**

Lent 4, Year B

The Lord be with you. **And also with you.**
Lift up your hearts. **We lift them to the Lord.**
Let us give thanks to the Lord our God. **It is right to give our thanks and praise.**

Blessed be your name, God of Moses, for you so love the world,
   and all that you so love you created to share life with you.
When your people were suffering as captives in Egypt
   you heard their cries, led them to freedom,
     and made with them a covenant life.
When your people were perishing in the poison of sin,
   you sent your only Son to take our trespasses into himself,
     to be our healing medicine.
Suffering his own death and rising in glory, he won our redemption
   and transformed the poison of our sin into your elixir of life.
And so we sing your praise with angels and archangels
   and all the company of heaven as we join the unending hymn.

Holy, holy, holy Lord, God of power and might.
Heaven and earth are full of your glory.
Hosanna in the highest.
Blessed is he who comes in the name of the Lord.
Hosanna in the highest.

Redeeming God, who sent your Son into the world
   not to condemn but so that the world might be saved through him,
     sanctify this everlasting feast and through it draw your church
       into your eternal, Triune life.
By your Spirit, bless these gifts of bread and wine that they may be for us
   the body and blood of our Lord Jesus Christ;
who, at supper with his disciples, took bread, gave you thanks,
   broke the bread, and gave it to them, saying,
     "Take, eat: this is my body which is given for you;

do this in remembrance of me."
After supper he took the cup.
Again he gave you thanks, and gave it to his disciples, saying,
"Drink this, all of you: this is my blood of the new covenant,
which is shed for you and for many for the forgiveness of sins.
Do this, as often as you drink it, in remembrance of me."

Great is the mystery of faith.
Christ has died; Christ is risen; Christ will come again.

Restoring God, whose Son was lifted up
that we might look upon him and live,
bring us through his cross to the glory of resurrection.
Shed your mercy on those who look upon malady and disease
and long for healing of body, mind, or spirit.
Deliver your children afflicted by the poison of enmity and strife
in their families, neighborhoods, or communities.
Hold your redeeming cross before eyes cast down by injustice.
Raise up in your church men and women of courage and discipleship.
Lift up in every heart the hope born of your passion
until all your children look upon the day
when the world that you so love is, at last, one with you in glory,
and together with the saints we drink the wine of your kingdom,
blessed and holy Trinity, now and forever. **Amen.**

Lent 4, Year C

The Lord be with you. **And also with you.**
Lift up your hearts. **We lift them to the Lord.**
Let us give thanks to the Lord our God. **It is right to give our thanks and praise.**

God of grace, you lift our hearts
   because, though we squandered your abundant gifts,
     you waited for us to turn back to you;
      and though we hardened our hearts to your mercy,
       you came to find us and draw us home to your banquet.
In Christ you made the journey into the far country of our exile from you,
   and in his death and resurrection you justify and sanctify us
     to stand in your presence and be reunited with your grace.
And so we give you thanks, gathering around the table of your kingdom
   with angels and archangels and all the company of heaven,
     singing your unending praise.

Holy, holy, holy Lord, God of power and might.
Heaven and earth are full of your glory.
Hosanna in the highest.
Blessed is he who comes in the name of the Lord.
Hosanna in the highest.

God of blessing, you are the host of our joy;
   in Christ you have made every preparation for this feast,
     even giving your own body that we might never be hungry again.
Send down your Holy Spirit,
   that we may once again belong in your house as your sons and daughters,
     and that these signs of sustaining bread and renewing wine
      may be for us the body and blood of your Son Jesus Christ;
who, at supper with his disciples, took bread, gave you thanks,
   broke the bread, and gave it to them, saying,
     "Take, eat: this is my body which is given for you;

do this in remembrance of me."
After supper he took the cup.
Again he gave you thanks, and gave it to his disciples, saying,
  "Drink this, all of you: this is my blood of the new covenant,
    which is shed for you and for many for the forgiveness of sins.
  Do this, as often as you drink it, in remembrance of me."

Great is the mystery of faith.
Christ has died; Christ is risen; Christ will come again.

Gathering God, when we languish with the pigs
  in a humiliation of our own making,
    may this broken body heal, restore, and renew our bodies.
When we lurk in the shadows in a resentment of our own devising,
  may this shed blood soften and cleanse and refresh our hearts.
Strengthen our hands, that we may seek a world
  where there is no hunger except hunger for you.
Empower our spirits, that we may strive for a world
  where there is no thirst except thirst for your righteousness.
    Hasten the day when this body shows us your desire for our well-being,
      and this blood reveals how far you go
        to save us from ourselves and restore us in the image of your Son,
          through whom, and with whom, and in whom
            all honor and glory are yours, now and forever. **Amen.**

Lent 5, Year A

The Lord be with you. **And also with you.**
Lift up your hearts. **We lift them to the Lord.**
Let us give thanks to the Lord our God. **It is right to give our thanks and praise.**

God of glory, you are worthy of thanks and praise,
   because you set humanity in a garden of delight
      to glorify and enjoy you forever.
When that garden turned into a valley of dry bones,
   you entered the valley in the form of Jesus Christ.
You breathed life into the dry bones and made them sing again.
You put your Spirit within us that we might live.
In the crucified Christ you became dry bones for us,
   and at Easter you showed us how to dance again.
And so as your resurrected people, with angels and archangels,
   and with all the company of heaven, we join in singing your unending praise.

Holy, holy, holy Lord, God of power and might.
Heaven and earth are full of your glory.
Hosanna in the highest.
Blessed is he who comes in the name of the Lord.
Hosanna in the highest.

Listening God, you heard your Son Jesus
   when he called on you in the face of Lazarus's death.
Hear us now as we call upon you
   to bring new life through this meal of memory and hope.
Come among us in the power of your Holy Spirit,
   that your people may be transformed
      from dry bones to your living body,
         and that these gifts of bread and wine may become for us
            the body and blood of your Son Jesus Christ;
who, at supper with his disciples, took bread, gave you thanks,

broke the bread, and gave it to them, saying,
"Take, eat: this is my body which is given for you;
do this in remembrance of me."
After supper he took the cup.
Again he gave you thanks, and gave it to his disciples, saying,
"Drink this, all of you: this is my blood of the new covenant,
which is shed for you and for many for the forgiveness of sins.
Do this, as often as you drink it, in remembrance of me."

Great is the mystery of faith.
Christ has died; Christ is risen; Christ will come again.

Resurrecting God,
where your people are in the valley of the shadow of death,
bring them your words of prophecy and hope;
where they are in the place of stench and decay,
give them the balm of your healing and forgiveness;
where they are under the weight of grief and depression,
roll away the stone.
Make us, your church, a place where dust can dream,
where dry bones become flesh, where nobodies become your body.
Reveal through Lazarus a foretaste of the resurrection of all creation,
when every tearful eye will gaze upon your consolation,
and every weary throat be filled with your song;
until every stone is rolled from every tomb and you sit in glory,
the resurrection and the life,
Father, Son, and Holy Spirit, now and forever. **Amen.**

Lent 5, Year B

The Lord be with you. **And also with you.**
Lift up your hearts. **We lift them to the Lord.**
Let us give thanks to the Lord our God. **It is right to give our thanks and praise.**

Glorious God, you created the heavens as the place for your glory to dwell
  and the earth as the theater for your glory to come among us.
You called your people to be a kingdom of priests
  and your church to be a priestly kingdom.
In Melchizedek you show us your people's vocation to be a righteous king,
  and in Jesus you show us true righteousness and true majesty.
You lift up your Son Jesus in cross and resurrection
  to draw all people to yourself.
And so we gladly thank you, with angels and archangels,
  and all the company of heaven, singing the hymn of your unending praise.

Holy, holy, holy Lord, God of power and might.
Heaven and earth are full of your glory.
Hosanna in the highest.
Blessed is he who comes in the name of the Lord.
Hosanna in the highest.

Righteous God, when the hour came for your Son to be glorified,
  he sat down with his disciples
    and reenacted the story of your liberating purpose for your people.
We gather as your disciples to reenact your liberating purpose
  in the death and resurrection of your Son.
Come among us now, that others may see you in us,
  and we may behold your glory, as these gifts of bread and wine
    become for us the body and blood of your Son Jesus Christ;
who, at supper with his disciples, took bread, gave you thanks,
  broke the bread, and gave it to them, saying,
    "Take, eat: this is my body which is given for you;

do this in remembrance of me."
After supper he took the cup.
Again he gave you thanks, and gave it to his disciples, saying,
  "Drink this, all of you: this is my blood of the new covenant,
    which is shed for you and for many for the forgiveness of sins.
  Do this, as often as you drink it, in remembrance of me."

Great is the mystery of faith.
Christ has died; Christ is risen; Christ will come again.

Heavenly God, you have glorified your name.
Glorify it again today, that those who stand before you
  with prayers and supplications made with loud cries and tears
    may find in you the solace for their aching,
      the joy of their desiring, and the goal of their yearning.
As you lifted up your Son through suffering to resurrected glory,
  lift up the wretched of the earth to find peace and rest
    at your side and in your heart.
Bring all who would see you face to face
  with your Son in the power of your Holy Spirit,
    until all injustice is transformed by your mercy,
      all deceit healed by your truth,
        and all oppression dismantled by your grace,
          until your kingdom is known on earth, now and forever. **Amen.**

Lent 5, Year C

The Lord be with you. **And also with you.**
Lift up your hearts. **We lift them to the Lord.**
Let us give thanks to the Lord our God. **It is right to give our thanks and praise.**

Extravagant God,
   you poured out your life in your covenant with your chosen people,
     and you poured out your life-blood
       in the ministry and death of your Son Jesus Christ.
You meet our meanness with your grace,
   our scarcity with your abundance,
     and our suspicion with your generous trust.
And so we give you thanks, with angels and archangels
   and all the company of heaven, singing the hymn of your unending praise.

Holy, holy, holy Lord, God of power and might.
Heaven and earth are full of your glory.
Hosanna in the highest.
Blessed is he who comes in the name of the Lord.
Hosanna in the highest.

Sharing God,
   in Jesus you attended a meal to celebrate Lazarus's resurrection,
     and so we gather today to celebrate Jesus' resurrection,
       in faith that even now you are preparing a feast
         to celebrate our resurrection with you.
Sanctify us, that even as our flesh and blood decay,
   our hearts are made ready that we may meet you face to face.
Send down your Holy Spirit, that this bread of sustenance and wine of joy
   may be for us the body and blood of your Son Jesus Christ;
who, at supper with his disciples, took bread, gave you thanks,
   broke the bread, and gave it to them, saying,
     "Take, eat: this is my body which is given for you;

do this in remembrance of me."
After supper he took the cup.
Again he gave you thanks, and gave it to his disciples, saying,
  "Drink this, all of you: this is my blood of the new covenant,
    which is shed for you and for many for the forgiveness of sins.
  Do this, as often as you drink it, in remembrance of me."

Great is the mystery of faith.
Christ has died; Christ is risen; Christ will come again.

Abundant God,
  when we know the price of everything and the value of nothing,
    may this meal remind us of the limitless joy you take in us.
When we are full of criticism of others and hatred of ourselves,
  may this sacrifice show us the goodness you see in us all.
Bless all our touching, that we may touch your gifts and one another
  as if we were touching your body and blood.
Bless all our desire, that in every craving and longing
  we may discover a deeper yearning for you.
Renew the hearts of all your people, that your whole church,
  seeking together the justice of your kingdom,
    may discover in the stranger the gifts that only come from you,
      through whom, and with whom, and in whom
        come all honor and glory, Father, Son, and Holy Spirit,
          one God, now and forever. **Amen.**

Palm Sunday

The Lord be with you. **And also with you.**
Lift up your hearts. **We lift them to the Lord.**
Let us give thanks to the Lord our God. **It is right to give our thanks and praise.**

It is our joy and destiny to praise you, Lord God,
   for in wondrous love you cast stars into space,
      and in meek obedience your Son surrendered to cruel nails.
With loving-kindness you called your people in Abraham,
   and in covenant with Moses you bound up your life in theirs.
Through exile you stayed close to them,
   and in Jesus you came among them
      bearing the fullness of grace and truth.
Your Son Jesus faced rejection, cruelty, and death,
   yet in resurrection you exalted him,
      and in sending your Spirit you shed glory on all people.
And so we rejoice with angels and archangels,
   and with all the company of heaven,
      singing the song of your unending praise.

Holy, holy, holy Lord, God of power and might.
Heaven and earth are full of your glory.
Hosanna in the highest.
Blessed is he who comes in the name of the Lord.
Hosanna in the highest.

Hosanna is our cry, Blessed One.
Your Son comes on a donkey in your name.
As Jesus entered Jerusalem to bear our sorrows and suffer for our sins,
   enter our hearts and confront our waywardness today.
Send your Holy Spirit upon us,
   that we may be your Son's crucified and risen body.
Send your Spirit upon this bread that it may be living bread,

and on this wine that it may be the cup of salvation, that together
    they may be for us the body and blood of your Son Jesus Christ;
who, at supper with his disciples, took bread, gave you thanks,
    broke the bread, and gave it to them, saying,
        "Take, eat: this is my body which is given for you;
            do this in remembrance of me."
After supper he took the cup.
Again he gave you thanks, and gave it to his disciples, saying,
    "Drink this, all of you: this is my blood of the new covenant,
        which is shed for you and for many for the forgiveness of sins.
    Do this, as often as you drink it, in remembrance of me."

Great is the mystery of faith.
Christ has died; Christ is risen; Christ will come again.

Humble God, your Son did not exploit his status but emptied himself.
Pour out your Spirit on all who are exploited, in world or church,
    on all who are humbled, by state or employer or family member,
    on all who are emptied of hope, faith, or love.
As you highly exalted your Son who had become a slave,
    highly exalt your children who suffer for righteousness,
        or grieve those they have cherished,
            or bend the knee to one who does not honor them.
Fill the earth with your justice and peace,
    until every heart shall sing and every tongue confess
        that you are the joy of their desiring, Father, Son, and Holy Spirit,
            ever one God, in all ages and forevermore. **Amen.**

Maundy Thursday

The Lord be with you. **And also with you.**
Lift up your hearts. **We lift them to the Lord.**
Let us give thanks to the Lord our God. **It is right to give our thanks and praise.**

Meek and majestic God,
   you set aside the perfection of your Trinitarian life
     to create the universe,
       and you called the children of Abraham to be your priestly kingdom.
You gave your people freedom in the parting of the sea
   and marked them for life with the blood of the Lamb.
In Jesus you laid aside the robe of your majesty
   and knelt among your children, facing humiliation and rejection.
In his agony in the garden and suffering on the cross
   you showed the world the extent of your love
     and your longing to bring us home to the throne
       where we shall join angels and archangels
         and all the company of heaven,
           praising your holy name in the unending hymn.

Holy, holy, holy Lord, God of power and might.
Heaven and earth are full of your glory.
Hosanna in the highest.
Blessed is he who comes in the name of the Lord.
Hosanna in the highest.

Self-giving God, in Jesus you became
   the Lamb who takes away the sins of the world,
     and the living bread, broken for the life of your children.
Come among us in the power of your Holy Spirit, that your people,
   as fragile and fitful as your disciples, may become your temple,
     and that these gifts of bread and wine may be for us
       the body and blood of your Son Jesus Christ;

who, at supper with his disciples, took bread, gave you thanks,
  broke the bread, and gave it to them, saying,
    "Take, eat: this is my body which is given for you;
      do this in remembrance of me."
After supper he took the cup.
Again he gave you thanks, and gave it to his disciples, saying,
  "Drink this, all of you: this is my blood of the new covenant,
    which is shed for you and for many for the forgiveness of sins.
  Do this, as often as you drink it, in remembrance of me."

Great is the mystery of faith.
Christ has died; Christ is risen; Christ will come again.

Blessed and broken God, be among your people
  who taste the bitter herbs of slavery and oppression;
    be close to your children who are poured out in grief and despair;
      remake the church, your Son's body,
        where it is broken by discord and dispute;
          and renew your creation in the joy of thanksgiving.
Spread your table in the face of friends and enemies,
  that all may know your peace and gather in the company of your saints,
    where you, in the presence of Christ
      and the companionship of the Holy Spirit, are all in all,
        one God, now and forever. **Amen.**

5. Easter

Easter Day

The Lord be with you. **And also with you.**
Lift up your hearts. **We lift them to the Lord.**
Let us give thanks to the Lord our God. **It is right to give our thanks and praise.**

Thanks and praise fill our hearts, Almighty God,
   for you are the Lord of creation and new creation,
     of covenant and new covenant.
You brought your people out of slavery to freedom in the Promised Land,
   and you brought your Son from the depth of death
     to the glory of resurrection life.
And so we gladly thank you,
   with your people on earth and all the company of heaven,
     singing the hymn of your unending praise.

Holy, holy, holy Lord, God of power and might.
Heaven and earth are full of your glory.
Hosanna in the highest.
Blessed is he who comes in the name of the Lord.
Hosanna in the highest.

Joy and gladness are our song, redeeming God,
   for in your conquest of death we see the destiny of every hope in you.
Come among us in the power of your Holy Spirit,
   that your children may be blessed with power and grace,
     and that this bread and cup may become for us
       the body and blood of your Son Jesus Christ;
who, at supper with his disciples, took bread, gave you thanks,
   broke the bread, and gave it to them, saying,
     "Take, eat: this is my body which is given for you;
       do this in remembrance of me."
After supper he took the cup.
Again he gave you thanks, and gave it to his disciples, saying,

"Drink this, all of you: this is my blood of the new covenant,
　　which is shed for you and for many for the forgiveness of sins.
　　Do this, as often as you drink it, in remembrance of me."

Great is the mystery of faith.
Christ has died; Christ is risen; Christ will come again.

Hope and glory are our breath, merciful God,
　　for you have rolled away the stone of despair,
　　　　the stone of oppression, the stone of lament, the stone of grief,
　　　　the stone of death, the stone of sin, the stone of fear.
Come and stand among us and breathe on us your peace,
　　breathe on us your power, breathe on us your eternal life,
　　　　that all who labor, all who stumble, all who hunger,
　　　　　　and all who fall shall meet you in the breaking of the bread
　　　　　　and be lifted up by your touch.
Shape your church to be your risen body;
　　make our scars beautiful like your scars,
　　　make our lives life-giving like your life,
　　　　and make our communion holy with your saints,
　　　　　until you come again in glory
　　　　　　and we eat with you in your kingdom,
　　　　　　　Father, Son, and Holy Spirit, ever one God. **Amen.**

Easter 2

The Lord be with you. **And also with you.**
Lift up your hearts. **We lift them to the Lord.**
Let us give thanks to the Lord our God. **It is right to give our thanks and praise.**

It is our duty and our joy to give you thanks and praise,
   Lord God of heaven and earth,
     because you are continually renewing your work of creation
      and transforming it to show your glory through resurrection.
With your touch you formed us from the dust of the earth.
You raised your people from slavery in Egypt;
   you bound them to you through your covenant on Sinai;
     and you made yourself known to them in exile and the Promised Land.
In the cross of Jesus you take into yourself the scars of our sin,
   and in his resurrected body you invite us to touch the wounds of your love.
And so we gladly thank you, with angels and archangels
   and all the company of heaven, singing the hymn of your unending praise.

Holy, holy, holy Lord, God of power and might.
Heaven and earth are full of your glory.
Hosanna in the highest.
Blessed is he who comes in the name of the Lord.
Hosanna in the highest.

Forgiving God, your Son's disciples cowered behind locked doors;
   and yet in him you visited them on the evening of resurrection
     and breathed on them the Spirit of peace.
Breathe that Holy Spirit upon us now,
   that your church may know the power of your forgiveness
     and these gifts of bread and wine may be for us
      the body and blood of your Son Jesus Christ;
who, at supper with his disciples, took bread, gave you thanks,
   broke the bread, and gave it to them, saying,

"Take, eat: this is my body which is given for you;
   do this in remembrance of me."
After supper he took the cup.
Again he gave you thanks, and gave it to his disciples, saying,
   "Drink this, all of you: this is my blood of the new covenant,
      which is shed for you and for many for the forgiveness of sins.
   Do this, as often as you drink it, in remembrance of me."

Great is the mystery of faith.
Christ has died; Christ is risen; Christ will come again.

Lord and God, intimate savior of our lives
   and cosmic ruler of the universe,
      in Jesus you are the substance of things hoped for
         and the knowledge of things unseen.
Visit any who struggle under the shadow of doubt;
   minister among all who suffer beneath the claims of oppressive rule;
      resurrect your children, your church, and your earth.
Bless those who have not seen and yet believe,
   and shape your wounded body the church
      to let the world see you through its scars.
Lift every voice to sing your Easter glory,
   until the day when all stand before your throne,
      in eternal communion with one another and with you,
         ever one God, Father, Son, and Holy Spirit. **Amen.**

Easter 3, Year A

The Lord be with you. **And also with you.**
Lift up your hearts. **We lift them to the Lord.**
Let us give thanks to the Lord our God. **It is right to give our thanks and praise.**

Blessing God, you walk with us from the Jerusalem of our failure
  to the Emmaus of your glorious revelation.
You made us to be your companions,
  and you gave us food and drink
    that we might share your substance with you.
You created us from the dust of the earth,
  and you re-created us by water and the Spirit.
You called your chosen people, you sent Moses and the prophets,
  and you came among us in Jesus
    that we might know you in his crucified and broken body
      and celebrate you in the everlasting joy of his resurrection.
And so we gladly thank you, with angels and archangels
  and all the company of heaven, singing the hymn of your unending praise.

Holy, holy, holy Lord, God of power and might.
Heaven and earth are full of your glory.
Hosanna in the highest.
Blessed is he who comes in the name of the Lord.
Hosanna in the highest.

Breaking God, when your Son sat at table with his crestfallen disciples,
  he was made known to them in the breaking of the bread.
Come among us now in the power of your Holy Spirit,
  that your people may discover you in the breaking of the bread,
    that you may stay with us and make your home among us,
      and that these gifts of bread and wine may become for us
        the body and blood of your Son Jesus Christ;
who, at supper with his disciples, took bread, gave you thanks,

broke the bread, and gave it to them, saying,
   "Take, eat: this is my body which is given for you;
      do this in remembrance of me."
After supper he took the cup.
Again he gave you thanks, and gave it to his disciples, saying,
   "Drink this, all of you: this is my blood of the new covenant,
      which is shed for you and for many for the forgiveness of sins.
   Do this, as often as you drink it, in remembrance of me."

Great is the mystery of faith.
Christ has died; Christ is risen; Christ will come again.

Sharing God, in the power of your Holy Spirit repeat among us
   your Son's actions of taking, blessing, breaking, and sharing,
      that you may take, bless, break, and share us,
         and that the world may recognize you
            in the way you act on our lives.
Breathe your Spirit on your church,
   that we might feel our hearts on fire as you talk with us
   and explain the scriptures to us.
Inspire all who stand still, looking sad.
Open the eyes of all who are kept from perceiving you.
Bring your bread of life
   to feed all who hunger in body, mind, or spirit,
      until the day when we live your life abundant
         with the communion of saints,
            in the presence and companionship of your Holy Trinity,
            Father, Son, and Holy Spirit, ever one God. **Amen.**

Easter 3, Year B

The Lord be with you. **And also with you.**
Lift up your hearts. **We lift them to the Lord.**
Let us give thanks to the Lord our God. **It is right to give our thanks and praise.**

Creator God, you made the wonder that is earth,
    inscribing soil, sky, and sea with life, energy, and glory.
Though we look upon you with eyes dimmed by the Fall,
  you gaze upon us with eyes filled with grace.
You breathe new air into our choking lungs,
  you bring life out of toxic soil,
    you turn polluted seas into the waters of baptism.
You parted the waters to liberate your captive people,
  and you rolled away the stone
    to bring us face to face with your resurrected Son.
You make us your Son's body, taken, blessed, and broken on the cross
  to be shared for the life of your world.
And so we gladly thank you, with angels and archangels,
  and all the company of heaven, singing the hymn of your unending praise.

Holy, holy, holy Lord, God of power and might.
Heaven and earth are full of your glory.
Hosanna in the highest.
Blessed is he who comes in the name of the Lord.
Hosanna in the highest.

Re-creating God,
  when your Son came to restore your purpose for the earth,
    he took the fruit of your abundance and the food of human labor.
Come among us now, and make us holy
  in the sharing of your gracious abundance and our faltering endeavor.
Take these gifts of bread and wine and make them for us
  the body and blood of your Son Jesus Christ;

who, at supper with his disciples, took bread, gave you thanks,
  broke the bread, and gave it to them, saying,
    "Take, eat: this is my body which is given for you;
      do this in remembrance of me."
After supper he took the cup.
Again he gave you thanks, and gave it to his disciples, saying,
  "Drink this, all of you: this is my blood of the new covenant,
    which is shed for you and for many for the forgiveness of sins.
  Do this, as often as you drink it, in remembrance of me."

Great is the mystery of faith.
Christ has died; Christ is risen; Christ will come again.

Ever-creating God,
  your Son Jesus invited his disciples to touch his risen body.
Come now in the power of your Holy Spirit,
  and touch all that is still to be resurrected.
Touch all who live in fear; touch any who know daily hunger;
  touch those who carry wounds and scars.
Touch all who are yet to see the salvation you bring through your Son;
  touch any who are stumbling and tentative in their faith;
    touch those who are disbelieving and still wondering.
Touch your whole church and make us one in you,
  that your scars may again proclaim your glory,
    and we may be united with your saints
      in the coming of your kingdom, ever one God,
        on earth as in heaven, Father, Son, and Holy Spirit. **Amen.**

Easter 3, Year C

The Lord be with you. **And also with you.**
Lift up your hearts. **We lift them to the Lord.**
Let us give thanks to the Lord our God. **It is right to give our thanks and praise.**

Worthy are you, Lord God, and worthy is the Lamb who was slain,
  to receive wisdom and might and glory and honor forever and ever.
From the pit of slavery you heard your people's cries
  and drew them up to freedom in your service.
Out of the snare of sin you saw the suffering of your creation
  and restored the life of your faithful ones.
From the grave of death you raised your Son to life on the third day.
In him you turn mourning into dancing;
  you remove the sackcloth of tears and clothe us with joy.
And so around your throne, with all you have gathered to yourself
  and raised to the company of heaven, we join in the eternal hymn of praise.

Holy, holy, holy Lord, God of power and might.
Heaven and earth are full of your glory.
Hosanna in the highest.
Blessed is he who comes in the name of the Lord.
Hosanna in the highest.

Providing God, your Son prepared a simple meal for his disciples
  which in your grace became a resurrection banquet.
As you revealed yourself to them, open our hearts
  to receive in this holy meal the miracle of his saving passion.
Send your Holy Spirit upon your church
  to make our life together a feast for all who hunger.
Sanctify this bread and cup that they may be for us
  the body and blood of your Son;
who, at supper with his disciples, took bread, gave you thanks,
  broke the bread, and gave it to them, saying,

"Take, eat: this is my body which is given for you;
  do this in remembrance of me."
After supper he took the cup.
Again he gave you thanks, and gave it to his disciples, saying,
  "Drink this, all of you: this is my blood of the new covenant,
    which is shed for you and for many for the forgiveness of sins.
  Do this, as often as you drink it, in remembrance of me."

Great is the mystery of faith.
Christ has died; Christ is risen; Christ will come again.

Great Shepherd, your Son is the holy Lamb,
  and by his blood you have made us your own flock.
Feed your sheep who hunger for the necessities of life,
  for safe food to eat and clean water to drink,
    for protection from fear, for shelter, and for warmth.
Tend your lambs when they long for love and acceptance
  and a place to belong.
Make your church a sheepfold of grace.
Shepherd all who have suffered harm
  and look to you for healing and hope.
Turn the sorrow of mourning into one eternal joy in your presence.
Bring us with all creation to that great day
  when we shall fall on our knees and worship the Lamb in glory,
    Holy Father, in the power of your Spirit. **Amen.**

Easter 4

The Lord be with you. **And also with you.**
Lift up your hearts. **We lift them to the Lord.**
Let us give thanks to the Lord our God. **It is right to give our thanks and praise.**

Shepherding God, we praise and thank you
  because you gathered your flock around Abraham,
    and through Moses and Joshua
      you brought your sheep to a place of safety.
In Jesus you came to us as a Passover Lamb
  to take away the sins of the world.
As our everlasting Good Shepherd you promise
  that those who hear your voice shall never be in want,
    for you know your sheep by name, and you call us your own
      and give to each of us a place in the sheepfold of your kingdom,
        where angels and archangels, and all the company of heaven,
          sing your unending praise.

Holy, holy, holy Lord, God of power and might.
Heaven and earth are full of your glory.
Hosanna in the highest.
Blessed is he who comes in the name of the Lord.
Hosanna in the highest.

Sustaining God, as you lead your sheep to green pastures
  and guide them beside still waters,
    so you have led us to this table
      where in bread and wine you restore our soul.
Send down your Holy Spirit and restore your church
  through the abundance of this sacred meal.
As we remember the story of your Son's life laid down for us,
  sanctify this bread and cup and make them be for us
    the body and blood of your Son Jesus Christ;

who, at supper with his disciples, took bread, gave you thanks,
  broke the bread, and gave it to them, saying,
    "Take, eat: this is my body which is given for you;
      do this in remembrance of me."
After supper he took the cup.
Again he gave you thanks, and gave it to his disciples, saying,
  "Drink this, all of you: this is my blood of the new covenant,
    which is shed for you and for many for the forgiveness of sins.
  Do this, as often as you drink it, in remembrance of me."

Great is the mystery of faith.
Christ has died; Christ is risen; Christ will come again.

Saving God, your rod and staff comfort all who look to you in faith.
Search out your sheep that are lost and bring them home.
When you find them in the valley of fear, gather them in your arms.
When they face evil in the presence of enemies,
  follow them with your goodness and mercy all the days of their life.
On that day when the shadow of death covers them,
  bring them to dwell in your house forever.
Shepherd us with all your saints of every age into your glorious presence,
  where we shall behold your Lamb in seated glory,
    most Holy Trinity, now and always. **Amen.**

Easter 5, Year A

The Lord be with you. **And also with you.**
Lift up your hearts. **We lift them to the Lord.**
Let us give thanks to the Lord our God. **It is right to give our thanks and praise.**

We rejoice to give you thanks and praise, God of love,
  because you called us to exist in your image,
    you filled the earth with wonder and beauty and life,
      and you made the children of Abraham your covenant people.
You made us a chosen race, a royal priesthood,
  a holy nation, your own people,
    and in the death and resurrection of Jesus
      you show us the way, the truth, and the life.
Once we were not a people, but now we are your people;
  once we had not received mercy, but now we have received mercy.
And so we gladly thank you, with angels and archangels
  and all the company of heaven, singing the hymn of your unending praise.

Holy, holy, holy Lord, God of power and might.
Heaven and earth are full of your glory.
Hosanna in the highest.
Blessed is he who comes in the name of the Lord.
Hosanna in the highest.

Living God, you prepare a place for us
  with the Holy Trinity in your kingdom banquet,
    and you set a place for us at this table as we anticipate your glory.
Come among us now, in the power of your Holy Spirit,
  that we may see your glory in the breaking of the bread,
    and that these gifts of bread and wine may become for us
      the body and blood of your Son Jesus Christ;
who, at supper with his disciples, took bread, gave you thanks,
  broke the bread, and gave it to them, saying,

"Take, eat: this is my body which is given for you;
   do this in remembrance of me."
After supper he took the cup.
Again he gave you thanks, and gave it to his disciples, saying,
  "Drink this, all of you: this is my blood of the new covenant,
    which is shed for you and for many for the forgiveness of sins.
  Do this, as often as you drink it, in remembrance of me."

Great is the mystery of faith.
Christ has died; Christ is risen; Christ will come again.

Glorious God, you promise
   that those who believe in you will do greater things than these.
Bestow upon your church the gifts of your Spirit,
   that your people may be with the hungry, do beautiful things,
     show grace amid hostility, witness to your story,
       and behold your glory.
Make us living stones and build us into a spiritual house,
   that we may be your holy priesthood and that all creation,
     suffering and flourishing, faithful and fallen,
       may be suffused with your glory and may overflow with your praise,
         Father, Son, and Holy Spirit, ever one God. **Amen.**

Easter 5, Year B

The Lord be with you. **And also with you.**
Lift up your hearts. **We lift them to the Lord.**
Let us give thanks to the Lord our God. **It is right to give our thanks and praise.**

Abiding God, you planted the vineyard of creation,
   and called your chosen people to be your vine,
     rooted and grounded in you.
In Jesus you gave us the true vine, turning earth into grapes
   and the water of life into the wine of eternal life.
Through your Son you abide in us, and in the power of your Holy Spirit
   you shape the branches of the vine to make fruit that will last.
Your Son was crucified on the vine of our sin,
   that the blood of his sacrifice
     might be the wine through which we may never be thirsty again.
In this meal of creation, of resurrection, and of everlasting life,
   you pour out the cup of your abundance to give us eternal joy in you.
And so we gladly thank you, with angels and archangels,
   and all the company of heaven, singing the hymn of your unending praise.

Holy, holy, holy Lord, God of power and might.
Heaven and earth are full of your glory.
Hosanna in the highest.
Blessed is he who comes in the name of the Lord.
Hosanna in the highest.

Transforming God,
   your Son took the ordinary substance of human flesh and bone;
     and on his last night with his friends
       he took the ordinary materials of bread and wine.
Come among us now, and make the ordinariness of our lives
   glow with the wonder of your eternal life.
Take these gifts of bread and wine and make them be for us

the body and blood of your Son Jesus Christ;
who, at supper with his disciples, took bread, gave you thanks,
  broke the bread, and gave it to them, saying,
    "Take, eat: this is my body which is given for you;
      do this in remembrance of me."
After supper he took the cup.
Again he gave you thanks, and gave it to his disciples, saying,
  "Drink this, all of you: this is my blood of the new covenant,
    which is shed for you and for many for the forgiveness of sins.
  Do this, as often as you drink it, in remembrance of me."

Great is the mystery of faith.
Christ has died; Christ is risen; Christ will come again.

Companionable God, you turn Word into flesh,
  and your perfect love casts out our fear.
You show us a way to love you
  by giving us brothers and sisters to love as we love you.
Abide with all whose lives are far from fruitful;
  remain with those who have experienced pruning;
    dwell with any who feel like branches that have been discarded.
Unite your whole church, living and departed,
  as branches of your one vine,
    and through being rooted and grounded in you,
      make us fruitful in body, mind, and spirit,
        until we stand before you, with your whole creation,
          and you are all in all, one God, Father, Son, and Holy Spirit. **Amen.**

Easter 5, Year C

The Lord be with you. **And also with you.**
Lift up your hearts. **We lift them to the Lord.**
Let us give thanks to the Lord our God. **It is right to give our thanks and praise.**

Creating God, you made the earth as a place of encounter.
Here you made a covenant with your chosen people.
When your children went astray
   you came among us in the form of your Son,
     showed your glory, and in his passion suffered for our sin.
In him you brought every aspect of creation to its purpose.
Your Son's resurrection empowered his disciples,
   and your Spirit's fire enlivens your church.
You promise us that when our story with you is completed,
   you will inaugurate a new heaven and a new earth
     where we shall enjoy life with you forever.
So with angels and archangels and all the company of heaven,
   anticipating your eternal praise, we bless you in everlasting song.

Holy, holy, holy Lord, God of power and might.
Heaven and earth are full of your glory.
Hosanna in the highest.
Blessed is he who comes in the name of the Lord.
Hosanna in the highest.

Redeeming God, you have prepared a banquet
   for us to share with you in your kingdom.
Send now your Holy Spirit, that we may taste that banquet today,
   that your Son may be present among us,
     and that this bread broken and wine outpoured
       may be for us his body and blood;
who, at supper with his disciples, took bread, gave you thanks,
   broke the bread, and gave it to them, saying,

"Take, eat: this is my body which is given for you;
  do this in remembrance of me."
After supper he took the cup.
Again he gave you thanks, and gave it to his disciples, saying,
  "Drink this, all of you: this is my blood of the new covenant,
    which is shed for you and for many for the forgiveness of sins.
  Do this, as often as you drink it, in remembrance of me."

Great is the mystery of faith.
Christ has died; Christ is risen; Christ will come again.

Transforming God, in Christ and in this holy meal
  you show us the shape of love.
In broken bread show us the cost of your love
  and inspire us to love like you.
In poured wine show us the constancy of your love
  and form us to love as truly as you love us.
Remake your earth that it may breathe your life.
Remake its people that they may resound with your glory.
Remake your church that it may look like your Son.
Wipe every tear from every eye; make death no more;
  and take away mourning and crying and pain,
    that all may find justice in your mercy
      and freedom in your service,
        until the beginning and the ending of all things are one in you,
          and you are all in all, one God, Father, Son, and Holy Spirit. **Amen.**

Easter 6, Year A

The Lord be with you. **And also with you.**
Lift up your hearts. **We lift them to the Lord.**
Let us give thanks to the Lord our God. **It is right to give our thanks and praise.**

Unknown yet revealing God,
   it is our duty and joy to thank and praise you,
      because from one ancestor you made all nations to inhabit the earth,
         and you allotted their times and boundaries,
            so they would search for you,
               in whom they live and move and have their being.
While our lives are circumscribed by the limitations of our minds and bodies,
   your life is beyond our reach and outside our imagining.
Yet in your mercy you embodied all your promises to your people
   in the sending of your Son, and through his dying and rising
      you have brought us to your throne of grace.
And so we gladly thank you, with angels and archangels,
   and all who with your ascended Son sit at your right hand on high,
      singing the hymn of your unending praise.

Holy, holy, holy Lord, God of power and might.
Heaven and earth are full of your glory.
Hosanna in the highest.
Blessed is he who comes in the name of the Lord.
Hosanna in the highest.

Sending and accompanying God, you do not leave us orphaned,
   but in Christ you make us your adopted children,
      and in your Spirit you send an Advocate to be with us forever.
By the power of that same Spirit, take the fragile flesh of your people
   and transform it into the resurrected glory of your church;
      and come down upon these gifts of bread and wine
         and make them be for us

the body and blood of your Son Jesus Christ;
who, at supper with his disciples, took bread, gave you thanks,
   broke the bread, and gave it to them, saying,
      "Take, eat: this is my body which is given for you;
         do this in remembrance of me."
After supper he took the cup.
Again he gave you thanks, and gave it to his disciples, saying,
   "Drink this, all of you: this is my blood of the new covenant,
      which is shed for you and for many for the forgiveness of sins.
   Do this, as often as you drink it, in remembrance of me."

Great is the mystery of faith.
Christ has died; Christ is risen; Christ will come again.

Sanctifying God, from the abundance of your limitless glory,
   bless your children who suffer for doing right.
Give to those who stand trial the gentleness and reverence of your Son.
As in Christ you proclaimed your word to the spirits in prison,
   make yourself known to all who find themselves
      incarcerated in body, mind, or spirit.
Be close to any who live with public shame,
   and all who carry the humiliation of others in their hearts.
Breathe your power upon your people
   where they face persecution, oppression, or false charge,
      that in truth you shall lead us to all truth,
         until that day when the whole earth is judged in righteousness
            by the one you have appointed and raised from the dead,
               and we stand before you, forgiven, loved, and free,
                  ever one God, Father, Son, and Holy Spirit. **Amen.**

Easter 6, Year B

The Lord be with you. **And also with you.**
Lift up your hearts. **We lift them to the Lord.**
Let us give thanks to the Lord our God. **It is right to give our thanks and praise.**

Wondrous and merciful God, we thank and praise you
  because we did not choose you but you chose us.
You destined us to become your friends
  from before the foundation of the world.
You showed steadfast love and faithfulness to your covenant people
  and remembered your promises in every generation.
Greater love hath no one than you, because in Christ
  you laid down your life and turned us from servants into friends,
    and by your Spirit you raise us up
      to be your beloved companions forever.
And so we gladly thank you, with angels and archangels,
  and all who with your risen and ascended Son
    sit at your right hand on high, singing the hymn of your unending praise.

Holy, holy, holy Lord, God of power and might.
Heaven and earth are full of your glory.
Hosanna in the highest.
Blessed is he who comes in the name of the Lord.
Hosanna in the highest.

God of joys and surprises, your Son's apostles
  were astounded that you sent your Holy Spirit upon the Gentiles
    and that all the earth was awakening to the praise of your name.
You invite us to join your company through baptism
  and sustain us in your fellowship through this meal of memory and hope.
Send your Holy Spirit upon your church
  that it may bear the image of your crucified and resurrected Son.
By the power of that same Spirit, bless this bread and this cup

that they may be for us the body and blood of your Son Jesus Christ;
who, at supper with his disciples, took bread, gave you thanks,
   broke the bread, and gave it to them, saying,
     "Take, eat: this is my body which is given for you;
       do this in remembrance of me."
After supper he took the cup.
Again he gave you thanks, and gave it to his disciples, saying,
   "Drink this, all of you: this is my blood of the new covenant,
     which is shed for you and for many for the forgiveness of sins.
   Do this, as often as you drink it, in remembrance of me."

Great is the mystery of faith.
Christ has died; Christ is risen; Christ will come again.

Overwhelming God,
   you give your children faith that celebrates your sovereignty.
Renew that faith among any who see your Son's continuing crucifixion
   more evidently than his glorious resurrection.
Restore and inspire all who, in the face of evil and suffering,
   feel less like conquerors and more like the conquered.
Walk with those who find your commandments a burden rather than a gift.
Hasten the day when all shall be drawn into the banquet of your kingdom,
   and you fill heaven and earth with the triumphs of your grace,
     ever one God, Father, Son, and Holy Spirit, now and forever. **Amen.**

Easter 6, Year C

The Lord be with you. **And also with you.**
Lift up your hearts. **We lift them to the Lord.**
Let us give thanks to the Lord our God. **It is right to give our thanks and praise.**

We lift our hearts in praise to you, God of glory,
   because in every time and place
     you have shown yourself to your people
      and revealed your purpose to dwell with them always.
In the wilderness you made your place of dwelling in a tabernacle.
In Jerusalem the temple became a theater of encounter with you.
In Jesus your Son you came among us,
   making your home in human flesh.
In his death he faced the consequences of our sin,
   and in his resurrection he made possible
     an everlasting home for us at your right hand.
You have prepared for us a holy city of heavenly lights
   where we will dwell with you forever.
So with angels and archangels
   we join the praises sung forevermore in that eternal city.

Holy, holy, holy Lord, God of power and might.
Heaven and earth are full of your glory.
Hosanna in the highest.
Blessed is he who comes in the name of the Lord.
Hosanna in the highest.

Lord God Almighty, from your throne flows the river of life.
Fed from that river,
   your tree of life bears fruit for the healing of the nations.
Nourish your church in this sacred meal,
   that the bread and wine we receive
     may be poured out through us as life abundant.

By the power of the Holy Spirit
  make your church a healing balm in places of suffering and sorrow.
Sanctify this bread and cup that they may be for us
  the body and blood of your Son;
who, at supper with his disciples, took bread, gave you thanks,
  broke the bread, and gave it to them, saying,
    "Take, eat: this is my body which is given for you;
      do this in remembrance of me."
After supper he took the cup.
Again he gave you thanks, and gave it to his disciples, saying,
  "Drink this, all of you: this is my blood of the new covenant,
    which is shed for you and for many for the forgiveness of sins.
  Do this, as often as you drink it, in remembrance of me."

Great is the mystery of faith.
Christ has died; Christ is risen; Christ will come again.

Revealing God, whose radiance is all holiness,
  make your face to shine upon us that we may be saved.
Look with mercy upon those who turn to you in hope
  and long for peace the world cannot give.
Hold in your light of compassion every troubled heart
  that waits for the dawn of your one eternal day.
Shine with the fullness of your love into every fear-filled soul,
  and make yourself known to all who long to see your face;
    until that hour when night is no more,
      and there is no need of lamp or sun, when you will be our light,
        and when in your eternal radiance
          you shall reign forever and ever, one God,
            Father, Son, and Holy Spirit. **Amen.**

Ascension of the Lord and Easter 7

The Lord be with you. **And also with you.**
Lift up your hearts. **We lift them to the Lord.**
Let us give thanks to the Lord our God. **It is right to give our thanks and praise.**

Glorious God, in Moses, the prophets, and the psalms you showed
   your purpose for your people and your love for your world.
In Jesus you fulfilled your promises and opened to us your heart.
In his passion and death we saw the consequences of our rejection
   and the depth of your yearning.
Yet you raised Jesus from the tomb.
In his resurrection you invite us into the company of your eternal joy,
   and in his ascension on high you seal as complete his work among us.
So with angels and archangels and all the company of heaven,
   we praise you forever, singing:

Holy, holy, holy Lord, God of power and might.
Heaven and earth are full of your glory.
Hosanna in the highest.
Blessed is he who comes in the name of the Lord.
Hosanna in the highest.

Gracious God, your Son at his ascension promised the disciples
   they would be clothed with power from on high.
Send now your Holy Spirit,
   that we may know the presence of your Son among us,
     and that bread broken, and wine outpoured,
       may be for us the body and blood of your Son Jesus Christ;
who, at supper with his disciples, took bread, gave you thanks,
   broke the bread, and gave it to them, saying,
     "Take, eat: this is my body which is given for you;
      do this in remembrance of me."
After supper he took the cup.

Again he gave you thanks, and gave it to his disciples, saying,
   "Drink this, all of you: this is my blood of the new covenant,
      which is shed for you and for many for the forgiveness of sins.
   Do this, as often as you drink it, in remembrance of me."

Great is the mystery of faith.
Christ has died; Christ is risen; Christ will come again.

Generous God, your Son told his disciples
   to stay in the city until they were clothed by the Spirit.
Give courage to those whom you call
   to stay in places of danger and confusion
      when their hearts are full of doubt and disillusion.
Your Son withdrew from the disciples
   when they did not know what the future would hold.
Be close to all who face an uncertain future
   and deeply know their need of you.
Your Son's disciples were continually in the temple praising you.
Give your church a fresh outpouring of your Spirit
   and make it a blessing to all the children of your earth;
      until the completion of your Son's ministry
         becomes the completion of your whole creation,
            and you are all in all, one God, Father, Son, and Holy Spirit. **Amen.**

Pentecost

The Lord be with you. **And also with you.**
Lift up your hearts. **We lift them to the Lord.**
Let us give thanks to the Lord our God. **It is right to give our thanks and praise.**

God of surprises, your Spirit brooded over the waters at creation
   and lived among your chosen people
     in wilderness, exile, and promised land.
Your Spirit filled Mary's womb at the moment of Jesus' conception
   and came upon him like a dove at his baptism.
When Christ died on the cross
   your power raised him from the tomb on the third day,
     and that same evening he breathed your forgiving grace
       on those who had deserted him.
On the day of Pentecost you sent your Spirit upon the fearful disciples,
   filling them with fire, with power, with wonder and joy,
     and making them your church.
And so we gladly thank you, with angels and archangels
   and all the company of heaven, singing the hymn of your unending praise.

Holy, holy, holy Lord, God of power and might.
Heaven and earth are full of your glory.
Hosanna in the highest.
Blessed is he who comes in the name of the Lord.
Hosanna in the highest.

God of comfort and strength, we look to your Holy Spirit
   to be with us in sorrow and in contentment,
     in crisis and in abiding stillness.
Come among us now through the power of your Spirit,
   that we may be transformed into your image,
     and that these gifts of bread and wine may become for us
       the body and blood of your Son Jesus Christ;

who, at supper with his disciples, took bread, gave you thanks,
  broke the bread, and gave it to them, saying,
    "Take, eat: this is my body which is given for you;
      do this in remembrance of me."
After supper he took the cup.
Again he gave you thanks, and gave it to his disciples, saying,
  "Drink this, all of you: this is my blood of the new covenant,
    which is shed for you and for many for the forgiveness of sins.
  Do this, as often as you drink it, in remembrance of me."

Great is the mystery of faith.
Christ has died; Christ is risen; Christ will come again.

God of dreams and prophecy, send down upon us
  your gifts of wisdom, knowledge, and faith;
    of healing, discernment, and interpretation,
      that your church may be built up in the likeness of your Son.
Let anyone who is hungry find in you the bread of life,
  and anyone who is thirsty find in you rivers of living water.
Speak your word to all who are alone and in fear or despair,
  and let each one of your children hear your voice in their own language,
    whether that language be art or science, work or play.
Sanctify your groaning creation,
  that your universe may breathe your breath and be filled with your life anew,
    that we may love what you love, and do what you would do,
      Father, Son, and Holy Spirit, ever one God. **Amen.**

6. Sundays after Pentecost (Summer)

Trinity Sunday

The Lord be with you. **And also with you.**
Lift up your hearts. **We lift them to the Lord.**
Let us give thanks to the Lord our God. **It is right to give our thanks and praise.**

Threefold and glorious God, in Fatherly joy you created all things
   through the grace of your Word and the wisdom of your Spirit.
In the depth of your love for the world you gave your only Son
   that all might come to new life in your Spirit.
You rolled away the stone by your Fatherly hand
   and in the power of your Spirit raised your incarnate Son from the dead.
In your Fatherly mercy you breathed your Spirit on the fearful disciples,
   giving them the fire of your love to live as the body of your Son.
And so, adoring you with apostles and prophets, with martyrs and saints,
   with angels and archangels, with cherubim and seraphim,
     and with all your glorious company in bright array,
       we celebrate the glory of your praise.

Holy, holy, holy Lord, God of power and might.
Heaven and earth are full of your glory.
Hosanna in the highest.
Blessed is he who comes in the name of the Lord.
Hosanna in the highest.

Lord God, there is none beside you;
   you are perfect in power, in love, and in purity.
You invite us to join you at your heavenly banquet that knows no end.
In this meal we recall the sacrifice of your Son
   and the sanctification of your Spirit.
Send that Spirit upon us now,
   that we may be made ready to be your companions,
     and on these gifts of bread and wine,
       that they may be for us

the body and blood of your Son, Jesus Christ our Lord;
who, at supper with his disciples, took bread, gave you thanks,
broke the bread, and gave it to them, saying,
"Take, eat: this is my body which is given for you;
do this in remembrance of me."
After supper he took the cup.
Again he gave you thanks, and gave it to his disciples, saying,
"Drink this, all of you: this is my blood of the new covenant,
which is shed for you and for many for the forgiveness of sins.
Do this, as often as you drink it, in remembrance of me."

Great is the mystery of faith.
Christ has died; Christ is risen; Christ will come again.

Triune God, in the dance of your love
we see your nature as utter relationship.
Be close to all who struggle in relationship at home,
in the workplace, across social divides and national thresholds.
As your three persons gaze in shared attention,
look upon those whose lives go unrecognized.
As your three members work together in true partnership,
uphold any who face the struggles of their life alone.
As your partners in threefold unity relish one another in deep delight,
revitalize those who live without joy or hope.
Make your church a community across time and space
that enjoys the gift of your life
and imitates the wonder of your love,
until all come into your presence and gaze upon your glory,
God in three persons, blessed Trinity. **Amen.**

June 5–11, Year A

The Lord be with you. **And also with you.**
Lift up your hearts. **We lift them to the Lord.**
Let us give thanks to the Lord our God. **It is right to give our thanks and praise.**

Lord Emmanuel, the with-us God, we thank and praise you
    because you called Abraham out of the dust of Haran
       and made him the father of many nations.
You blessed him and blessed those who blessed him,
    and called his nation one in whom all peoples would find a blessing.
You reckoned his faith as righteousness.
In Jesus you fulfilled that blessing and, in his dying and rising,
    opened out that covenant to your whole creation.
And so we celebrate the wonders of your grace,
    with all the host of heaven, singing your unending hymn.

Holy, holy, holy Lord, God of power and might.
Heaven and earth are full of your glory.
Hosanna in the highest.
Blessed is he who comes in the name of the Lord.
Hosanna in the highest.

God of ever-presence, Abraham built an altar in the desert
    because you had appeared to him.
Appear to us now as we gather around this holy table in your name.
As your Son pitched his tent in our midst,
    so through your Holy Spirit make him present to us
       and make us holy through him, that we might behold your glory.
Sanctify by that same Spirit this bread and wine,
    that they may be for us the body and blood of your Son, Jesus Christ our Lord;
who, at supper with his disciples, took bread, gave you thanks,
    broke the bread, and gave it to them, saying,
       "Take, eat: this is my body which is given for you;

do this in remembrance of me."
After supper he took the cup.
Again he gave you thanks, and gave it to his disciples, saying,
    "Drink this, all of you: this is my blood of the new covenant,
        which is shed for you and for many for the forgiveness of sins.
    Do this, as often as you drink it, in remembrance of me."

Great is the mystery of faith.
Christ has died; Christ is risen; Christ will come again.

Infectious God, in touching the hem of your Son's garment
    a woman was restored to wholeness and community.
In this sacrament give us grace to touch the hem of your garment
    and so find life and truth and peace.
Heal all who find themselves excluded
    by prejudice, discrimination, or bigotry.
Restore to your company any who have withdrawn
    through shame or fear or regret.
Lift up those who are invisible
    because of cruelty or imprisonment or suppression.
Visit your children who are close to death or dismayed by grief.
Gather to yourself a kingdom of sinner and sage, exile and exalted,
    that the body, mind, and spirit of your groaning creation
        may leap for joy and sing in your heart forever,
            Father, Son, and Holy Spirit. **Amen.**

June 5–11, Year B

The Lord be with you. **And also with you.**
Lift up your hearts. **We lift them to the Lord.**
Let us give thanks to the Lord our God. **It is right to give our thanks and praise.**

Faithful God, we rejoice in spirit and in truth
   to celebrate the weight of your glory,
     for even when we perceive you with foolish and self-seeking hearts,
      you still redeem our waywardness with your grace.
You destined us from before the foundation of the world
   to be your companions through your Son Jesus Christ;
     and though your chosen people sought to be like other nations
      and though your church forgets that its foundation and purpose is you,
       still you do not forget us.
Through your Son's cross you dismantled the power of sin and death
   and made a new family of all who do your will.
And so with glad and grateful hearts we sing your unending praise,
with angels and archangels and all the company of heaven.

Holy, holy, holy Lord, God of power and might.
Heaven and earth are full of your glory.
Hosanna in the highest.
Blessed is he who comes in the name of the Lord.
Hosanna in the highest.

God of incarnation, in Jesus you made an earthly tent
   in which to dwell among us;
     you raised him from the dead
      that we might tabernacle with you forever.
Make yourself known among us today
   in this tent of meeting you set up with us.
Through your Holy Spirit make the crucified and risen Lord present to us.
Make us holy through him that we might behold your glory.

By that same Spirit sanctify this bread and wine,
   that they may be for us the body and blood of your Son Jesus Christ;
who, at supper with his disciples, took bread, gave you thanks,
   broke the bread, and gave it to them, saying,
      "Take, eat: this is my body which is given for you;
         do this in remembrance of me."
After supper he took the cup.
Again he gave you thanks, and gave it to his disciples, saying,
   "Drink this, all of you: this is my blood of the new covenant,
      which is shed for you and for many for the forgiveness of sins.
      Do this, as often as you drink it, in remembrance of me."

Great is the mystery of faith.
Christ has died; Christ is risen; Christ will come again.

Liberating God, visit your children
   who are enslaved by the harshness of others.
Raise up your people when their sons are pressed into servitude
   and their daughters are made playthings of the powerful.
Transform the hearts of rulers
   that they may use their power to set people free
      and exert their influence to promote flourishing life
         for all under their authority.
Unshackle any who live under the shadow of oppression
   and let them go,
      until the day you bring us into your one eternal presence,
         transforming every sorrow and sin and suffering
            in the fullness of your glory beyond all measure,
               Father, Son, and Holy Spirit, ever one God, now and forever. **Amen.**

June 5–11, Year C

The Lord be with you. **And also with you.**
Lift up your hearts. **We lift them to the Lord.**
Let us give thanks to the Lord our God. **It is right to give our thanks and praise.**

All our days we open our lips in praise to you, Lord God.
From the moment of our birth you breathe into us our very life,
   and in making us your disciples you breathe your Spirit upon us.
At the beginning of time you put into Adam your breath of life,
   and when your people were bowed low in sin,
     you put into the mouths of prophets your word of truth.
As you gave your prophet Elijah power to raise a widow's son,
   so you gave your Son power to raise up those who had died;
     and on the third day you raised from the dead the crucified one
       in the power of your Spirit.
And so with all who live and breathe your Spirit,
   with angels and archangels and all the company of heaven,
     we praise your name and join the unending hymn.

Holy, holy, holy Lord, God of power and might.
Heaven and earth are full of your glory.
Hosanna in the highest.
Blessed is he who comes in the name of the Lord.
Hosanna in the highest.

Ever-giving God, as you transformed the widow's small provision,
   in her jar of meal and jug of oil,
     into earthly sustenance by your eternal grace,
      take these simple ingredients
        and feed us with the bread of heaven and the cup of salvation.
Pour your Holy Spirit upon your church gathered around this table
   that we may know your unfailing presence
     and become food for your hungry world.

Sanctify this bread and cup that they may be for us
　　the body and blood of your Son;
who, at supper with his disciples, took bread, gave you thanks,
　　broke the bread, and gave it to them, saying,
　　　　"Take, eat: this is my body which is given for you;
　　　　　　do this in remembrance of me."
After supper he took the cup.
Again he gave you thanks, and gave it to his disciples, saying,
　　"Drink this, all of you: this is my blood of the new covenant,
　　　　which is shed for you and for many for the forgiveness of sins.
　　Do this, as often as you drink it, in remembrance of me."

Great is the mystery of faith.
Christ has died; Christ is risen; Christ will come again.

Reviving God, you keep faith forever, raising up the forgotten,
　　restoring the fallen, and remembering the foreigner.
Watch over your people who endure through famine and drought;
　　strengthen all who hunger and thirst for daily provision.
Sustain those who are far from home, looking for a way to survive.
Lift up any who are bowed low by sighs too deep for words.
Uphold children who lack parents to love them
　　or a family to call their own;
　　　　be merciful to mourning parents who grieve the loss of a child.
Breathe your Spirit upon all flesh,
　　and bring us to the day when we shall be raised up
　　　　and made one with you and with one another in Christ Jesus,
　　　　　　when tears and sorrow and sighing shall be no more,
　　　　　　　　and there shall be one life, one hope, and one joy shared in you,
　　　　　　　　　　most Holy Trinity, now and forever. **Amen.**

June 12–18, Year A

The Lord be with you. **And also with you.**
Lift up your hearts. **We lift them to the Lord.**
Let us give thanks to the Lord our God. **It is right to give our thanks and praise.**

Trinity of grace and love, we thank and praise you,
   for you purposed before the foundation of the world
      to open your dance of delight to include even us,
         and you shaped your very life to incorporate us in your dance forever.
While we were yet sinners,
   Christ not only came among us but died at our hands.
In the glory of his resurrection
   he called ones like us to be his apostles
      and spread the good news of his mercy to all the world.
And so with apostles and saints and angels
   and every creature in whose heart your song is sung,
      we join our voices in your eternal praise.

Holy, holy, holy Lord, God of power and might.
Heaven and earth are full of your glory.
Hosanna in the highest.
Blessed is he who comes in the name of the Lord.
Hosanna in the highest.

Abiding God, in three visitors
   you appeared to Abraham in the heat of the day,
      and before him you broke bread
         and made your glorious purpose known.
Come among your people today, that in the sharing of food
   we may be made bearers of your covenant of grace.
Send your Holy Spirit
   on the bread that we break and the cup that we share,
      that they may be for us

the body and blood of your Son, Jesus Christ our Lord;
who, at supper with his disciples, took bread, gave you thanks,
   broke the bread, and gave it to them, saying,
      "Take, eat: this is my body which is given for you;
         do this in remembrance of me."
After supper he took the cup.
Again he gave you thanks, and gave it to his disciples, saying,
   "Drink this, all of you: this is my blood of the new covenant,
      which is shed for you and for many for the forgiveness of sins.
   Do this, as often as you drink it, in remembrance of me."

Great is the mystery of faith.
Christ has died; Christ is risen; Christ will come again.

Sustaining God, as your servant Paul
   and his Lord Christ before him suffered and endured,
      strengthen your church and hasten your kingdom
         through the witness of your people under persecution.
When your children are oppressed, give them courage to endure.
When they find strength to endure,
   produce in them character to reflect your truth.
When they develop character,
   manifest in them hope of your deliverance.
When they grow in hope, do not disappoint them,
   but roll down justice like a never-failing stream,
      until that day when a new heaven and a new earth
         engulf the longings of your aching people,
            God of eternity, Father, Son, and Holy Spirit. **Amen.**

June 12–18, Year B

The Lord be with you. **And also with you.**
Lift up your hearts. **We lift them to the Lord.**
Let us give thanks to the Lord our God. **It is right to give our thanks and praise.**

Glorious God, we praise and thank you,
　because you destined us to be your children,
　　and when you bring us to faith in your Son Jesus Christ
　　　you make a new creation.
Your people longed for a leader,
　and out of Bethlehem you gave them David;
　　when they yearned for a Savior,
　　　out of Bethlehem you gave them Jesus.
In your Son's life and death you showed us the extent of your love,
　and in his resurrection and ascension you showed us our future in you.
And so with all the company of heaven
　we rejoice to sing the praise of your glory.

Holy, holy, holy Lord, God of power and might.
Heaven and earth are full of your glory.
Hosanna in the highest.
Blessed is he who comes in the name of the Lord.
Hosanna in the highest.

True and living God, you do not judge by outward appearances
　but look upon the heart.
You came among us in your Son Jesus Christ,
　whose appearance was one with us,
　　and whose heart was one with you.
You call your church in human form;
　send upon us your Holy Spirit
　　that we may become one with you in faith and hope and love.
By that same Spirit take this food and drink,

whose outward appearance is bread and wine,
    and make them be for us the body and blood of your Son Jesus Christ;
who, at supper with his disciples, took bread, gave you thanks,
    broke the bread, and gave it to them, saying,
        "Take, eat: this is my body which is given for you;
            do this in remembrance of me."
After supper he took the cup.
Again he gave you thanks, and gave it to his disciples, saying,
    "Drink this, all of you: this is my blood of the new covenant,
        which is shed for you and for many for the forgiveness of sins.
    Do this, as often as you drink it, in remembrance of me."

Great is the mystery of faith.
Christ has died; Christ is risen; Christ will come again.

Promising God, you set our hearts to anticipate your harvest,
    in which all that turns to you is transformed into glory,
        and all that shrinks from you is turned to dust.
Uphold all who live in the midst of famine,
    that the bread of your eternal banquet
        may bring hope to the hungry.
Strengthen any who walk in the desert of despair,
    that the wine of your kingdom
        may give sustenance to those who thirst.
Bless all who labor and are heavy laden,
    that the sacrifice you made once for all may inspire them
        to walk with you until the time for tears is done,
            and you fill heaven and earth
                with the ever-rolling stream of your righteousness,
                    ever one God, Father, Son, and Holy Spirit, now and forever. **Amen.**

June 12–18, Year C

The Lord be with you. **And also with you.**
Lift up your hearts. **We lift them to the Lord.**
Let us give thanks to the Lord our God. **It is right to give our thanks and praise.**

Creating and re-creating God, you planted the vineyard of Israel
  and tended it with prophets, priests, and kings.
In the fullness of time you came among us in Jesus,
  our prophet, our priest, and our king.
In his life he was a prophet of your kingdom,
   in his death he was a priest who released us from sin,
    and in his resurrection he was king over all that oppresses us.
You make a new creation when we come to you in search of forgiveness,
  and you show us our destiny
    when we take our place with those around your throne,
      joining angels and archangels and all the company of heaven,
       singing the hymn of your unending praise.

Holy, holy, holy Lord, God of power and might.
Heaven and earth are full of your glory.
Hosanna in the highest.
Blessed is he who comes in the name of the Lord.
Hosanna in the highest.

God of life and new life,
  you meet us in our waywardness and restore us by your faithfulness.
When we join in the feast of your kingdom
  we expect to be transformed by your grace.
You have brought from the soil our daily bread
  and from the vineyard our wine of rejoicing.
Now send down your Holy Spirit,
  that they may be for us the body and blood of your Son Jesus Christ;
who, at supper with his disciples, took bread, gave you thanks,

broke the bread, and gave it to them, saying,
  "Take, eat: this is my body which is given for you;
    do this in remembrance of me."
After supper he took the cup.
Again he gave you thanks, and gave it to his disciples, saying,
  "Drink this, all of you: this is my blood of the new covenant,
    which is shed for you and for many for the forgiveness of sins.
  Do this, as often as you drink it, in remembrance of me."

Great is the mystery of faith.
Christ has died; Christ is risen; Christ will come again.

Redeeming God,
  as you have turned grain through ground flour into bread;
    as you have turned vines through crushed grapes into wine;
      as through your Holy Spirit you have brought Jesus
        through crucified agony into glorious resurrection,
          bring all your people
            through times of doubt and despair and desolation
            to the joy of your eternal kingdom.
As this bread becomes your body,
  and as your body becomes the shape of your church,
    feed the deepest hungers of our hearts and of your world
      and meet the yearning thirst
        of all who seek water, love, or justice,
          until the day when we are filled
            with the abundant fruits of your Spirit in union with Christ,
            ever one God. **Amen.**

June 19–25, Year A

The Lord be with you. **And also with you.**
Lift up your hearts. **We lift them to the Lord.**
Let us give thanks to the Lord our God. **It is right to give our thanks and praise.**

We lift our hearts and souls to you, Lord God,
  for you made creation out of nothing,
    and in Abraham you called a people to be your own.
You crafted a destiny for your children
  from the barrenness of despair and the wilderness of sin.
You made an everlasting covenant
  that bound you and humanity to be with one another forever.
In Jesus you made a new covenant
  that embodied humankind's full presence before you
    and your full presence before humankind.
And so we gladly thank you, with angels and archangels,
  and all the company of heaven, singing the hymn of your unending glory.

Holy, holy, holy Lord, God of power and might.
Heaven and earth are full of your glory.
Hosanna in the highest.
Blessed is he who comes in the name of the Lord.
Hosanna in the highest.

Uniting God, you bind yourself to us in Christ's death,
  and you bind us to yourself in Christ's resurrection.
In him we are dead to sin and alive to you.
Send now your Holy Spirit upon us
  and upon this meal in his memory,
    that we might be a ransomed, healed, restored, and forgiven people
      delivered from the curse of slavery,
        and that this bread and wine may be for us
          the body and blood of your Son Jesus Christ;

who, at supper with his disciples, took bread, gave you thanks,
   broke the bread, and gave it to them, saying,
      "Take, eat: this is my body which is given for you;
         do this in remembrance of me."
After supper he took the cup.
Again he gave you thanks, and gave it to his disciples, saying,
   "Drink this, all of you: this is my blood of the new covenant,
      which is shed for you and for many for the forgiveness of sins.
   Do this, as often as you drink it, in remembrance of me."

Great is the mystery of faith.
Christ has died; Christ is risen; Christ will come again.

Jealous God, you want us for yourself
   and you teach us to shape all our loves as ways of loving you.
Give your consolation to all who live with no peace, but only a sword.
Dwell with those who find their household divided,
   son against father, mother against daughter;
      and any who find it hard to love you
         and to cherish their family members too.
Restore your church
   that it may discover you on the way of the cross
      and find its life by losing it for your sake,
         until the day when you are the joy of our desiring
            and we the joy of yours,
               when every eye shall behold you
                  and every tongue confess you as Lord,
                     one and holy God, Father, Son, and Holy Spirit. **Amen.**

June 19–25, Year B

The Lord be with you. **And also with you.**
Lift up your hearts. **We lift them to the Lord.**
Let us give thanks to the Lord our God. **It is right to give our thanks and praise.**

It is our joy to praise and thank you, Lord God,
   because you called your chosen people
      to be a wily David in the face of the Goliath of the nations.
You equipped them with smooth stones of wisdom and faithfulness.
Even when your children forgot your will
   and sought to become Goliath,
      you recalled them to their true identity
         and raised up among them a Son of David
            to face the Goliath of sin and death with your word of truth alone.
And still today you call your church
   away from the threats and temptations of being Goliath
      to the risk and wonder of being remade
         to be like David, in the image of Jesus.
And so with angels and archangels and all the company of heaven
   we join the unending song of your glory.

Holy, holy, holy Lord, God of power and might.
Heaven and earth are full of your glory.
Hosanna in the highest.
Blessed is he who comes in the name of the Lord.
Hosanna in the highest.

Faithful God, in Christ you speak to us amid the storm of our fear
   and dwell with us when our faith is weak.
You are with us
   even when we lament our peril and doubt our destiny.
Come upon your church today in the power of your Spirit
   that your people may be reborn

as children of hope and courage and endurance.
Send that same Spirit upon this bread and this cup,
   that we may find in them the joy of your presence
      and they may be for us
         the body and blood of your Son Jesus Christ;
who, at supper with his disciples, took bread, gave you thanks,
   broke the bread, and gave it to them, saying,
      "Take, eat: this is my body which is given for you;
         do this in remembrance of me."
After supper he took the cup.
Again he gave you thanks, and gave it to his disciples, saying,
   "Drink this, all of you: this is my blood of the new covenant,
      which is shed for you and for many for the forgiveness of sins.
   Do this, as often as you drink it, in remembrance of me."

Great is the mystery of faith.
Christ has died; Christ is risen; Christ will come again.

Sustaining God, inspire all whom you call to serve you
   to realize that now is the day of salvation.
Infuse your church with purity, knowledge, patience,
   kindness, holiness of spirit, and genuine love.
When your disciples face afflictions, hardships,
   calamities, imprisonments, and hunger,
      make them possessors of all things in you,
         until that day when dishonor and distrust and death are no more
            and your Spirit fills your creation with the glory of your risen Son,
               eternal Father, forever and ever. **Amen.**

June 19–25, Year C

The Lord be with you. **And also with you.**
Lift up your hearts. **We lift them to the Lord.**
Let us give thanks to the Lord our God. **It is right to give our thanks and praise.**

Blessed are you, God and Father of all.
Through creation and covenant, prophet and promise,
 you have called us your own and made us your children.
You pledged yourself to Abraham and Sarah and their offspring forever.
Through the law you showed your people the path of life;
 when they rejected your ways, you did not forsake them
  but sent prophets to bring them home to you.
In the fullness of time you sent your Son,
 making us heirs according to the promise made to Abraham,
  and adopting us as your children through faith.
In Christ you gather to yourself all your people in an eternal embrace
 where there is neither Jew nor Greek, slave nor free, male nor female.
In his dying and rising you take away our sin
 and open to us the gift of everlasting life.
And so with angels and archangels and all the company of heaven
 enfolded in the bonds of your love,
  we praise your name and join the unending hymn.

Holy, holy, holy Lord, God of power and might.
Heaven and earth are full of your glory.
Hosanna in the highest.
Blessed is he who comes in the name of the Lord.
Hosanna in the highest.

Bounteous God, as you fed Elijah in the wilderness
 that he might draw near to your holy mountain
  and come into your presence,
   make this bread for the journey

our place of encounter with you.
Send your Holy Spirit upon your church,
   and in the strength of this food
      draw us near to the least and the lost.
Sanctify this bread and cup that they may be for us
   the body and blood of your Son;
who, at supper with his disciples, took bread, gave you thanks,
   broke the bread, and gave it to them, saying,
      "Take, eat: this is my body which is given for you;
         do this in remembrance of me."
After supper he took the cup.
Again he gave you thanks, and gave it to his disciples, saying,
   "Drink this, all of you: this is my blood of the new covenant,
      which is shed for you and for many for the forgiveness of sins.
   Do this, as often as you drink it, in remembrance of me."

Great is the mystery of faith.
Christ has died; Christ is risen; Christ will come again.

Everlasting God, in whom deep calls to deep,
   you speak your word of life into the fullness of silence.
Calm the fury of destruction
   around any caught up in tornado or hurricane, earthquake or fire.
Come to those who yearn for peace or protection.
Quiet every troubled spirit and strengthen every soul cast down.
Silence in us all clamoring for attention that is not your own.
Give us courage to hear the sound of sheer silence,
   that we may know your still, small voice.
Bring us at the last into your holy presence,
   and gather us with your saints around the altar of your praise,
      when all who belong to Christ shall be one in you, eternal Father,
         in the power of the Holy Spirit, forever and ever. **Amen.**

June 26–July 2, Year A

The Lord be with you. **And also with you.**
Lift up your hearts. **We lift them to the Lord.**
Let us give thanks to the Lord our God. **It is right to give our thanks and praise.**

God of mercy and grace,
   we praise and thank you in spirit and in truth;
     for you have asked everything of us,
       and at the same time you have given us
         everything you ask of us.
In Abraham you called a people
   and invited them to entrust their future to you.
In the sacrifice of Isaac and the provision of the ram
   you foretold your gracious redemption of the world.
You sent Jesus, your own Lamb,
   as the new Isaac, the true offering,
     that we might belong in your company forever.
In his death and resurrection
   we know you to be the Lord who provides.
And so we rejoice with angels and archangels,
   and with all the company of heaven,
     singing the song of your unending praise.

Holy, holy, holy Lord, God of power and might.
Heaven and earth are full of your glory.
Hosanna in the highest.
Blessed is he who comes in the name of the Lord.
Hosanna in the highest.

Freely giving God,
   in Christ you deliver us from the wages of sin
     and invite us into eternal life.
Sanctify your people gathered around your holy table,

that every heart may offer you welcome.
Send your Holy Spirit upon this bread and cup,
   that they may be for us the body and blood of your Son Jesus Christ;
who, at supper with his disciples, took bread, gave you thanks,
   broke the bread, and gave it to them, saying,
      "Take, eat: this is my body which is given for you;
         do this in remembrance of me."
After supper he took the cup.
Again he gave you thanks, and gave it to his disciples, saying,
   "Drink this, all of you: this is my blood of the new covenant,
      which is shed for you and for many for the forgiveness of sins.
   Do this, as often as you drink it, in remembrance of me."

Great is the mystery of faith.
Christ has died; Christ is risen; Christ will come again.

God of creation and covenant,
   you order your world in springtime and harvest,
      and restore your world in resurrection and final glory.
Put a song in every weary throat and hope in every troubled heart.
Uphold your little ones
   where they face hardship, sorrow, or abandonment.
Bless parents who have lost the trust of their children,
   and children who live outside the care of loving arms.
Make this meal a sign of your abundance in a world of scarcity
   and your companionship in a world of loneliness.
Make us heralds of your kingdom
   and fill our hearts with longing for your heavenly banquet,
      where you will be all in all,
         one God, Father, Son, and Holy Spirit, for evermore. **Amen.**

June 26–July 2, Year B

The Lord be with you. **And also with you.**
Lift up your hearts. **We lift them to the Lord.**
Let us give thanks to the Lord our God. **It is right to give our thanks and praise.**

Transforming God,
    we return unending gratitude for your limitless generosity.
In the crucified and risen Christ
    you show us the extent and cost of your love.
Though he was rich, yet for our sake he became poor,
    so that by his poverty we might become rich.
He became what we are,
    that in the power of your Holy Spirit
      we might become what he is.
You destined from the beginning
    that we might become your companions forever.
And so we delight to join saints and angels
    and all the company of heaven,
      gathered around your glorious throne,
        singing the never-ending praise of your name.

Holy, holy, holy Lord, God of power and might.
Heaven and earth are full of your glory.
Hosanna in the highest.
Blessed is he who comes in the name of the Lord.
Hosanna in the highest.

Cleansing God, your touch and word turned death to life
    in the body of a young girl,
      and when a suffering woman touched the hem of your garment
        you proclaimed that her faith had made her well.
Come among us now in that same word and touch,
    and restore the body, mind, and spirit of your church to life in your name.

In the power of your Holy Spirit
 speak over and touch this bread and this cup,
  that we may find in them your healing and resurrection,
   and they may be for us the body and blood of your Son Jesus Christ;
who, at supper with his disciples, took bread, gave you thanks,
 broke the bread, and gave it to them, saying,
  "Take, eat: this is my body which is given for you;
   do this in remembrance of me."
After supper he took the cup.
Again he gave you thanks, and gave it to his disciples, saying,
 "Drink this, all of you: this is my blood of the new covenant,
  which is shed for you and for many for the forgiveness of sins.
 Do this, as often as you drink it, in remembrance of me."

Great is the mystery of faith.
Christ has died; Christ is risen; Christ will come again.

Healing God, when your Son raised the daughter of Jairus,
 he ordered that she be given something to eat.
Make this meal one that anticipates the coming of your kingdom,
 where fear is turned to belief, sickness becomes wholeness,
  ridicule is changed into worship, and grief is transformed into dancing.
Instill hope in your church, raise up the fallen and disgraced,
 lift up the downtrodden,
  and renew your whole creation in the ways of justice and peace,
   that all the world may come to enjoy
    the glorious resurrection of your Son Jesus Christ,
     in the grace of your Holy Spirit,
      in union with you, Father most merciful,
       one God, now and forever. **Amen.**

June 26–July 2, Year C

The Lord be with you. **And also with you.**
Lift up your hearts. **We lift them to the Lord.**
Let us give thanks to the Lord our God. **It is right to give our thanks and praise.**

God of the whirlwind, you created all things out of nothing;
   you called your chosen people out of the wilderness;
     and in your Son's dying and rising
       you re-created us out of the chaos of our sin.
You passed your mantle from Elijah to Elisha,
   and in the power of your Holy Spirit
     you passed the mantle of Jesus to the apostles and to your church.
So now we celebrate the call of your grace
   in the company of saints and angels, and all the chorus of heaven,
     singing the hymn of your unending praise.

Holy, holy, holy Lord, God of power and might.
Heaven and earth are full of your glory.
Hosanna in the highest.
Blessed is he who comes in the name of the Lord.
Hosanna in the highest.

God of the journey,
   your Son Jesus Christ had nowhere to lay his head,
     but still he sets a table in our wilderness
      and meets us in the sustenance of bread and wine.
Now send down your Holy Spirit,
   that in them we may find our home in you,
     and that these gifts of the earth and human hands
      may be for us the body and blood of your Son Jesus Christ;
who, at supper with his disciples, took bread, gave you thanks,
   broke the bread, and gave it to them, saying,
     "Take, eat: this is my body which is given for you;

do this in remembrance of me."
After supper he took the cup.
Again he gave you thanks, and gave it to his disciples, saying,
"Drink this, all of you: this is my blood of the new covenant,
which is shed for you and for many for the forgiveness of sins.
Do this, as often as you drink it, in remembrance of me."

Great is the mystery of faith.
Christ has died; Christ is risen; Christ will come again.

Ever-gracious God, as Elisha asked Elijah for a double share of his spirit,
so now we seek a double share of your Spirit.
Fill our bodies with your heavenly food,
fill your church with truth and grace,
fill your world with righteousness and peace,
and fill your whole creation with the praise of your glory,
that our deepest hungers may be met in you,
the deepest thirst of all who struggle through each day
may be met in the coming of your kingdom,
and the deepest needs of all who are oppressed may be met
in the never-failing stream of your liberating love,
until the day when we are filled forever
with the abundant fruits of your Spirit
in union with Christ, ever one God. **Amen.**

July 3–9, Year A

The Lord be with you. **And also with you.**
Lift up your hearts. **We lift them to the Lord.**
Let us give thanks to the Lord our God. **It is right to give our thanks and praise.**

Father, Lord of heaven and earth,
   we gladly lift our hearts to you in thanksgiving and praise,
     because you have hidden your story of salvation
       from the wise and intelligent and revealed it to infants.
You have disclosed your mercy to the outcast Hagar,
   to the barren Sarah, to the shunned Rahab,
     to the childless Hannah, and to the unmarried Mary.
In Jesus you became a child for us,
   through whom we might discover the secrets of your glory.
Again and again you revealed your sacred purpose
   through those your world despises, demeans, or ignores.
Finally you made your purpose known through your Son,
   cursed by our sin as he hung on the cross.
And so we rejoice with angels and archangels,
   and with all the company of heaven,
     singing the song of your unending praise.

Holy, holy, holy Lord, God of power and might.
Heaven and earth are full of your glory.
Hosanna in the highest.
Blessed is he who comes in the name of the Lord.
Hosanna in the highest.

Overflowing God,
   as you led your children to meet their destinies at the well,
     you become in Christ the well of life that replenishes us
       that we may never be thirsty again.
Fill your church with your abundant grace

that it may be a cup that runneth over with your mercy.
Send your Holy Spirit upon this food and drink,
   that they may be for us the body and blood of your Son Jesus Christ;
who, at supper with his disciples, took bread, gave you thanks,
   broke the bread, and gave it to them, saying,
      "Take, eat: this is my body which is given for you;
         do this in remembrance of me."
After supper he took the cup.
Again he gave you thanks, and gave it to his disciples, saying,
   "Drink this, all of you: this is my blood of the new covenant,
      which is shed for you and for many for the forgiveness of sins.
   Do this, as often as you drink it, in remembrance of me."

Great is the mystery of faith.
Christ has died; Christ is risen; Christ will come again.

God of the weary and heavy laden, God of the tired, the poor,
   the huddled masses yearning to breathe free,
      God of the homeless and the tempest-tossed,
         bring rest to all who labor today.
Set your gentle yoke upon them, for you are gentle and humble in heart.
Be a shining golden light in the souls
   of all who struggle in body, mind, or spirit,
      with demons within or without,
         with fears about the future or regrets about the past.
Through this communion with you
   in union with Christ in the power of your Spirit,
      write on our hearts a new law
         that draws us to walk with you across the storms of suffering,
            the tremors of temptation, and the pangs of persecution.
And on the last day, bring us home to you forever. **Amen.**

July 3–9, Year B

The Lord be with you. **And also with you.**
Lift up your hearts. **We lift them to the Lord.**
Let us give thanks to the Lord our God. **It is right to give our thanks and praise.**

Humble God, we rejoice to worship and enjoy you forever,
   for your grace is sufficient for us,
     and your power is made perfect in weakness.
You created the world as a theater for your companionship,
   and you raised up a people
     through whom all nations would find a blessing.
In David you brought together all the hopes of your chosen people.
When your covenant was neglected and betrayed
   you sent Jesus, Son of David.
In his death and resurrection he restored the hopes of your people
   and the promise of your glory.
Though we forget you, never do you forget us.
And so with all the company of heaven
   we lift up the song of your everlasting praise.

Holy, holy, holy Lord, God of power and might.
Heaven and earth are full of your glory.
Hosanna in the highest.
Blessed is he who comes in the name of the Lord.
Hosanna in the highest.

Mysterious and holy God, when your Son came to his hometown
   the people could not believe that one like them
     could be so much like you.
Yet in wisdom and power he showed your face despite their unbelief.
Send your Holy Spirit upon your church
   that all who gather in your name
     may find in you the joy of their desiring.

Send that same Spirit on these ordinary gifts of bread and wine,
   that they may be for us the body and blood of your Son Jesus Christ;
who, at supper with his disciples, took bread, gave you thanks,
   broke the bread, and gave it to them, saying,
      "Take, eat: this is my body which is given for you;
         do this in remembrance of me."
After supper he took the cup.
Again he gave you thanks, and gave it to his disciples, saying,
   "Drink this, all of you: this is my blood of the new covenant,
      which is shed for you and for many for the forgiveness of sins.
   Do this, as often as you drink it, in remembrance of me."

Great is the mystery of faith.
Christ has died; Christ is risen; Christ will come again.

Patient God, in Christ you endured weaknesses,
   insults, hardships, persecutions, and calamities for our sake;
      you became weak, that we might find our true strength lies in you.
As you equipped your servant Paul
   through every challenge to share your gospel,
      send your Holy Spirit on all who are weak,
         that they may be upheld in your power;
            on any who are insulted,
               that they may hear you calling their name;
                  on those who are persecuted,
                     that they may know your justice, your vindication, and your peace.
Hasten the day when your tired, poor, homeless, and tempest-tossed
   may breathe free, lift their lamp beside your golden door,
      and celebrate the banquet of your kingdom,
         liberating God, Father, Son, and Holy Spirit. **Amen.**

July 3–9, Year C

The Lord be with you. **And also with you.**
Lift up your hearts. **We lift them to the Lord.**
Let us give thanks to the Lord our God. **It is right to give our thanks and praise.**

Exalted is your name always and everywhere, Lord God,
   for you created all things.
By your grace you wash away our sin and make all things new.
When your people crossed the Jordan into the Promised Land,
   you washed away their bondage and betrayals
     and gave them a new life with you.
Your prophet Elisha sent Naaman into this same water
   to wash in humility and be cleansed of his leprosy.
When your Son came to be baptized by John at the Jordan,
   you brought him up out of the waters
     to usher in your new creation, your kingdom.
And so we rejoice with all who are water-washed and Spirit-born,
   and in the company of those who have crossed over Jordan
     into the promised land of everlasting life with you,
       with angels and archangels and all the company of heaven,
         as we join their unending hymn.

Holy, holy, holy Lord, God of power and might.
Heaven and earth are full of your glory.
Hosanna in the highest.
Blessed is he who comes in the name of the Lord.
Hosanna in the highest.

God of the harvest, you sowed among us the seed of your only Son.
When he died for our salvation, he was buried in the earth
   and raised on the third day to be the firstfruits of resurrection.
Send down your Holy Spirit upon your church
   to go as laborers into your fields,

to reap the bountiful harvest of your kingdom.
Sanctify this bread and cup
   that they may be for us the body and blood of your Son;
who, at supper with his disciples, took bread, gave you thanks,
   broke the bread, and gave it to them, saying,
      "Take, eat: this is my body which is given for you;
         do this in remembrance of me."
After supper he took the cup.
Again he gave you thanks, and gave it to his disciples, saying,
   "Drink this, all of you: this is my blood of the new covenant,
      which is shed for you and for many for the forgiveness of sins.
   Do this, as often as you drink it, in remembrance of me."

Great is the mystery of faith.
Christ has died; Christ is risen; Christ will come again.

Glorious God, you have revealed to us your creative joy
   in a tapestry of spacious skies, amber waves of grain,
      purple mountain majesties, and fruited plains.
Shed your grace upon all who call this land home,
   from those in high places to the least of these.
Have mercy wherever the beauty of the land has been stripped and sold.
Strengthen all who work for the dream of brotherhood
   from sea to shining sea.
Bring us, together with your children from every nation,
   to the day when we shall enter your heavenly city
      undimmed by human tears
         and rejoice in every gain divine,
            all-holy God, Father, Son, and Holy Spirit. **Amen.**

July 10–16, Year A

The Lord be with you. **And also with you.**
Lift up your hearts. **We lift them to the Lord.**
Let us give thanks to the Lord our God. **It is right to give our thanks and praise.**

Creator God, you made this earth of paths and rocks and thorns and soil.
To Abraham you promised fertile land,
   and to Moses you offered blessing and freedom.
In your prophets you called your people
   to cultivate the promises of your land
      and cherish the blessings of your freedom.
In Jesus you gave us your superabundant soil.
In his cross he was plowed and broken open,
   that we might be restored, replenished, and renewed,
      to be planted again as your good seed in this earth.
And so we gladly thank you,
   with angels and archangels and all the company of heaven,
      singing the hymn of your unending praise.

Holy, holy, holy Lord, God of power and might.
Heaven and earth are full of your glory.
Hosanna in the highest.
Blessed is he who comes in the name of the Lord.
Hosanna in the highest.

Abundant God, from your good soil you make enough and plenty
   to feed and inspire all your children,
      and out of your earth you bring the glory of resurrection life.
Come among us now through the power of your Spirit,
   that we may be transformed into your likeness,
      and that these gifts of bread and wine
         may become for us the body and blood of your Son Jesus Christ;
who, at supper with his disciples, took bread, gave you thanks,

broke the bread, and gave it to them, saying,
  "Take, eat: this is my body which is given for you;
    do this in remembrance of me."
After supper he took the cup.
Again he gave you thanks, and gave it to his disciples, saying,
  "Drink this, all of you: this is my blood of the new covenant,
    which is shed for you and for many for the forgiveness of sins.
  Do this, as often as you drink it, in remembrance of me."

Great is the mystery of faith.
Christ has died; Christ is risen; Christ will come again.

Transforming God,
  where your children are in the grip of evil and bewilderment,
    bring them your courage and clarity.
Where they are without deep root and facing trouble or persecution,
  give them patience and endurance.
Where they are burdened by the cares of the world
  and tempted by the lure of wealth,
    offer them wisdom and understanding.
And where they bear fruit and yield,
  make that fruit so plentiful that it may feed all in your world
    who hunger for faith, for hope, or for love.
Sanctify your groaning creation,
  that your universe may breathe your breath
    and be filled with your life anew,
      that we may love what you love, and do what you would do,
        Father, Son, and Holy Spirit, ever one God. **Amen.**

July 10–16, Year B

The Lord be with you. **And also with you.**
Lift up your hearts. **We lift them to the Lord.**
Let us give thanks to the Lord our God. **It is right to give our thanks and praise.**

Orchestrating God, we rejoice to thank you,
   for in Christ you have made known to us the mystery of your will,
     according to your good pleasure.
You have shown us your plan for the fullness of time,
   to gather up all things in your Son,
     things in heaven and things on earth.
In Christ you have bestowed upon us an inheritance that we,
   who set our hope on him, might live for the praise of your glory.
You have marked those who believe
   with the seal of the promised Holy Spirit
     as the pledge of your redemption.
And so we anticipate that fullness and that glory
   by joining the angels in the everlasting song of praise.

Holy, holy, holy Lord, God of power and might.
Heaven and earth are full of your glory.
Hosanna in the highest.
Blessed is he who comes in the name of the Lord.
Hosanna in the highest.

Blessed be you, God our Father,
   for you chose us in Christ before the foundation of the world
     to be holy and blameless before you in love.
You destined us for adoption as your children.
Send down your Spirit on your people that,
   through the power of your Son's dying and rising,
     we might know forgiveness of our sins in the riches of your grace.
As you bring us redemption through the blood of our Savior,

sanctify this bread and this cup,
   that in them we may meet you
      in the body and blood of your Son Jesus Christ;
who, at supper with his disciples, took bread, gave you thanks,
   broke the bread, and gave it to them, saying,
      "Take, eat: this is my body which is given for you;
         do this in remembrance of me."
After supper he took the cup.
Again he gave you thanks, and gave it to his disciples, saying,
   "Drink this, all of you: this is my blood of the new covenant,
      which is shed for you and for many for the forgiveness of sins.
   Do this, as often as you drink it, in remembrance of me."

Great is the mystery of faith.
Christ has died; Christ is risen; Christ will come again.

Covenanting God, in David you show us
   the ecstatic joy of being your companion,
      and the coruscating delight of being your child.
As David knew the scorn of his wife Michal,
   bring solace to any who live with the disdain or contempt
      of family, neighbors, or colleagues.
As your prophet John the Baptist
   faced the price of his courage and Herod's folly,
      give perseverance and hope to all who face danger
         because of their faith or their witness.
Raise up prophets among your people
   who can see and name what does not belong with you
      and can shine the light of your truth
         in the nighttime of fear and oppression,
            until the day when all sorrow is turned to dancing
               and all creation emanates the praise of your glory,
                  three-in-one God, Father, Son, and Holy Spirit,
                     forever and ever. **Amen.**

July 10–16, Year C

The Lord be with you. **And also with you.**
Lift up your hearts. **We lift them to the Lord.**
Let us give thanks to the Lord our God. **It is right to give our thanks and praise.**

God our savior, we give you thanks and praise,
  that when the nations had strayed far from your ways
    you called Abraham,
      and when your people were lost and oppressed
        you sent Jesus,
      and when we are defeated, downcast, and desolate,
        in the power of the Holy Spirit you make Jesus present to us.
You pick us up from our failure, our oppression, and our sin
  and journey with us and bring us to safety and promise to return.
In the death and resurrection of Christ
  you heal the wounds of the past
    and offer the gift of an everlasting future with you.
So now we celebrate the wonders of your grace
  with saints and angels, and all the company of heaven,
    singing the hymn of your unending praise.

Holy, holy, holy Lord, God of power and might.
Heaven and earth are full of your glory.
Hosanna in the highest.
Blessed is he who comes in the name of the Lord.
Hosanna in the highest.

God our redeemer, on our journey with you,
  you turn us from your burden
    into carriers of one another's burdens.
On the way you feed us with the bread of life and the cup of salvation.
Now send down your Holy Spirit,
  that we may be made holy as you are holy,

and that these gifts of the earth and human hands
    may be for us the body and blood of your Son Jesus Christ;
who, at supper with his disciples, took bread, gave you thanks,
  broke the bread, and gave it to them, saying,
    "Take, eat: this is my body which is given for you;
      do this in remembrance of me."
After supper he took the cup.
Again he gave you thanks, and gave it to his disciples, saying,
  "Drink this, all of you: this is my blood of the new covenant,
    which is shed for you and for many for the forgiveness of sins.
  Do this, as often as you drink it, in remembrance of me."

Great is the mystery of faith.
Christ has died; Christ is risen; Christ will come again.

Merciful God, in Jesus, through story, miracle, and example,
  you turn us and all creation upside down.
Direct our hearts in the ways we should go,
  visit the downtrodden and set them on their feet again,
    and restore the land, sea, and air of your creation,
      that all things and creatures and people
        may fulfill their created purpose
          in reflecting your glory and singing your praise,
            until the day when you are all in all, in union with Christ,
              ever one God. **Amen.**

July 17–23, Year A

The Lord be with you. **And also with you.**
Lift up your hearts. **We lift them to the Lord.**
Let us give thanks to the Lord our God. **It is right to give our thanks and praise.**

Glory and praise are yours, majestic God,
   for you make a ladder between heaven and earth;
     in Jesus you descend that ladder to bring us into your presence,
       and in his death and resurrection you bring us with him,
         ascending the ladder to your throne of grace.
You set creation free from its bondage to decay
   and bestow upon your children
     the freedom of the glory of your redemption.
You call your people to be a blessing to all the families of the earth.
And so we join the ladder of angels and archangels,
   ascending and descending with all the company of heaven,
     singing the song of your unending praise.

Holy, holy, holy Lord, God of power and might.
Heaven and earth are full of your glory.
Hosanna in the highest.
Blessed is he who comes in the name of the Lord.
Hosanna in the highest.

Liberating God, through the sonship of Jesus
   you send your Spirit to create among your children
     the joy of adoption
       and bestow upon us the gift of being your heirs.
Send that Spirit upon us now,
   that we might be what we eat, Christ's body in your world;
     and sanctify this bread and this cup,
       that they may be for us the blessed body and blood
         of your Son Jesus Christ;

who, at supper with his disciples, took bread, gave you thanks,
   broke the bread, and gave it to them, saying,
      "Take, eat: this is my body which is given for you;
         do this in remembrance of me."
After supper he took the cup.
Again he gave you thanks, and gave it to his disciples, saying,
   "Drink this, all of you: this is my blood of the new covenant,
      which is shed for you and for many for the forgiveness of sins.
   Do this, as often as you drink it, in remembrance of me."

Great is the mystery of faith.
Christ has died; Christ is risen; Christ will come again.

God of patience and hope, sower of all good seeds,
   show those who suffer
      the incomparable glory of what you have in store for them.
When your children's field is interlaced with weeds among the wheat,
   when the labor pains of creation groan to highest heaven,
      give us your heart to live in your time
         and abide in the truth of what we do not yet see.
Bless your people that they may know that you are with them
   and will keep them wherever they go,
      that they shall exclaim that surely you are among them,
         though they did not know it.
Bring all creation into the eternal joy of abiding in an awesome place,
   your very house, the gate of heaven,
      where you dwell forever, Father, Son, and Holy Spirit,
         through all ages with power and glory. **Amen.**

July 17–23, Year B

The Lord be with you. **And also with you.**
Lift up your hearts. **We lift them to the Lord.**
Let us give thanks to the Lord our God. **It is right to give our thanks and praise.**

Father of mercy, we give you thanks and praise
  because we who once were far off
    have been brought near by the blood of Christ.
He is our peace;
  in his flesh he has broken down the dividing wall of hostility
    between Jew and Gentile and between you and us.
He has created in himself one new humanity
  and reconciled us to you in one body through the cross.
So we gladly thank you, no longer as strangers and aliens,
  but as citizens with the saints and members of your household,
    proclaiming with the company of heaven the praise of your glory.

Holy, holy, holy Lord, God of power and might.
Heaven and earth are full of your glory.
Hosanna in the highest.
Blessed is he who comes in the name of the Lord.
Hosanna in the highest.

God of peace, you brought again from the dead your Son Jesus Christ,
  and made in him a holy temple where we could be one with you.
Send your Spirit upon your people
  that we may be built together into your dwelling place.
As you promised your children
  that you would build a house to abide with them,
    sanctify this bread and this cup,
      that they may be for us a dwelling place for your Son,
        the body and blood of Christ Jesus our Lord;
who, at supper with his disciples, took bread, gave you thanks,

broke the bread, and gave it to them, saying,
  "Take, eat: this is my body which is given for you;
    do this in remembrance of me."
After supper he took the cup.
Again he gave you thanks, and gave it to his disciples, saying,
  "Drink this, all of you: this is my blood of the new covenant,
    which is shed for you and for many for the forgiveness of sins.
  Do this, as often as you drink it, in remembrance of me."

Great is the mystery of faith.
Christ has died; Christ is risen; Christ will come again.

Resurrecting and restoring God,
  your Son had compassion on the crowd,
    for they were like sheep without a shepherd.
As he made the journey across the lake
  to be with your people in their distress,
    so you sent him to be incarnate among us
      and share our human struggle.
Bless all who long to touch the fringe of his cloak today.
Comfort any who are at sea in body, mind, or spirit.
Visit those who rely on others to bring them to you.
Strengthen your servants who need to retreat
  to a deserted place all by themselves and rest a while.
Cherish your children who have crossed over the lake to be with you,
  and give hope to those who stand fearfully on the shore;
    until the day when healing becomes salvation,
      and salvation becomes your company,
        and your company is the fullness of joy,
          ever one God, Father, Son, and Holy Spirit. **Amen.**

July 17–23, Year C

The Lord be with you. **And also with you.**
Lift up your hearts. **We lift them to the Lord.**
Let us give thanks to the Lord our God. **It is right to give our thanks and praise.**

Resounding praise belongs to you, Alpha and Omega,
   for yours is the beginning and ending of all things.
Through your Word you created the visible and the invisible,
   and in him all things hold together.
By shaping a people bound in love,
   you fashioned a covenant that would never end.
In the fullness of time your Word became flesh;
   you sent among us the firstborn of all creation,
     pleased to dwell in human form.
Through him you have reconciled all things in heaven and earth,
   making peace through the blood of his cross.
Before every beginning and beyond every ending
   you call us to be your disciples and destine us to be your saints.
And so we give you thanks in the company of angels and archangels
   as we join the everlasting hymn.

Holy, holy, holy Lord, God of power and might.
Heaven and earth are full of your glory.
Hosanna in the highest.
Blessed is he who comes in the name of the Lord.
Hosanna in the highest.

God our companion,
   as you drew Mary of Bethany to your Son's feet, hungry for his word,
     so bring us to this table, hungry for Jesus.
As your church remembers Christ's saving passion,
   come upon your church in the power of your Holy Spirit
     to dwell with us in the fullness of your presence,

and feed us till we want no more.
Sanctify this bread and cup
    that they may be for us the body and blood of your Son;
who, at supper with his disciples, took bread, gave you thanks,
    broke the bread, and gave it to them, saying,
        "Take, eat: this is my body which is given for you;
            do this in remembrance of me."
After supper he took the cup.
Again he gave you thanks, and gave it to his disciples, saying,
    "Drink this, all of you: this is my blood of the new covenant,
        which is shed for you and for many for the forgiveness of sins.
    Do this, as often as you drink it, in remembrance of me."

Great is the mystery of faith.
Christ has died; Christ is risen; Christ will come again.

God of Mary and Martha,
    your resurrected Son has the words of eternal life.
Give your church grace like Mary to linger where Jesus is.
Grant us patience to abide among those
    who look to you in trust and hope,
        and to stand with any who have no one to stay by their side.
Where your children hunger and thirst for companionship,
    bring them new friends in Christ.
Where they suffer from famine, be their bread of life.
Open your heaven,
    that the one who has reconciled all things in his death and resurrection
        may present us holy and blameless before you,
            and your Word made flesh may welcome us
                to the banquet of the riches of your glory,
                    in the power of your Spirit, Holy Father, now and forever. **Amen.**

July 24–30, Year A

The Lord be with you. **And also with you.**
Lift up your hearts. **We lift them to the Lord.**
Let us give thanks to the Lord our God. **It is right to give our thanks and praise.**

Sovereign God, you foreknew us, before the universe was created.
In Abraham and Moses you called us to be your people.
You predestined us through the power of your Holy Spirit
  to be conformed to the image of your crucified and risen Son.
In Jesus you justified us by your grace,
  and on the last day you will glorify us to live with you forever.
And so we gladly thank you,
    with angels and archangels and all the company of heaven,
      singing the hymn of your unending praise.

Holy, holy, holy Lord, God of power and might.
Heaven and earth are full of your glory.
Hosanna in the highest.
Blessed is he who comes in the name of the Lord.
Hosanna in the highest.

You, Lord God, are like a merchant who sacrifices everything
  because you above all want us, your pearl,
    buried in the world's field.
And in that field also you grow grain and grape
  to feed us from your heart now and forever.
Come among us now through the power of your Spirit,
  that we may be transformed into your likeness,
    and that these gifts of bread and wine may become for us
      the body and blood of your Son Jesus Christ;
who, at supper with his disciples, took bread, gave you thanks,
  broke the bread, and gave it to them, saying,
    "Take, eat: this is my body which is given for you;

do this in remembrance of me."
After supper he took the cup.
Again he gave you thanks, and gave it to his disciples, saying,
"Drink this, all of you: this is my blood of the new covenant,
which is shed for you and for many for the forgiveness of sins.
Do this, as often as you drink it, in remembrance of me."

Great is the mystery of faith.
Christ has died; Christ is risen; Christ will come again.

Everlasting God, you have promised
that nothing can separate us from your love.
Be with your children who know hardship, distress, or persecution;
visit your beloved who experience famine, nakedness, peril, or sword;
abide with us in death, as in life;
give us nothing to fear from angels or rulers,
from things present, or things to come,
or in the face of powers, or height, or depth,
or anything else in all creation.
Knowing that you did not withhold your own Son,
but gave him up for all of us,
inscribe in us faith that you will with him
bestow upon us everything else as well.
We pray in union with Christ in the power of your Holy Spirit,
who helps us in our weakness,
and intercedes with sighs too deep for words,
Father of all, now and forever. **Amen.**

July 24–30, Year B

The Lord be with you. **And also with you.**
Lift up your hearts. **We lift them to the Lord.**
Let us give thanks to the Lord our God. **It is right to give our thanks and praise.**

We bow our knees before you, Father,
 from whom every family in heaven and on earth takes its name.
We thank and praise you, for in Christ you had compassion on our scarcity
 and turned it into your abundance.
You call us to bring to you
 the needs and fruits of your people and your world.
You commission us as your Son's disciples
 to distribute the blessings of his grace and the benefits of his passion.
He took our human nature
 in order to bless it in his incarnation and ministry;
  he was broken on the cross
   in order that your everlasting life might be shared through resurrection.
And so we gladly render to you the praise of your glory,
 joining the company of heaven in the everlasting song.

Holy, holy, holy Lord, God of power and might.
Heaven and earth are full of your glory.
Hosanna in the highest.
Blessed is he who comes in the name of the Lord.
Hosanna in the highest.

Revealing God, in your Son you fed the multitudes
 and so showed your power to turn the water of our existence
  into the wine of eternal life with you.
Strengthen your people through your Holy Spirit
 that they might be rooted and grounded in love.
As your Son held the loaves and through them made his glory known,
 send down your Holy Spirit on this bread and this wine

that they may be for us the body and blood of Jesus Christ;
who, at supper with his disciples, took bread, gave you thanks,
  broke the bread, and gave it to them, saying,
    "Take, eat: this is my body which is given for you;
      do this in remembrance of me."
After supper he took the cup.
Again he gave you thanks, and gave it to his disciples, saying,
  "Drink this, all of you: this is my blood of the new covenant,
    which is shed for you and for many for the forgiveness of sins.
  Do this, as often as you drink it, in remembrance of me."

Great is the mystery of faith.
Christ has died; Christ is risen; Christ will come again.

Glorious God, in Christ you disclose
  the breadth and length and height and depth
    of a love that surpasses knowledge.
You come toward us across the rough sea of our anxiety
  and in the nighttime of our fear,
    and counsel us to be not afraid.
Walk alongside any who experience deep hunger
  and know not where to turn;
    bless those who have been deeply betrayed,
      and who live with the consequences
        of another's ruthlessness or conspiring;
          stretch out your hand to all who search for someone to trust.
To you, who by the power at work within us
  are able to accomplish abundantly more
    than all we can ask or imagine,
      to you be glory in the church and in Christ Jesus to all generations,
        in the fellowship of the Holy Spirit, one God now and ever. **Amen.**

July 24–30, Year C

The Lord be with you. **And also with you.**
Lift up your hearts. **We lift them to the Lord.**
Let us give thanks to the Lord our God. **It is right to give our thanks and praise.**

Hallowed be your name, heavenly Father,
  for yours is the kingdom and the power and the glory now and forever.
You formed a people for yourself and called them your children.
You delivered them from evil and saved them in the time of trial.
Once we were no people, but now we are your people,
  because in the fullness of time you sent your Son
    to forgive us our trespasses through the blood of his cross,
      and in your Holy Spirit you give us power
        to forgive those who trespass against us.
And so we gladly praise you with your people on earth
  and all the company of heaven as we join the unending hymn.

Holy, holy, holy Lord, God of power and might.
Heaven and earth are full of your glory.
Hosanna in the highest.
Blessed is he who comes in the name of the Lord.
Hosanna in the highest.

God of blessing, you promise that as you give us our daily bread,
  so you shall feed us with the bread of life for eternity.
Come down upon your church in the power of your Holy Spirit,
  that as we remember your Son's saving passion and resurrection
    and share this holy meal,
      we may become bread for your hungry world.
Sanctify this bread and cup that they may be for us
  the body and blood of your Son;
who, at supper with his disciples, took bread, gave you thanks,
  broke the bread, and gave it to them, saying,

"Take, eat: this is my body which is given for you;
   do this in remembrance of me."
After supper he took the cup.
Again he gave you thanks, and gave it to his disciples, saying,
   "Drink this, all of you: this is my blood of the new covenant,
      which is shed for you and for many for the forgiveness of sins.
   Do this, as often as you drink it, in remembrance of me."

Great is the mystery of faith.
Christ has died; Christ is risen; Christ will come again.

Giver of every good and perfect gift,
   you promise that everyone who asks will receive,
      everyone who seeks will find,
         and to everyone who knocks the door will be opened.
Send your blessing upon those who ask for what you alone can give.
Pour your grace upon any who search and upon all who long to be found.
Give perseverance to those who knock at the door of justice.
As you dwelt bodily in your Son in all your fullness,
   dwell in your church today,
      that by the power of the Holy Spirit
         those who are called the children of the living God
            may know your resurrecting power,
               until the day when your kingdom comes and your will is done
                  on earth as it is in heaven,
                     most holy God, Father, Son, and Holy Spirit. **Amen.**

July 31–August 6, Year A

The Lord be with you. **And also with you.**
Lift up your hearts. **We lift them to the Lord.**
Let us give thanks to the Lord our God. **It is right to give our thanks and praise.**

It is our delight and our privilege
  to lift our hearts to you, our Lord and God,
    because in this Eucharistic feast
      you give us the pattern of our salvation.
In the inadequacy of loaves and fishes
  we see our paltry offerings from the gift of your creation;
    but just as in incarnation, cross, and resurrection
      you took, and blessed, and broke,
        and shared our human nature in Jesus,
          so he took, and blessed, and broke,
            and shared the loaves and fish
              to be an overflowing banquet of glory for your hungry people.
Through the abundance of twelve baskets left over
  you restore Israel's twelve tribes to service in your kingdom,
    and you invite us to share your feast, with angels and archangels,
      and all the company of heaven,
        singing the hymn of your unending praise.

Holy, holy, holy Lord, God of power and might.
Heaven and earth are full of your glory.
Hosanna in the highest.
Blessed is he who comes in the name of the Lord.
Hosanna in the highest.

Out of nothing, God of mercy, you made your creation;
  and out of slavery and wilderness you called your chosen people.
Out of flesh and blood and dust and ashes
  you summon us to be your church.

Send your Holy Spirit upon us now,
  that we may become holy, even as you are holy.
Sanctify this bread and this wine,
  that they may transform our hearts and minds and souls and voices
    as they become for us the body and blood of your blessed Son our Lord;
who, at supper with his disciples, took bread, gave you thanks,
  broke the bread, and gave it to them, saying,
    "Take, eat: this is my body which is given for you;
      do this in remembrance of me."
After supper he took the cup.
Again he gave you thanks, and gave it to his disciples, saying,
  "Drink this, all of you: this is my blood of the new covenant,
    which is shed for you and for many for the forgiveness of sins.
  Do this, as often as you drink it, in remembrance of me."

Great is the mystery of faith.
Christ has died; Christ is risen; Christ will come again.

God of all who struggle, you wrestled with Jacob until daybreak.
Open the eyes of all who fight all night,
  to learn if their battle is indeed with you.
Visit the hearts of any who limp because of an old wound,
  to understand if that wound was part of your redemption.
As you gave Jacob a new name,
  and as in baptism you seal each one of us with your name
    as your adopted children,
      bless those who search to find their true identity
        or to discover who you truly want them to be.
Come among all who are oppressed,
  that they may see you face to face
    and in you find life and hope,
      until the day when your glory is fully revealed
        and you are all in all, ever one God,
          Father, Son, and Holy Spirit, our living Lord. **Amen.**

July 31–August 6, Year B

The Lord be with you. **And also with you.**
Lift up your hearts. **We lift them to the Lord.**
Let us give thanks to the Lord our God. **It is right to give our thanks and praise.**

Forgiving and restoring God, we thank and praise you
  because you make the gifts of your creation
    into the means of our redemption,
      and you turn our fallen folly into the occasion of your risen glory.
In Christ the Lamb you gave us everything you had.
Though we strayed from your ways and slayed your holy one,
  yet you set before us this gracious banquet
    in which that crucified and risen Lamb reconciles us with you.
And so we live in gratitude for your mercy
  and in praise of your grace,
    joining the company of heaven in their constant hymn.

Holy, holy, holy Lord, God of power and might.
Heaven and earth are full of your glory.
Hosanna in the highest.
Blessed is he who comes in the name of the Lord.
Hosanna in the highest.

Faithful Father, in Christ you give us the food
  that will never perish but endures for eternal life.
Give us this bread always,
  that coming to you your people will never be hungry,
    and believing in you your people will never be thirsty.
Bless us with the unity of the Spirit in the bond of peace,
  that this bread and this wine may be for us
    the body and blood of our Lord Jesus Christ;
who, at supper with his disciples, took bread, gave you thanks,
  broke the bread, and gave it to them, saying,

"Take, eat: this is my body which is given for you;
   do this in remembrance of me."
After supper he took the cup.
Again he gave you thanks, and gave it to his disciples, saying,
   "Drink this, all of you: this is my blood of the new covenant,
      which is shed for you and for many for the forgiveness of sins.
   Do this, as often as you drink it, in remembrance of me."

Great is the mystery of faith.
Christ has died; Christ is risen; Christ will come again.

God and Father of all, who is above all and through all and in all,
   make your church humble, gentle, and patient,
      living a life worthy of its calling.
You summon apostles, prophets, evangelists, pastors, and teachers
   to equip the saints for the work of ministry,
      for building up the body of Christ.
Empower your people for service, and build your church up in love.
Draw all who look to you with hope into unity of faith,
   growing together into the full stature of Christ.
Renew your servants in the gifts of ministry
   and bless any who labor and are heavy laden
      by surrounding them with the joyous companionship of your saints,
         until all who share in one Lord, one faith, and one baptism
            are one in unity before your throne,
               everlasting God, Trinity of perpetual peace. **Amen.**

July 31–August 6, Year C

The Lord be with you. **And also with you.**
Lift up your hearts. **We lift them to the Lord.**
Let us give thanks to the Lord our God. **It is right to give our thanks and praise.**

Blessed be your name, Father most holy,
   for your steadfast love endures forever.
You called Israel to be your child,
   and out of Egypt you brought forth your son.
When Israel turned away and refused you,
   your compassion grew warm and strong
     and ruled over your anger,
       and you led him with cords of kindness
         and wrapped him in bands of love.
Because you could not withdraw, in your great mercy,
   you sent your infant Son, eternally begotten of you,
     not only for the children of Israel
       but for all whom you would embrace as your daughters and sons.
By his sacrifice you turned toward the whole world in everlasting love.
And so we give you thanks with angels and archangels
   and all the company of heaven, joining the unending hymn.

Holy, holy, holy Lord, God of power and might.
Heaven and earth are full of your glory.
Hosanna in the highest.
Blessed is he who comes in the name of the Lord.
Hosanna in the highest.

Inexhaustible God, you have not stored up treasure for yourself
   but instead have been rich toward us;
     you did not keep your Son in heaven
       but sent him among us to share your boundless inheritance of grace.
Send your Spirit upon your church,

that grace freely received may be freely shared.
Sanctify this bread and cup
   that they may be for us the body and blood of your Son;
who, at supper with his disciples, took bread, gave you thanks,
   broke the bread, and gave it to them, saying,
      "Take, eat: this is my body which is given for you;
         do this in remembrance of me."
After supper he took the cup.
Again he gave you thanks, and gave it to his disciples, saying,
   "Drink this, all of you: this is my blood of the new covenant,
      which is shed for you and for many for the forgiveness of sins.
   Do this, as often as you drink it, in remembrance of me."

Great is the mystery of faith.
Christ has died; Christ is risen; Christ will come again.

Creating God, in Christ you make a new family of faith
   where there is neither Jew nor Greek, slave nor free.
Revive your church in the very places
   where human differences threaten to keep your disciples divided.
Wherever your church is in dispute with itself
   and your disciples are in conflict with one another,
      stir our hearts to repentance,
         give us humility to discover what love means,
            and open our imaginations to the life made possible in you.
Renew us and all creation in your image,
   until the day when Christ is all and is in all,
      Trinity of love and power, one God, now and forever. **Amen.**

August 7–13, Year A

The Lord be with you. **And also with you.**
Lift up your hearts. **We lift them to the Lord.**
Let us give thanks to the Lord our God. **It is right to give our thanks and praise.**

It is right to lift our hearts to you, Almighty God,
   for your Spirit brooded over the waters
      before the foundation of the world,
         your pillar of fire led your people to freedom
           through the waters of the Red Sea,
              and your Son Jesus came to his disciples
                across the stormy waves of Galilee.
In his agonizing death we see how far we stray from you,
   and in his resurrection we see how you draw us close
      despite our betrayals and failures.
We long for the day when all the saints adore thee,
   casting down their golden crowns around the glassy sea,
      with angels and archangels and all the company of heaven,
         singing the hymn of your unending praise.

Holy, holy, holy Lord, God of power and might.
Heaven and earth are full of your glory.
Hosanna in the highest.
Blessed is he who comes in the name of the Lord.
Hosanna in the highest.

We thank and praise you, Lord God,
   because in Jesus you come to us, call us to you,
      lift us up when we fear and fail and fall,
         and stay with us through the storm.
Come among us now through the power of your Spirit,
   that we may be transformed into your likeness,
      and that these gifts of bread and wine may become for us

the body and blood of your Son Jesus Christ;
who, at supper with his disciples, took bread, gave you thanks,
  broke the bread, and gave it to them, saying,
    "Take, eat: this is my body which is given for you;
      do this in remembrance of me."
After supper he took the cup.
Again he gave you thanks, and gave it to his disciples, saying,
  "Drink this, all of you: this is my blood of the new covenant,
    which is shed for you and for many for the forgiveness of sins.
  Do this, as often as you drink it, in remembrance of me."

Great is the mystery of faith.
Christ has died; Christ is risen; Christ will come again.

Everlasting God, you promise us the righteousness that comes from faith,
  and you assure us that everyone who calls upon your name will be saved.
Be close to all who struggle to believe,
  make yourself known to any who have never heard,
    empower those who are called to proclaim,
      and bless the ones you have sent.
Visit those who are hungry:
  be among them as the bread of life.
Comfort any who are thirsty:
  restore them with your fountain of living water.
Strengthen all who are at sea in the trials and travails of life:
  come to them across the waters and make your home with them.
We pray in union with Christ in the power of your Holy Spirit,
  who helps us in our weakness,
    and intercedes with sighs too deep for words,
      Father of all, now and forever. **Amen.**

August 7–13, Year B

The Lord be with you. **And also with you.**
Lift up your hearts. **We lift them to the Lord.**
Let us give thanks to the Lord our God. **It is right to give our thanks and praise.**

God of the living and the dead,
   it is our joy to give you thanks and praise
      because, though we are your rebellious creation,
         you love us and go to every length to bring us home to you.
As your servant David's son Absalom
   was left hanging between heaven and earth,
      your Son Jesus hung on the cross for our salvation.
As the young men struck David's son and killed him,
   so Jesus, the Son of David, had a spear thrust into his side.
And as David cried, "Would that I had died instead of you!"
   we recall that in Christ you did die instead of us,
      your wayward children.
And so with humble, thankful hearts we join the angels and archangels
   to sing the hymn of your endless glory.

Holy, holy, holy Lord, God of power and might.
Heaven and earth are full of your glory.
Hosanna in the highest.
Blessed is he who comes in the name of the Lord.
Hosanna in the highest.

True and living God,
   in Christ you send us the bread that comes down from heaven,
      and you promise that whoever eats of this bread will live forever.
Sanctify your people
   that they may be marked with a seal for the day of redemption
      and be raised up on the last day.
Send your Holy Spirit on this bread and this cup,

that they may be for us the body and blood of our Lord Jesus Christ;
who, at supper with his disciples, took bread, gave you thanks,
    broke the bread, and gave it to them, saying,
        "Take, eat: this is my body which is given for you;
            do this in remembrance of me."
After supper he took the cup.
Again he gave you thanks, and gave it to his disciples, saying,
    "Drink this, all of you: this is my blood of the new covenant,
        which is shed for you and for many for the forgiveness of sins.
    Do this, as often as you drink it, in remembrance of me."

Great is the mystery of faith.
Christ has died; Christ is risen; Christ will come again.

Faithful God, you call us to imitate you
    in truth-telling, honesty, grace, kindness, forgiveness, and tender love.
Show your people when to be angry,
    and how not to let the sun go down on their anger.
Come among any who are entangled in bitterness and wrath
    and wrangling and malice and slander.
Bring healing to all who are estranged from a family member
    or one to whom they were once bound in love.
Build up those who are cast down by harshness or cruelty or violence.
Usher every willing heart into the banquet of your kingdom,
    that all your creation may share the wonder of your mercy,
        Father, Son, and Holy Spirit, now and forever. **Amen.**

August 7–13, Year C

The Lord be with you. **And also with you.**
Lift up your hearts. **We lift them to the Lord.**
Let us give thanks to the Lord our God. **It is right to give our thanks and praise.**

God of time and eternity, we give you thanks and praise,
  that you weave the fabric of your purpose
    through the warp of our faith and the weft of our faithlessness.
You meet us as you met Isaac and Jacob in the tents of our transience
  and prepare us as you prepared Abraham for the city of your joy.
We make ourselves strangers and foreigners to you,
  but you greet us in your Son;
    in his death and resurrection you bring us home
      to be the people of your possession.
And so we gladly thank you, with saints and angels,
  and all the company of heaven,
    singing the hymn of your unending praise.

Holy, holy, holy Lord, God of power and might.
Heaven and earth are full of your glory.
Hosanna in the highest.
Blessed is he who comes in the name of the Lord.
Hosanna in the highest.

Loving God, you call us your treasure,
  and you tell us that where your treasure is,
    there your heart is also.
In Jesus you lodge your heart among us,
  and in this sharing of your holy meal
    you place that heart at the heart of our lives.
Now send down your Holy Spirit,
  that we may become holy as you are holy,
    and that these gifts of bread and wine may be for us

the body and blood of your Son Jesus Christ;
who, at supper with his disciples, took bread, gave you thanks,
   broke the bread, and gave it to them, saying,
      "Take, eat: this is my body which is given for you;
         do this in remembrance of me."
After supper he took the cup.
Again he gave you thanks, and gave it to his disciples, saying,
   "Drink this, all of you: this is my blood of the new covenant,
      which is shed for you and for many for the forgiveness of sins.
   Do this, as often as you drink it, in remembrance of me."

Great is the mystery of faith.
Christ has died; Christ is risen; Christ will come again.

Revealing God, as we perceive your Son,
   in the power of your Spirit, to be present in this bread and this wine,
      open our eyes to see your presence
         in the places and people wherein you make known your glory,
            so that when you come again on the last day,
               we shall recognize you by the company you keep,
                  and you shall recognize us by the company we keep.
Just as you have shown us that your heart is always with us,
   wherever our hearts stray,
      so now draw our hearts always to be where your heart is.
As you have made us your treasure on earth,
   transform us and your whole creation into your treasure in heaven,
      until the day when all hearts are drawn to you
         in the harmony of your praise,
            ever one God, our savior and our friend. **Amen.**

August 14–20, Year A

The Lord be with you. **And also with you.**
Lift up your hearts. **We lift them to the Lord.**
Let us give thanks to the Lord our God. **It is right to give our thanks and praise.**

Thanks and praise be to you, Lord God of mercy and grace,
   for you entered into covenant trust with your chosen people,
     and bestowed on them boundless gifts and an irrevocable calling.
In Jesus you take your children's food and give it to all creation,
   even we who lurk in the shadows,
     hoping for the crumbs of your eternal glory.
You have lifted us from the floor to your table,
   and from a place beyond redemption to the joy of your heart.
And so we gladly thank you,
   with angels and archangels and all the company of heaven,
     singing the hymn of your unending praise.

Holy, holy, holy Lord, God of power and might.
Heaven and earth are full of your glory.
Hosanna in the highest.
Blessed is he who comes in the name of the Lord.
Hosanna in the highest.

Cleansing God, in Christ you come among us in infectious purity,
   and heal us from the inside out.
You give us eternal food that, in you,
   we may never be hungry again.
Send your Holy Spirit upon us now,
   that we may become people who take in the holiness of your mercy,
     and give out the abundance of your grace.
Sanctify this bread and this wine, that they may become for us
   the body and blood of your Son, Jesus Christ our Lord;
who, at supper with his disciples, took bread, gave you thanks,

broke the bread, and gave it to them, saying,
  "Take, eat: this is my body which is given for you;
    do this in remembrance of me."
After supper he took the cup.
Again he gave you thanks, and gave it to his disciples, saying,
  "Drink this, all of you: this is my blood of the new covenant,
    which is shed for you and for many for the forgiveness of sins.
Do this, as often as you drink it, in remembrance of me."

Great is the mystery of faith.
Christ has died; Christ is risen; Christ will come again.

Forgiving God, you sent Joseph to Egypt,
  through the conspiracy of his brothers,
    to redeem your people from the curse of famine.
You sent your Son Jesus to the cross,
  through the corruption of our human will,
    to liberate us from sin and death.
Raise up among us children of hope,
  of courage, of truth, and of vision,
    who embody your will to turn our evil into your good.
Transform the lives of all who live under famine today;
  visit any who are excluded by envy or prejudice or fear;
    and lift the hearts of those who are weighed down
      under burdens too great to bear.
Gather at your resurrection banquet
  your whole church, living and departed,
    that all creation may feast with eyes and ears and touch and tongue
      on the effervescence of your glory,
        ever one God, Father, Son, and Holy Spirit, forever. **Amen.**

August 14–20, Year B

The Lord be with you. **And also with you.**
Lift up your hearts. **We lift them to the Lord.**
Let us give thanks to the Lord our God. **It is right to give our thanks and praise.**

God of great and steadfast love, we thank and praise you
  because you open your life that we may abide in you.
You called Abraham and made your home
  in the midst of the people whom you had chosen,
    a great people, so numerous they could not be numbered or counted.
In Jesus, son of David, you walked before us
  in faithfulness, in righteousness, and in uprightness of heart.
You crowned him king and ushered in a reign that has no end;
  and in your grace you invite us to gather around his heavenly throne,
    joining all the company of heaven, singing your unending hymn of glory.

Holy, holy, holy Lord, God of power and might.
Heaven and earth are full of your glory.
Hosanna in the highest.
Blessed is he who comes in the name of the Lord.
Hosanna in the highest.

Ever-present God, through meals
  you show your people your faithfulness in the wilderness,
    your persistence in times of famine,
      and your will to be our companion forever.
Your Son shared a meal the night before he died for our salvation,
  and on the day he rose for our redemption.
Send your Holy Spirit on your people,
  that those who eat the flesh of your Son and drink his blood
    may have eternal life.
Sanctify this bread and this wine, that they may be for us
  the body and blood of our Lord Jesus Christ;

who, at supper with his disciples, took bread, gave you thanks,
   broke the bread, and gave it to them, saying,
      "Take, eat: this is my body which is given for you;
         do this in remembrance of me."
After supper he took the cup.
Again he gave you thanks, and gave it to his disciples, saying,
   "Drink this, all of you: this is my blood of the new covenant,
      which is shed for you and for many for the forgiveness of sins.
   Do this, as often as you drink it, in remembrance of me."

Great is the mystery of faith.
Christ has died; Christ is risen; Christ will come again.

Steadfast God, you offered your servant Solomon
   any gift he needed to take up the mantle of leading your people.
When he chose an understanding mind,
   able to discern between good and evil,
      you gave him also those things for which he had not asked.
You bestow on us so much more than we desire or deserve.
Send upon your people the gift of wisdom,
   that your children may know the paths that lead to peace,
      your church may be renewed in the ways of gentleness,
         and your kingdom may come near in grace and truth.
Build up rulers and leaders in the virtues of discernment and mercy.
Show your face to those who ache
   for your overturning day of reversal,
      and hasten the coming of your just and righteous reign,
         Triune God, now and forever. **Amen.**

August 14–20, Year C

The Lord be with you. **And also with you.**
Lift up your hearts. **We lift them to the Lord.**
Let us give thanks to the Lord our God. **It is right to give our thanks and praise.**

It is a good and joyful thing to give our thanks to you, faithful God,
   because you have surrounded us with so great a cloud of witnesses
      who have followed the path of your promises.
By faith your people crossed the Red Sea
   when you brought them out of slavery.
By faith your Son endured the cross, disregarding its shame.
By faith your apostles endured chains and imprisonment,
   testifying to the gospel.
By faith your martyrs suffered mockery and death for your glory alone.
And so with this cloud of witnesses from every age and time
   we praise you with angels and archangels and all the company of heaven
      as we join the unending hymn.

Holy, holy, holy Lord, God of power and might.
Heaven and earth are full of your glory.
Hosanna in the highest.
Blessed is he who comes in the name of the Lord.
Hosanna in the highest.

Righteous God, whose Son is the pioneer and perfecter of our faith,
   make your church a vineyard of justice and peace.
Nourish your people with this fruit of the vine
   and sanctify us with your Holy Spirit,
      that we may bring forth the perfect fruit of your kingdom.
Send your Holy Spirit upon this bread and cup,
   that they may be for us the body and blood of your Son;
who, at supper with his disciples, took bread, gave you thanks,
   broke the bread, and gave it to them, saying,

"Take, eat: this is my body which is given for you;
   do this in remembrance of me."
After supper he took the cup.
Again he gave you thanks, and gave it to his disciples, saying,
   "Drink this, all of you: this is my blood of the new covenant,
      which is shed for you and for many for the forgiveness of sins.
   Do this, as often as you drink it, in remembrance of me."

Great is the mystery of faith.
Christ has died; Christ is risen; Christ will come again.

Redeeming God,
   whose Son for the sake of heavenly joy won our salvation,
      strengthen us to run with perseverance the race set before us.
Liberate your people in the midst of every sorrow
   that they may hold fast to your unfailing mercy.
Raise up into your unending glory
   every soul weighed heavy with struggle.
Give your children a heart to see through every trial of life
   to a deeper joy that is possible only in you.
Grant us wisdom in the midst of conflict
   to discern your ways of peace.
Bring us all to the day when we are made perfect in your love
   and rejoice in your promises fulfilled,
      beholding Christ our Lord seated at your right hand on high
         in the power of the Holy Spirit, one God, now and always. **Amen.**

August 21–27, Year A

The Lord be with you. **And also with you.**
Lift up your hearts. **We lift them to the Lord.**
Let us give thanks to the Lord our God. **It is right to give our thanks and praise.**

We lift our hearts and give our thanks and praise to you,
   God of our mothers and fathers,
      because you brought order out of chaos,
         you called a people to be your own,
            and in Moses you saw the misery of your people
               and heard their cries.
In Elijah and the prophets you pleaded with your people
   to be true to their identity as your chosen ones,
      and finally in Jesus you came down to deliver us
         from sin and death and oppression
            through the obedience of the cross and the glory of the resurrection.
And so we gladly thank you,
   joining with angels and archangels and all the company of heaven
      to sing the hymn of your unending praise.

Holy, holy, holy Lord, God of power and might.
Heaven and earth are full of your glory.
Hosanna in the highest.
Blessed is he who comes in the name of the Lord.
Hosanna in the highest.

We thank and praise you, Lord God,
   because in the power of your Holy Spirit
      you give us everything we need to follow you—
         gifts of prophecy, ministry, exhortation,
            generosity, leadership, and compassion.
Send down your Holy Spirit upon us now,
   that we may be not conformed to your world

but transformed by your renewing grace.
Give us your very self in these gifts of bread and wine
  and make them for us the body and blood of your Son Jesus Christ;
who, at supper with his disciples, took bread, gave you thanks,
  broke the bread, and gave it to them, saying,
    "Take, eat: this is my body which is given for you;
      do this in remembrance of me."
After supper he took the cup.
Again he gave you thanks, and gave it to his disciples, saying,
  "Drink this, all of you: this is my blood of the new covenant,
    which is shed for you and for many for the forgiveness of sins.
  Do this, as often as you drink it, in remembrance of me."

Great is the mystery of faith.
Christ has died; Christ is risen; Christ will come again.

God of deliverance, you open up the gift of your scripture
  to reveal who you are and who we are.
Through the gift of your holy communion,
  bring your whole creation into the form of your likeness.
Have mercy on those who are oppressed,
  be close to all who live under hostile regimes,
    and hear the cries of all whose children are in constant danger.
Make us a subversive people who incubate your exodus
  and practice divine disobedience,
    until the day comes when all the world praises your name
      and is filled with your justice and peace.
We pray in union with Christ in the power of your Holy Spirit,
  God of glory, forever and ever. **Amen.**

August 21–27, Year B

The Lord be with you. **And also with you.**
Lift up your hearts. **We lift them to the Lord.**
Let us give thanks to the Lord our God. **It is right to give our thanks and praise.**

Holy God, whom neither earth nor heaven can contain,
   we gather around the mystery of your grace.
You called your chosen people to abide with you
   in covenant and steadfast love,
     and through them you called all the peoples of the earth
       to know your name and come before you in godly fear.
When your children wondered if you would indeed dwell upon the earth,
   you embodied and renewed your covenant
     in the flesh of your Son Jesus Christ.
And so we thank and praise you,
   joining with cherubim and seraphim and the company of heaven,
     singing the never-ending hymn of your glory.

Holy, holy, holy Lord, God of power and might.
Heaven and earth are full of your glory.
Hosanna in the highest.
Blessed is he who comes in the name of the Lord.
Hosanna in the highest.

Faithful God, there is no one else to whom we can go;
   you alone have the power of resurrection and the words of eternal life.
Your Son promised that those who eat his flesh and drink his blood
   abide in him, and he in them.
Sanctify your people that they may come to believe and know
   that you are the Holy One.
Send down your Holy Spirit on this bread and this cup,
   that they may be for us the body and blood of our Lord Jesus Christ;
who, at supper with his disciples, took bread, gave you thanks,

broke the bread, and gave it to them, saying,
  "Take, eat: this is my body which is given for you;
    do this in remembrance of me."
After supper he took the cup.
Again he gave you thanks, and gave it to his disciples, saying,
  "Drink this, all of you: this is my blood of the new covenant,
    which is shed for you and for many for the forgiveness of sins.
  Do this, as often as you drink it, in remembrance of me."

Great is the mystery of faith.
Christ has died; Christ is risen; Christ will come again.

God our stronghold, give your people the power
  to stand firm in faith clothed in the armor of your Spirit.
Uphold any who are oppressed by rulers, authorities,
  cosmic powers, or spiritual forces.
Be the belt of truth for those who live amid lies,
  and the breastplate of righteousness for all who are exploited.
Put shoes on the feet of your children who proclaim the gospel of peace,
  and guard all who seek refuge behind the shield of faith.
Equip any who face hostility with the helmet of salvation
  and the sword of your Spirit.
As your Son's agonizing cross came before his glorious resurrection,
  follow the travails of your people with the wondrous coming of your kingdom,
    that every tear-filled eye may bask in the joy of your Triune majesty,
      one God, Father, Son, and Holy Spirit. **Amen.**

August 21–27, Year C

The Lord be with you. **And also with you.**
Lift up your hearts. **We lift them to the Lord.**
Let us give thanks to the Lord our God. **It is right to give our thanks and praise.**

God of Sinai and Zion, you have met us on a mountain
   of blazing fire and gloom and tempest,
      and in Moses you made a covenant with your chosen people.
When we were faithless, you remained faithful.
Yet in Jesus you renew that covenant not in anger but in gentleness,
   not in grief but in joy, not in terror but in trust.
And so you lead us in thanksgiving to Mount Zion,
   to the spirits of the righteous made perfect,
      to the assembly of the firstborn enrolled in your company,
         and to angels and archangels in festal gathering,
            singing the hymn of your unending praise.

Holy, holy, holy Lord, God of power and might.
Heaven and earth are full of your glory.
Hosanna in the highest.
Blessed is he who comes in the name of the Lord.
Hosanna in the highest.

God beyond our imaginings,
   in Jesus you make yourself a being who may be touched,
      and in this sacrament of bread and wine
         you allow us to touch your heart.
In your Son's death he was nailed to a cross,
   and in his resurrection the disciples touched his hands and side.
Come close to us in the power of your Spirit
   and make us worthy to stand in your presence and serve you.
Send down that same Spirit, that these gifts of bread and wine
   may be for us the body and blood of your Son Jesus Christ;

who, at supper with his disciples, took bread, gave you thanks,
broke the bread, and gave it to them, saying,
"Take, eat: this is my body which is given for you;
do this in remembrance of me."
After supper he took the cup.
Again he gave you thanks, and gave it to his disciples, saying,
"Drink this, all of you: this is my blood of the new covenant,
which is shed for you and for many for the forgiveness of sins.
Do this, as often as you drink it, in remembrance of me."

Great is the mystery of faith.
Christ has died; Christ is risen; Christ will come again.

God our savior, in Jesus you healed the woman crippled for many years,
and likewise in Jesus you transform your world so long crippled by sin.
As you make yourself present in the power of your Spirit
in this bread and this wine,
alert us to perceive your presence and transforming love
wherever we see ourselves or others crippled
by sin or suffering or sadness or oppression.
Touch us in our places of despair,
touch all your people in their woundedness and grief,
and touch your whole creation
as it groans in eager longing for your coming again,
that we may come face to face with you,
and you may know us in the likeness of your Son,
ever one God, Father, Son, and Holy Spirit. **Amen.**

August 28–September 3, Year A

The Lord be with you. **And also with you.**
Lift up your hearts. **We lift them to the Lord.**
Let us give thanks to the Lord our God. **It is right to give our thanks and praise.**

Blessed be your holy name, God of Abraham, Isaac, and Jacob,
   for you have revealed yourself to be the only, the eternal, the great I AM.
From the flames of the burning bush you anointed Moses
   to lead your people out of hardship and bondage to the land of promise.
In the fire of the prophets you spoke of a day
    when every sin and sorrow would be burned away
     and all the earth would be ablaze with your glory.
In the fullness of time you revealed your way of overcoming evil
    in the crucible of your Son's passion and death;
      through his resurrection you proclaimed once again
        that you are the great I AM for all generations.
And so we give you thanks with your church on earth
    and all the company of heaven, as we join the unending hymn.

Holy, holy, holy Lord, God of power and might.
Heaven and earth are full of your glory.
Hosanna in the highest.
Blessed is he who comes in the name of the Lord.
Hosanna in the highest.

Lord God, as you made the earth beneath Moses's feet into holy ground,
   sanctify this meal to bring us into your sacred presence.
As we remember your Son's saving mercies,
   send down your Spirit to anoint your church for ministry.
By that same Spirit bless this bread and cup
   that they may be for us the body and blood of our Savior Jesus Christ;
who, at supper with his disciples, took bread, gave you thanks,
   broke the bread, and gave it to them, saying,

"Take, eat: this is my body which is given for you;
   do this in remembrance of me."
After supper he took the cup.
Again he gave you thanks, and gave it to his disciples, saying,
   "Drink this, all of you: this is my blood of the new covenant,
      which is shed for you and for many for the forgiveness of sins.
   Do this, as often as you drink it, in remembrance of me."

Great is the mystery of faith.
Christ has died; Christ is risen; Christ will come again.

Sending God, who commissioned Moses
   for a purpose beyond his comprehension,
      send forth your church with an imagination shaped for your kingdom.
Give your disciples grace to bless those who persecute them,
   to be patient in suffering, to persevere in prayer, and to rejoice in hope.
Stretch every heart to find life in you by losing it,
   and strengthen your people with courage and wisdom
      to take up their cross and follow your Son.
Make your people on earth ready for a purpose beyond our imagining,
   a life beyond our deserving, a glory beyond our reckoning,
      until your kingdom comes on earth as it is in heaven
         and you bring us with the saints onto eternal holy ground,
            aflame with your love, most holy Trinity, now and forever. **Amen.**

August 28–September 3, Year B

The Lord be with you. **And also with you.**
Lift up your hearts. **We lift them to the Lord.**
Let us give thanks to the Lord our God. **It is right to give our thanks and praise.**

We gladly and joyfully thank and praise you, our Lord and God,
    for you created all things from the overflowing of your goodness
        and made us your beloved in your covenant of grace.
Out of the long winter of our estrangement
    you called us to arise and come away with you,
        because the springtime of our salvation was at hand.
In fulfillment of your own purpose
    you gave us birth by your Word of truth,
        so that we would become the firstfruits of his creatures.
In your Son Jesus you set us as a seal upon your heart,
    and in his cross and resurrection
        you showed that your love was stronger than death.
And so we join our voices with the heavenly throng,
    singing the hymn of your eternal glory.

Holy, holy, holy Lord, God of power and might.
Heaven and earth are full of your glory.
Hosanna in the highest.
Blessed is he who comes in the name of the Lord.
Hosanna in the highest.

Transforming God, you long for us to become holy like you.
Through this gathering of reconciliation
    and word of truth and embodiment of peace
        you fill us with bread for the journey.
In the power of your Holy Spirit,
    make all who participate in this blessed meal
        doers of your word, and not hearers only.

By your same Spirit, bless this food and drink
    that they may be for us the body and blood of our Lord Jesus Christ;
who, at supper with his disciples, took bread, gave you thanks,
    broke the bread, and gave it to them, saying,
        "Take, eat: this is my body which is given for you;
            do this in remembrance of me."
After supper he took the cup.
Again he gave you thanks, and gave it to his disciples, saying,
    "Drink this, all of you: this is my blood of the new covenant,
        which is shed for you and for many for the forgiveness of sins.
    Do this, as often as you drink it, in remembrance of me."

Great is the mystery of faith.
Christ has died; Christ is risen; Christ will come again.

Gentle God, you call us to be quick to listen and slow to speak.
Embolden all who have no one to listen to them,
    that in their distress, or dismay, or disease
        they may meet friends, receive justice, and find you.
Give wisdom to any who have something to say,
    that they may speak your words, live your hope,
        and draw others to your truth.
Bless those who struggle with anger,
    that their frustration may turn to good work,
        and their sense of deep wrong yield a pursuit of righteousness.
Hasten the day when there is no more grief or sorrow,
    but you are all in all, ever one God, Father, Son, and Holy Spirit. **Amen.**

August 28–September 3, Year C

The Lord be with you. **And also with you.**
Lift up your hearts. **We lift them to the Lord.**
Let us give thanks to the Lord our God. **It is right to give our thanks and praise.**

Exalted above all is your name, God of Jacob,
   for you feed your people, not only for today but for eternity,
      with your food that truly satisfies.
When your people hungered,
   you longed to feed them with finest wheat,
      and through the grace of your servant Joseph
         turned famine into abundant provision.
When you brought your children out of slavery,
   you filled their mouths with good things
      and led them to life in a land of plenty.
In the fullness of time, your Son gave us a place of honor
   at the banquet of salvation,
      which is more than we could ever deserve.
And so we rejoice with all who feed on him by faith with thanksgiving,
   with angels and archangels and all the company of heaven,
      as we join the unending hymn.

Holy, holy, holy Lord, God of power and might.
Heaven and earth are full of your glory.
Hosanna in the highest.
Blessed is he who comes in the name of the Lord.
Hosanna in the highest.

Transforming God, as you exalt the humble and humble the exalted,
   pour your grace upon your church
      gathered to remember the dying and rising of your Son.
Send your Spirit upon this bread and this cup,
   that they may be for us the body and blood of our Lord Jesus Christ;

who, at supper with his disciples, took bread, gave you thanks,
  broke the bread, and gave it to them, saying,
    "Take, eat: this is my body which is given for you;
      do this in remembrance of me."
After supper he took the cup.
Again he gave you thanks, and gave it to his disciples, saying,
  "Drink this, all of you: this is my blood of the new covenant,
    which is shed for you and for many for the forgiveness of sins.
    Do this, as often as you drink it, in remembrance of me."

Great is the mystery of faith.
Christ has died; Christ is risen; Christ will come again.

Inviting God, as in your Son you beckon
  the poor and the crippled and the blind and the lame,
    visit your church where it is poor,
      and make it reflect the wonder of your love;
    renew your people where they are crippled,
      that your power may be made perfect in weakness;
    empower your children where they are blind,
      that they may know you more truly;
    and uphold your saints where they are lame,
      that they may find friends gracious in support and strength
        with whom they may never be afraid.
Make your church a place of hospitality,
  that it may entertain angels unawares.
For in Christ you are the same yesterday, today, and forever,
  and in the power of your Spirit we shall never walk alone,
    heavenly Father, radiant in glory. **Amen.**

7. Sundays after Pentecost (Fall)

September 4–10, Year A

The Lord be with you. **And also with you.**
Lift up your hearts. **We lift them to the Lord.**
Let us give thanks to the Lord our God. **It is right to give our thanks and praise.**

We glorify and enjoy you now and forever, gracious God,
  because you created the universe as your work of art,
    and set us in the midst of it.
When the canvas of your kindness was torn by our sin,
  you crafted a work of even more depth and beauty
    from the damage we had done.
When your Son's body was scarred and pierced,
  you raised him to glorious life.
In your chosen people you drew out a song of thankfulness and praise,
  and in your church you give us voices to shout and dance
    and sculpt and inscribe the wonders of your love.
And so we rejoice to join with angels and archangels
  and all the company of heaven,
    singing the hymn of your unending praise.

Holy, holy, holy Lord, God of power and might.
Heaven and earth are full of your glory.
Hosanna in the highest.
Blessed is he who comes in the name of the Lord.
Hosanna in the highest.

We lift our hearts to you, Lord God,
  because you draw your whole creation
    into the celebration of your glory.
Send down your Holy Spirit upon us now,
  that every part of every one of us
    might become an instrument of your peace.
Give us your very self in these gifts of bread and wine

and make them be for us
    the body and blood of your Son Jesus Christ;
who, at supper with his disciples, took bread, gave you thanks,
    broke the bread, and gave it to them, saying,
        "Take, eat: this is my body which is given for you;
           do this in remembrance of me."
After supper he took the cup.
Again he gave you thanks, and gave it to his disciples, saying,
    "Drink this, all of you: this is my blood of the new covenant,
        which is shed for you and for many for the forgiveness of sins.
    Do this, as often as you drink it, in remembrance of me."

Great is the mystery of faith.
Christ has died; Christ is risen; Christ will come again.

God of justice, make us a prophetic people,
    whose every work and every act
        is a proclamation of the new order found in you
           and worthy of your kingdom.
Holy God, make us a priestly people,
    whose lives are so transparent with your truth
        that we become a place of encounter between you
           and your beloved children.
Reigning God, make us a kingly people,
    whose hearts are filled with worship and wonder,
        and who seek to bring every one of your gifts to fruition
           in the power of your Spirit.
We pray in union with Christ in the power of your Holy Spirit,
    God of glory, forever and ever. **Amen.**

September 4–10, Year B

The Lord be with you. **And also with you.**
Lift up your hearts. **We lift them to the Lord.**
Let us give thanks to the Lord our God. **It is right to give our thanks and praise.**

Maker and redeemer of all, we lift our hearts to thank you,
    because you open our ears to hear your voice
        and release our tongue to sing your praise.
You created the earth as a place of encounter
    between you and your creatures.
You called your people from slavery and wilderness
    to covenant and abundant life.
You gave your children manna to share,
    and from the crumbs that fell from their table
        you made a banquet to welcome the Gentiles
            to the joy of your companionship.
You made the body of your crucified and risen Son
    the altar of your mercy and of our redemption.
And so we zealously proclaim the triumphs of your grace,
    joining with angels and archangels and all the company of heaven
        in the hymn of your eternal glory.

Holy, holy, holy Lord, God of power and might.
Heaven and earth are full of your glory.
Hosanna in the highest.
Blessed is he who comes in the name of the Lord.
Hosanna in the highest.

Life-giving God, you share your bread with the poor,
    and you make this banquet the place
        where in the power of your Spirit
            we are united as one body in your Son.
Make this meal a moment of reconciliation

between you and your people,
and let those who share in it be ambassadors of reconciliation
within your wounded world.
Send your Holy Spirit upon this bread and this cup,
that they may be for us the body and blood of our Lord Jesus Christ;
who, at supper with his disciples, took bread, gave you thanks,
broke the bread, and gave it to them, saying,
"Take, eat: this is my body which is given for you;
do this in remembrance of me."
After supper he took the cup.
Again he gave you thanks, and gave it to his disciples, saying,
"Drink this, all of you: this is my blood of the new covenant,
which is shed for you and for many for the forgiveness of sins.
Do this, as often as you drink it, in remembrance of me."

Great is the mystery of faith.
Christ has died; Christ is risen; Christ will come again.

God of the afflicted, you have chosen the poor in the world
to be rich in faith and to be heirs of the kingdom
that you have promised to those who love you.
Make your church rich as you are rich,
in compassion and mercy, in wisdom and grace;
and make your people poor as you are poor,
in sharing the calamity of those who endure injustice
and knowing the pain of all who live with the world's anger.
Take away the mask of poverty, that all may see with joy
the riches of those the world calls poor,
and remove the mask of wealth, that all may see with love
the poverty of those the world calls rich.
Hasten the day when your gentle mercy
triumphs over the world's harsh judgment,
and all find a place at the feast of your kingdom,
ever one God, Father, Son, and Holy Spirit. **Amen.**

September 4–10, Year C

The Lord be with you. **And also with you.**
Lift up your hearts. **We lift them to the Lord.**
Let us give thanks to the Lord our God. **It is right to give our thanks and praise.**

Praise be unto you, God of the prophets,
   for you have taken in your own two hands
     the redemption of your world
      and refashioned us from brokenness into life everlasting with you.
Like a potter you fashioned your chosen people,
   making them into a vessel worthy of your glory.
When that vessel was spoiled you called your people to repentance
   and sent prophets to renew their faith.
In the fullness of time, through the death and resurrection of your Son,
   you reworked the clay like a potter at a wheel,
     and remade a vessel revealing your goodness and grace
      through the forgiveness of sins, raising us up
       from the dust of the earth to the hope of everlasting life.
And so with angels and archangels and all the company of heaven
   we praise your name and join their unending hymn.

Holy, holy, holy Lord, God of power and might.
Heaven and earth are full of your glory.
Hosanna in the highest.
Blessed is hc who comes in the name of the Lord.
Hosanna in the highest.

God of love, you welcome us at this table
   as brothers and sisters in a new family.
Shape our life together by the way we belong to one another in you.
Send your Holy Spirit upon your church
   to make us faithful witnesses to your beloved community.
Sanctify this bread and cup

that they may be for us the body and blood of your Son;
who, at supper with his disciples, took bread, gave you thanks,
   broke the bread, and gave it to them, saying,
      "Take, eat: this is my body which is given for you;
         do this in remembrance of me."
After supper he took the cup.
Again he gave you thanks, and gave it to his disciples, saying,
   "Drink this, all of you: this is my blood of the new covenant,
      which is shed for you and for many for the forgiveness of sins.
   Do this, as often as you drink it, in remembrance of me."

Great is the mystery of faith.
Christ has died; Christ is risen; Christ will come again.

Creating and re-creating God, you are the potter and we are the clay.
Renew your church today in the touch of your hands.
Search and know the places that are broken
   and the hearts that long to be mended.
Form your people in faithfulness to Jesus.
Shape us to be his disciples, to take up our cross and follow him.
Have your own way with us, Lord:
   mold us and make us, search us and try us, touch us and heal us,
      till all shall see Christ only, always, living in us.
Bring us at last to the blessed day when we are one
   with the family of saints gathered around your throne,
      in the company of the Holy Spirit, in union with Christ,
         Father most holy, now and always. **Amen.**

September 11–17, Year A

The Lord be with you. **And also with you.**
Lift up your hearts. **We lift them to the Lord.**
Let us give thanks to the Lord our God. **It is right to give our thanks and praise.**

It is good and joyful to sing your praise,
   God of Moses and Miriam, for you are majestic in holiness,
      awesome in splendor, and glorious in power.
You rejoice in all you have made,
   and you have created all things to ring out your joy.
When your children were shackled as Pharaoh's slaves,
   you heard their cries, divided the waters of the sea,
      and opened a path to lead them to freedom on dry ground.
When your people were captive to the bondage of sin,
   you sent your Son, full of your forgiving mercies,
      to release us and to send us to share with others
         the grace we have ourselves received.
And so we give you thanks and extol your holy name,
   with angels and archangels and all the company of heaven,
      as we join the unending hymn.

Holy, holy, holy Lord, God of power and might.
Heaven and earth are full of your glory.
Hosanna in the highest.
Blessed is he who comes in the name of the Lord.
Hosanna in the highest.

Delivering God, through your Son's dying and rising,
   you have released us from the debt of sin
      into the company of the forgiven.
Sanctify us, who share this meal, to be a sign of jubilee hope
   in your freeing, redeeming, life-giving promise.
Send your Spirit upon this bread and this cup of blessing

to be for us the body and blood of our Lord Jesus Christ;
who, at supper with his disciples, took bread, gave you thanks,
  broke the bread, and gave it to them, saying,
    "Take, eat: this is my body which is given for you;
      do this in remembrance of me."
After supper he took the cup.
Again he gave you thanks, and gave it to his disciples, saying,
  "Drink this, all of you: this is my blood of the new covenant,
    which is shed for you and for many for the forgiveness of sins.
  Do this, as often as you drink it, in remembrance of me."

Great is the mystery of faith.
Christ has died; Christ is risen; Christ will come again.

God of mercy, shape your church
  to embody the forgiveness you make possible in Christ.
Have compassion upon your sons and daughters
  who suffer the isolation of shame or disgrace.
Give courage and conviction to any who find it difficult to forgive
  a brother or sister from the heart,
    and console your children whose pleas for clemency are unheeded.
Bring your kingdom near in every place
  where financial debt weighs down nation or household.
Draw us into your eternal life,
    that heralding your emancipation and proclaiming your liberation
      together with your people of every age,
        we may be bound to you forever in one perfect freedom,
          everlasting God, Father, Son, and Holy Spirit. **Amen.**

September 11–17, Year B

The Lord be with you. **And also with you.**
Lift up your hearts. **We lift them to the Lord.**
Let us give thanks to the Lord our God. **It is right to give our thanks and praise.**

God of wisdom and truth,
   we give you heartfelt thanks for the joy of your creation,
     and abundant praise for the grace of your liberating love.
You gathered the twelve tribes of Israel
   and spoke your word to Elijah and your prophets.
In the fullness of time your Son gathered twelve disciples
   and walked the way of the cross
     that John the Baptist had prepared for him.
After his great passion and suffering,
   he rose to glory on the third day.
And so with the host of heaven we gather around your throne,
   singing your eternal hymn of glory.

Holy, holy, holy Lord, God of power and might.
Heaven and earth are full of your glory.
Hosanna in the highest.
Blessed is he who comes in the name of the Lord.
Hosanna in the highest.

Suffering God, your Son knew betrayal, and denial, and pain, and death.
In his broken body we see the extent of your love for us
   and the depths of our rejection of you.
Send your Spirit upon those gathered here,
   that this meal may be an outpouring of your love
     and a healing of our rejection.
Send that same Spirit upon this bread and wine, that they may be for us
   the body and blood of our Lord Jesus Christ;
who, at supper with his disciples, took bread, gave you thanks,

broke the bread, and gave it to them, saying,
"Take, eat: this is my body which is given for you;
do this in remembrance of me."
After supper he took the cup.
Again he gave you thanks, and gave it to his disciples, saying,
"Drink this, all of you: this is my blood of the new covenant,
which is shed for you and for many for the forgiveness of sins.
Do this, as often as you drink it, in remembrance of me."

Great is the mystery of faith.
Christ has died; Christ is risen; Christ will come again.

Expectant God, in your Son you were denied,
and you call us to deny ourselves:
be close to all who have been denied
by those they had come to trust.
In Christ you took up a cross:
give strength to all who carry his cross today.
You call us to follow in the way of life, and truth, and peace:
draw near to any who dwell amid hostility and discord.
As your Son lost his life in order to save us,
show your church where it should cease to save
and be free to lose, and where it should gladly lose,
in order the more wondrously to save and be saved.
Put a song in every weary throat
that celebrates the day of your coming,
and open our eyes to see that great day,
when with the holy angels the Son of Man comes
in the power of the Spirit and the glory of the Father. **Amen.**

September 11–17, Year C

The Lord be with you. **And also with you.**
Lift up your hearts. **We lift them to the Lord.**
Let us give thanks to the Lord our God. **It is right to give our thanks and praise.**

Honor and glory be to you, Lord God, king of the ages,
   because you created the world and called a people;
      yet when your people became skilled in doing evil
         and forgot how to do good,
           you displayed the utmost patience,
             and your grace overflowed with love.
When your sheep wandered away from their sheepfold,
   you searched high and low,
     and in Jesus you came among your people
       to bring them home to you.
Just so, when we wander away,
   you come to us in the crucified and risen Jesus
     and place us on your shoulders and rejoice to bring us home.
And so we enter that joy in the presence of angels and archangels
   and all the company of heaven,
     singing the hymn of your unending praise.

Holy, holy, holy Lord, God of power and might.
Heaven and earth are full of your glory.
Hosanna in the highest.
Blessed is he who comes in the name of the Lord.
Hosanna in the highest.

God of grace, in Christ you came into the world
   to save sinners, to welcome them, and to eat with them.
You spread a table in our sight and invite us to join you in glory.
Now send down your Holy Spirit,
   that your people who have strayed like lost sheep

may dwell in the paths of righteousness,
    and that these gifts of bread and wine may be for us
        the body and blood of your Son Jesus Christ;
who, at supper with his disciples, took bread, gave you thanks,
    broke the bread, and gave it to them, saying,
        "Take, eat: this is my body which is given for you;
            do this in remembrance of me."
After supper he took the cup.
Again he gave you thanks, and gave it to his disciples, saying,
    "Drink this, all of you: this is my blood of the new covenant,
        which is shed for you and for many for the forgiveness of sins.
    Do this, as often as you drink it, in remembrance of me."

Great is the mystery of faith.
Christ has died; Christ is risen; Christ will come again.

Searching and yearning God,
    in Christ you enter the wilderness
        and sweep the dark corners of our world
            because you hate nothing you have made
                and long to draw us back to your heart.
Find those who are lost; reach any who have strayed;
    pursue all who seem determined to wander
        further and further from your fold.
Heal your earth: where the fruitful land is waste and void,
    where the mountains are quaking,
        and the birds of the air have fled,
            bring hope, transformation, and deliverance.
Immortal, invisible Father,
    redeem your creation in the power of your Spirit,
        and draw all things through the free gift of your Son
            into the glory of your presence. **Amen.**

September 18–24, Year A

The Lord be with you. **And also with you.**
Lift up your hearts. **We lift them to the Lord.**
Let us give thanks to the Lord our God. **It is right to give our thanks and praise.**

We lift our hearts to you, gracious God,
   because you made the dazzling creation out of nothing,
      yet made us to share eternity with you.
In covenant love you called your chosen people to an imagination
   as plentiful as the stars in the sky and the sands of the desert.
Your Son Jesus transformed our hearts
   from the scarcity of mammon to the wondrous abundance of manna,
      and through the church you gather us to share in the holy feast
         where your grace abounds for all, forever.
His cross and resurrection turn the emptiness of sin
   into the fullness of everlasting life.
And so we join with angels and archangels
   and all the company of heaven,
      singing the hymn of your unending praise.

Holy, holy, holy Lord, God of power and might.
Heaven and earth are full of your glory.
Hosanna in the highest.
Blessed is he who comes in the name of the Lord.
Hosanna in the highest.

We give you thanks and praise, Lord God,
   for in your Son Jesus you became the true bread from heaven,
      the manna sustaining us in every wilderness,
         the bread of abundant life that never runs out.
Send down your Holy Spirit upon us now,
   that we might become living bread for your hungry world.
Give us your very self in these gifts of bread and wine

and make them for us the body and blood of your Son Jesus Christ;
who, at supper with his disciples, took bread, gave you thanks,
  broke the bread, and gave it to them, saying,
    "Take, eat: this is my body which is given for you;
      do this in remembrance of me."
After supper he took the cup.
Again he gave you thanks, and gave it to his disciples, saying,
  "Drink this, all of you: this is my blood of the new covenant,
    which is shed for you and for many for the forgiveness of sins.
  Do this, as often as you drink it, in remembrance of me."

Great is the mystery of faith.
Christ has died; Christ is risen; Christ will come again.

Ever-bountiful God, listen to the hunger of your children
  and nourish their true life in you.
Draw near to those who toil for daily wages
  and all who wonder where they will find daily bread.
Bless any whose days are spent looking for work or waiting for hire.
Give each of your sons and daughters a place in your kingdom
  and fruitful work in your vineyard,
    not only for a passing day but for eternity.
By your Holy Spirit in your holy church,
  make the labors of our hands tell the good news
    of your harvest of plenty,
      and hasten the day when in one great sharing around your table
        with your people throughout the ages
          we shall taste and see that you are good.
Through Christ and with Christ and in Christ,
  all honor and glory are yours,
    Almighty Father, now and forever. **Amen.**

September 18–24, Year B

The Lord be with you. **And also with you.**
Lift up your hearts. **We lift them to the Lord.**
Let us give thanks to the Lord our God. **It is right to give our thanks and praise.**

God of good fruits, it is right to give you thanks and praise
   because you place your life in our hands,
      that we may share it and enjoy it.
In your Son Jesus you set a little child among us,
   and embodied your promises to your chosen people.
In his betrayal and crucifixion
   we see the cost of your entrusting your very self to us;
      and the still-scarred hands of his resurrection
         reveal how deep and irresistible is your love.
In his ascension on high we rejoice to see him raised up to glory
   and seated at your right hand.
And so we join with angels and archangels
   and with all the company of heaven,
      singing the hymn of your eternal glory.

Holy, holy, holy Lord, God of power and might.
Heaven and earth are full of your glory.
Hosanna in the highest.
Blessed is he who comes in the name of the Lord.
Hosanna in the highest.

Wisdom from above, despite all we have done to you,
   still in this holy meal when we stretch out our hands
      you fill them with your life and love.
Send your Spirit upon your people,
   that hands which have received such precious things
      may be made holy in faith and service.
By that same Spirit, sanctify this bread and this cup

that they may be for us the body and blood of our Lord Jesus Christ;
who, at supper with his disciples, took bread, gave you thanks,
 broke the bread, and gave it to them, saying,
  "Take, eat: this is my body which is given for you;
   do this in remembrance of me."
After supper he took the cup.
Again he gave you thanks, and gave it to his disciples, saying,
 "Drink this, all of you: this is my blood of the new covenant,
  which is shed for you and for many for the forgiveness of sins.
 Do this, as often as you drink it, in remembrance of me."

Great is the mystery of faith.
Christ has died; Christ is risen; Christ will come again.

Joy-giving God, make your people worthy of your trust.
Open our hearts to the poor, and stretch out our hands to the needy.
Open our mouths with gentleness born of wisdom,
 and put the teaching of kindness on our tongues.
Give us a share in the fruit of your hands,
 that all the world may praise the wonders of your grace.
Give your church the trust and confidence
 to be last of all and servant of all;
  until that day when you welcome the last to be the first
   and draw your children with all creation near to your heart,
    making all things new,
     ever one God, Father, Son, and Holy Spirit. **Amen.**

September 18–24, Year C

The Lord be with you. **And also with you.**
Lift up your hearts. **We lift them to the Lord.**
Let us give thanks to the Lord our God. **It is right to give our thanks and praise.**

God of wonder and love, we thank and praise you
  because we and all creation were your debtors;
    your Son Jesus Christ forgave our debts
      at the price of his own blood
        and showed us what your grace could do.
When your people cried out for healing balm,
  you restored their soul,
    sending your only Son to be the steward
      who turned justice into mercy
       and in spite of our failure
         made us welcome in your eternal home
          as your companions forever.
He transforms us from resentful antagonists
  and anxious sinners into joyful friends,
    and in his glorious resurrection opens the way to life with you.
And so with angels and archangels and the company of heaven,
  we join the everlasting song of praise.

Holy, holy, holy Lord, God of power and might.
Heaven and earth are full of your glory.
Hosanna in the highest.
Blessed is he who comes in the name of the Lord.
Hosanna in the highest.

God our savior, you desire everyone to be saved
  and to come to the knowledge of the truth;
    and in Christ Jesus you have given us
      the one mediator between yourself and humankind.

Receive the supplications and thanksgivings of your church,
   that by the power of your Spirit your people may be made holy
      in the likeness of your Son.
By that same Holy Spirit, bless these gifts of bread and wine,
   that they may be for us the body and blood of our Lord Jesus Christ;
who, at supper with his disciples, took bread, gave you thanks,
   broke the bread, and gave it to them, saying,
      "Take, eat: this is my body which is given for you;
         do this in remembrance of me."
After supper he took the cup.
Again he gave you thanks, and gave it to his disciples, saying,
   "Drink this, all of you: this is my blood of the new covenant,
      which is shed for you and for many for the forgiveness of sins.
   Do this, as often as you drink it, in remembrance of me."

Great is the mystery of faith.
Christ has died; Christ is risen; Christ will come again.

God of compassion, bring hope to any whose joy is gone,
   who find grief is upon them, whose heart is sick.
Come near to all who find you far away, who have waited long,
   whose sadness is deep, who have been taken hold of by dismay,
      whose eyes are a fountain of tears.
Be their balm in Gilead. Be the physician of their soul and body.
Restore the well-being of your people.
Give them faith, lend them patience, fill them with courage,
   and heal every sin-sick soul.
Bring your whole creation to the day
   when your saints enjoy the glory of your kingdom,
      and you are all in all, one God, Father, Son, and Holy Spirit. **Amen.**

September 25–October 1, Year A

The Lord be with you. **And also with you.**
Lift up your hearts. **We lift them to the Lord.**
Let us give thanks to the Lord our God. **It is right to give our thanks and praise.**

We exalt you, Lord God, for the holy extravagance of your salvation.
Worthy are you to whom we bow,
   for in your Son you have knelt before us in humility.
You have looked with favor upon your servant Israel;
   you have scattered the proud in the thoughts of their hearts
     and have lifted up the lowly.
Your Son, though of the same love and same mind as you,
   did not regard equality with you as something to be exploited,
     but emptied himself, taking the form of a slave.
Being born in human likeness, he humbled himself
   even unto death on a cross.
You lifted him up in resurrection glory,
   and exalted him to your right hand on high.
And so, on bended knee, we confess him as Lord,
   with angels and archangels and all the company of heaven,
     joining the unending hymn.

Holy, holy, holy Lord, God of power and might.
Heaven and earth are full of your glory.
Hosanna in the highest.
Blessed is he who comes in the name of the Lord.
Hosanna in the highest.

Communing God, make your joy complete
   by uniting those who share this meal
     with the same mind that was in Christ Jesus.
As we remember his saving mercies,
   make us to be of the same love, the same heart,

sharing in the same Spirit;
and sanctify this bread and cup that they may be for us
the body and blood of your Son Jesus Christ;
who, at supper with his disciples, took bread, gave you thanks,
broke the bread, and gave it to them, saying,
"Take, eat: this is my body which is given for you;
do this in remembrance of me."
After supper he took the cup.
Again he gave you thanks, and gave it to his disciples, saying,
"Drink this, all of you: this is my blood of the new covenant,
which is shed for you and for many for the forgiveness of sins.
Do this, as often as you drink it, in remembrance of me."

Great is the mystery of faith.
Christ has died; Christ is risen; Christ will come again.

God of every consolation, bring your kingdom among your children
who are bowed low under the weight of oppression.
Send your Spirit of truth into places
where servanthood has turned to exploitation,
service has turned to slavery,
or humility has turned to bonded labor.
Empty your church of all that obscures its witness to the cross of Christ.
Make us ready for that one eternal day
when we shall kneel around your throne,
together with prophets, apostles, and martyrs,
in the company of Jesus our Lord,
giving all praise and glory to you,
God our Father, forever and ever. **Amen.**

September 25–October 1, Year B

The Lord be with you. **And also with you.**
Lift up your hearts. **We lift them to the Lord.**
Let us give thanks to the Lord our God. **It is right to give our thanks and praise.**

Redeeming God, we delight
  to praise you for the triumphs of your grace
    and to thank you for the wonders of your love.
You created all things to fulfill your longing
  to be in covenant relationship with us.
When that trust was broken,
  you visited your children in the exile of Babylon
    and upheld them in a foreign place.
Again in Christ you came closer to your people through suffering
  than they had been to you in times of plenty.
Because his resurrection was for us and our salvation,
  we call upon your holy name in the hope that never disappoints us,
    and we celebrate your glory,
      joining with the host of heaven in the never-ending song.

Holy, holy, holy Lord, God of power and might.
Heaven and earth are full of your glory.
Hosanna in the highest.
Blessed is he who comes in the name of the Lord.
Hosanna in the highest.

Renewing God, in Christ you reveal to us the heart of your life,
  and you show us how to live the life of your heart.
He is the wonder of you, standing before us,
  and the reality of us, standing before you.
Send your Holy Spirit upon your children,
  that they may be shaped by your love and joy and peace.
Bless this bread and wine by the power of that same Spirit,

that they may be for us the body and blood of our Lord Jesus Christ;
who, at supper with his disciples, took bread, gave you thanks,
   broke the bread, and gave it to them, saying,
      "Take, eat: this is my body which is given for you;
         do this in remembrance of me."
After supper he took the cup.
Again he gave you thanks, and gave it to his disciples, saying,
   "Drink this, all of you: this is my blood of the new covenant,
      which is shed for you and for many for the forgiveness of sins.
   Do this, as often as you drink it, in remembrance of me."

Great is the mystery of faith.
Christ has died; Christ is risen; Christ will come again.

Restoring God, visit today all who are sick:
   send them companions to abide with them,
      faithful friends to pray with them,
         forgiving disciples to be close to them in their suffering,
            and prophets to raise them from sadness and pain.
As your servant Elijah prayed fervently for rain
   and found his answer in you,
      look with mercy on all who live
         in distress or scarcity or doubt or despair,
            and hear the cry of all who have found a stumbling block
               in those they had cause to trust.
Turn our sorrow into dancing and our grief into hope,
   until your kingdom comes, your will is finally done,
      and you are all in all, God the three in one. **Amen.**

September 25–October 1, Year C

The Lord be with you. **And also with you.**
Lift up your hearts. **We lift them to the Lord.**
Let us give thanks to the Lord our God. **It is right to give our thanks and praise.**

Immortal God of unapproachable light,
   honor and dominion be unto you,
     for you invite us to dine with you at the heavenly banquet
      with your Son Jesus Christ, the blessed and only Sovereign,
       King of kings and Lord of lords.
When in Christ you were incarnate among us,
   you came not as the proud and haughty rich man
    but lived and died as the poor man at the gate.
He laid down his life that we might be reconciled with you
   and in his resurrection showed us your love and your power.
And so we celebrate your glory, with all the company of heaven,
   singing the everlasting song.

Holy, holy, holy Lord, God of power and might.
Heaven and earth are full of your glory.
Hosanna in the highest.
Blessed is he who comes in the name of the Lord.
Hosanna in the highest.

Trusting God, your servant Jeremiah believed
   the exile of your people would come to an end,
    and so he bought a field that would one day reward his faith in you.
In this meal of earthly bread and heavenly wine
   you make a promise to us that though our time on earth be short,
    our abiding with you in heaven will be forever.
By the power of your Holy Spirit,
   make us rich in good works, generous, and ready to share,
    that we may take hold of the life that lies in you.

By that same Spirit make this bread and cup be for us
   the body and blood of your Son Jesus Christ;
who, at supper with his disciples, took bread, gave you thanks,
   broke the bread, and gave it to them, saying,
      "Take, eat: this is my body which is given for you;
         do this in remembrance of me."
After supper he took the cup.
Again he gave you thanks, and gave it to his disciples, saying,
   "Drink this, all of you: this is my blood of the new covenant,
      which is shed for you and for many for the forgiveness of sins.
   Do this, as often as you drink it, in remembrance of me."

Great is the mystery of faith.
Christ has died; Christ is risen; Christ will come again.

Generous and ever-giving God,
   make money an instrument of your peace.
Where your children are too wealthy,
   make them content with food and clothing,
      not placing their hopes in the uncertainty of riches.
Where your people long to have more,
   free them from the harmful desires
      that might plunge them into ruin and destruction.
Where money causes a great chasm of division,
   bring partnership, understanding, and kindness.
Visit all who are in agony
   through pain or humiliation or regret or abandonment,
      and set our eyes on you
         who provide us so richly with everything for our enjoyment;
         until the day when you are all in all,
            ever one God, Father, Son, and Holy Spirit. **Amen.**

October 2–8, Year A

The Lord be with you. **And also with you.**
Lift up your hearts. **We lift them to the Lord.**
Let us give thanks to the Lord our God. **It is right to give our thanks and praise.**

It is our duty and our joy to thank and praise you, Father of mercies,
   because when the gift of your grace was rejected by your creation people
     you offered it to your chosen people,
      and when it was rejected by your chosen people
       you offered it once more in your Son.
When your Son was rejected and crucified you came not in wrath
   but in the power of your Holy Spirit
     to spread the good news
      of restoration, reconciliation, and resurrection,
       beginning in Jerusalem and on to the ends of the earth.
And so we stand before you
   not in fear of your judgment but rejoicing in your abundant mercy,
     joining with angels and archangels and all the company of heaven,
      to sing the hymn of your unending praise.

Holy, holy, holy Lord, God of power and might.
Heaven and earth are full of your glory.
Hosanna in the highest.
Blessed is he who comes in the name of the Lord.
Hosanna in the highest.

You give us so much, gracious God,
   but everything we have is loss
     compared to the wondrous love we see in your Son Jesus Christ.
On the night before your Son died
   we took away everything you gave us in him,
     and yet you gave us a meal.
Now in this wonderful sacrament

we give you everything we know how to give you,
   praying that you will give us Christ in the form of this meal.
Send down your Holy Spirit upon us now,
   that we might become the body of Christ that you give us to eat.
Give us your very self in these gifts of bread and wine
   and make them for us the body and blood of your Son Jesus Christ;
who, at supper with his disciples, took bread, gave you thanks,
   broke the bread, and gave it to them, saying,
     "Take, eat: this is my body which is given for you;
       do this in remembrance of me."
After supper he took the cup.
Again he gave you thanks, and gave it to his disciples, saying,
   "Drink this, all of you: this is my blood of the new covenant,
     which is shed for you and for many for the forgiveness of sins.
   Do this, as often as you drink it, in remembrance of me."

Great is the mystery of faith.
Christ has died; Christ is risen; Christ will come again.

God the Alpha and Omega,
   you are the wisdom from which we come,
     and you are the destiny to which we are going.
You abide among us, between us, and within us.
Where your servants are rejected, sustain them.
Where your messengers are beaten, renew them.
Where your children are cast out, give them hope of justice and vindication.
Where your vineyard is in the hands of headstrong tenants,
   bring your liberation, bring your transformation,
     bring your righteousness, until the day comes
       when we and your suffering people see you face to face,
         ever one God, Father, Son, and Holy Spirit. **Amen.**

October 2–8, Year B

The Lord be with you. **And also with you.**
Lift up your hearts. **We lift them to the Lord.**
Let us give thanks to the Lord our God. **It is right to give our thanks and praise.**

Rightly we give you thanks and praise, gracious God,
  for whom and through whom all things exist,
    because you made us little lower than the angels
      and crowned us with glory and honor.
Long ago you spoke to us through the prophets,
  but now you have revealed yourself through your Son,
    heir of all things, reflection of your glory,
      and exact imprint of your very being.
Through him you sustain all creation by your powerful Word.
In him you made purification for sins:
  as your servant he tasted death for everyone.
And so we gladly thank you,
  with saints and angels and the whole host of heaven,
    singing your eternal song.

Holy, holy, holy Lord, God of power and might.
Heaven and earth are full of your glory.
Hosanna in the highest.
Blessed is he who comes in the name of the Lord.
Hosanna in the highest.

Merciful Father, you sent your Son as the pioneer of our salvation.
Though we do not yet see everything in subjection to him,
  we do see Jesus crowned with honor because of his suffering death.
Through this holy meal in your company, show us Jesus today.
In the midst of this congregation,
  raise up your Spirit of love and joy and peace.
Send that same Spirit on this bread and this wine,

that they may be for us the body and blood of our Lord Jesus Christ;
who, at supper with his disciples, took bread, gave you thanks,
    broke the bread, and gave it to them, saying,
        "Take, eat: this is my body which is given for you;
            do this in remembrance of me."
After supper he took the cup.
Again he gave you thanks, and gave it to his disciples, saying,
    "Drink this, all of you: this is my blood of the new covenant,
        which is shed for you and for many for the forgiveness of sins.
    Do this, as often as you drink it, in remembrance of me."

Great is the mystery of faith.
Christ has died; Christ is risen; Christ will come again.

Transforming God, visit all today
    who dwell in the throes of suffering, sorrow, pain, or distress.
Give them courage to withstand and patience to persist.
Take away all that would prevent your children from coming to you,
    and give your church grace to receive your kingdom like a little child.
Receive into your arms of mercy
    any who have been dismissed or excluded
        or treated as objects of shame.
Melt all hardness of heart into the wonder of a people
    united in your inseparable love,
        until heaven and earth are joined in the banquet of your glory,
            ever one God, Father, Son, and Holy Spirit. **Amen.**

October 2–8, Year C

The Lord be with you. **And also with you.**
Lift up your hearts. **We lift them to the Lord.**
Let us give thanks to the Lord our God. **It is right to give our thanks and praise.**

It is our duty and our joy to thank you,
   Lord God, our hope and our foundation,
      because you made this sunrise of wonder
         and you established the heavens in bright array.
With great joy, you called a people and set them free.
Finally in your Son Jesus you came among your people
   and let loose the power of your Spirit.
In Jesus' death and resurrection
   you transformed our meanness and cruelty
      into your unfailing joy and grace.
And so we praise you with angels and archangels
   and all the company of heaven,
      singing the hymn of your unending praise.

Holy, holy, holy Lord, God of power and might.
Heaven and earth are full of your glory.
Hosanna in the highest.
Blessed is he who comes in the name of the Lord.
Hosanna in the highest.

Exhilarating God,
   in Jesus you have given us the architect of our salvation,
      and in this meal you show us your willingness
         to be broken and poured out to win us back to you.
Send down your Holy Spirit,
   that your people may be sanctified by your grace,
      and these gifts of bread and wine may be for us
         the body and blood of your Son Jesus Christ;

who, at supper with his disciples, took bread, gave you thanks,
  broke the bread, and gave it to them, saying,
    "Take, eat: this is my body which is given for you;
      do this in remembrance of me."
After supper he took the cup.
Again he gave you thanks, and gave it to his disciples, saying,
  "Drink this, all of you: this is my blood of the new covenant,
    which is shed for you and for many for the forgiveness of sins.
    Do this, as often as you drink it, in remembrance of me."

Great is the mystery of faith.
Christ has died; Christ is risen; Christ will come again.

Generous God, as you fill us with the bread of life,
  renew our hope that not only we but all your people
    may never be hungry again.
Make us heralds and apostles and teachers,
  that we may know your power to save,
    be called to spread your grace and mercy,
      and build one another up in the ways of righteousness and peace;
        that our tradition may be renewed in trust,
          deepened in suffering, and resolute amid shame,
            until we see you face to face,
              and your justice shines throughout the earth,
              and all people rise to enjoy your glory,
                ever one God, Father, Son, and Holy Spirit. **Amen.**

October 9–15, Year A

The Lord be with you. **And also with you.**
Lift up your hearts. **We lift them to the Lord.**
Let us give thanks to the Lord our God. **It is right to give our thanks and praise.**

Worthy of all praise are you, God of Moses,
   for you made humankind in your image;
      male and female you created us,
         in your likeness, to reveal your glory.
When your chosen people lost faith
   and cast a false image for themselves in the form of a golden calf,
      you reminded them that they were created in your likeness.
In the fullness of time, when we sought after lesser gods,
   you cast yourself in human form, as one of us,
      to reshape in us your divine image
         through the cross of your Son and the power of the Holy Spirit,
            to make us holy as you are holy, reflecting your eternal glory.
And so with your people on earth and all the company of heaven,
   we join the unending hymn.

Holy, holy, holy Lord, God of power and might.
Heaven and earth are full of your glory.
Hosanna in the highest.
Blessed is he who comes in the name of the Lord.
Hosanna in the highest.

Feasting God,
   as we share in this wedding banquet of Christ and your church,
      draw heaven and earth together as one in you.
Send your Holy Spirit upon us to clothe us in perfecting grace
   for joining the feast of saints.
Sanctify this bread and cup to make them be for us
   the body and blood of our Savior Jesus Christ;

who, at supper with his disciples, took bread, gave you thanks,
  broke the bread, and gave it to them, saying,
    "Take, eat: this is my body which is given for you;
      do this in remembrance of me."
After supper he took the cup.
Again he gave you thanks, and gave it to his disciples, saying,
  "Drink this, all of you: this is my blood of the new covenant,
    which is shed for you and for many for the forgiveness of sins.
  Do this, as often as you drink it, in remembrance of me."

Great is the mystery of faith.
Christ has died; Christ is risen; Christ will come again.

Faithful God, receive the supplications of your church
  and bestow upon your children
    the peace that passes all understanding.
Empower your people to embody
  whatever is true, whatever is honorable, whatever is just.
Inspire your sons and daughters to pursue
  whatever is pure, whatever is pleasing, whatever is commendable.
Shape the life of your church around
  whatever is excellent and worthy of praise.
Hasten the day when every heart and mind in union with Christ Jesus
  shall rejoice in that perfect peace of your coming kingdom
    and be made eternally new in your image,
      Trinity of every grace, now and forever. **Amen.**

October 9–15, Year B

The Lord be with you. **And also with you.**
Lift up your hearts. **We lift them to the Lord.**
Let us give thanks to the Lord our God. **It is right to give our thanks and praise.**

We lift our hearts to you with thanks and praise, Almighty God,
  for nothing is impossible with you.
You brought the universe to life
  and called a people to be your own.
In Jesus you came and laid bare your purpose
  for us and for all creation.
In him you parted with all your possessions,
  came close to the poor, and lived humbly with us.
He is our great high priest who has passed through the heavens;
  he sympathizes with our weaknesses
    and was tempted as we are, yet without sin.
Because of his dying and rising
  we approach your throne with boldness,
    that we may receive mercy and find grace in time of need.
And so with the whole host of heaven, we join in singing your eternal song.

Holy, holy, holy Lord, God of power and might.
Heaven and earth are full of your glory.
Hosanna in the highest.
Blessed is he who comes in the name of the Lord.
Hosanna in the highest.

Reconciling God, in baptism you ask us
  to let go of family, friends, and all security;
    but from you we receive back a hundredfold
      in brothers and sisters, mothers and children,
        and, in the age to come, eternal life.
As your church offers this food to you,

give us back your glory, your wisdom, and your power,
   that we may be your Son's body in the world.
Send your Holy Spirit upon these gifts of bread and wine,
   that they may be for us the body and blood of our Lord Jesus Christ;
who, at supper with his disciples, took bread, gave you thanks,
   broke the bread, and gave it to them, saying,
      "Take, eat: this is my body which is given for you;
         do this in remembrance of me."
After supper he took the cup.
Again he gave you thanks, and gave it to his disciples, saying,
   "Drink this, all of you: this is my blood of the new covenant,
      which is shed for you and for many for the forgiveness of sins.
   Do this, as often as you drink it, in remembrance of me."

Great is the mystery of faith.
Christ has died; Christ is risen; Christ will come again.

Living and active God, your Word divides soul from spirit,
   joint from marrow.
Speak your truth into the lives
   of all who plead for your saving power today.
Hear the cries of those whose complaint is bitter;
   comfort any whose voices are weighed down with groaning;
      bless your children when they wish they could vanish
         and when they long for thick darkness to cover them.
When our salvation seems as impossible
   as a camel passing through the eye of a needle,
      come among us with the joy and power of your Son's resurrection,
         and astound us with your grace,
            until that day when every eye shall see you
               and every tongue shall tell
                  how great is your mercy and how wondrous your glory,
                     Holy Trinity of love. **Amen.**

October 9–15, Year C

The Lord be with you. **And also with you.**
Lift up your hearts. **We lift them to the Lord.**
Let us give thanks to the Lord our God. **It is right to give our thanks and praise.**

Trusting and abiding God, we lift our hearts to thank and praise you,
　because even when we are faithless toward you,
　　you are always faithful toward us.
In creation you made a myriad of wonders for us to enjoy;
　yet in our sin we saw scarcity rather than abundance.
In Israel you made a people for your own heart;
　but your people longed to be like other nations.
In exile you taught your prophets and priests
　to seek the welfare of the city where you had sent them.
There in a foreign land
　you made yourself known to your people in a new way,
　　so that when your Son Jesus Christ was crucified for our salvation
　　　his disciples saw in his servanthood the pattern of your suffering love.
And so with all the company of heaven we rejoice in the eternal song.

Holy, holy, holy Lord, God of power and might.
Heaven and earth are full of your glory.
Hosanna in the highest.
Blessed is he who comes in the name of the Lord.
Hosanna in the highest.

Restoring God, as in Christ you made a new community out of exiles,
　so today you gather to your table
　　the leper, the outcast, and the wounded.
Send your Spirit upon your church
　that it may be a community of reconciliation and truth.
Sanctify these gifts of bread and wine:
　make them be for us the body and blood of our Lord Jesus Christ;

who, at supper with his disciples, took bread, gave you thanks,
   broke the bread, and gave it to them, saying,
      "Take, eat: this is my body which is given for you;
         do this in remembrance of me."
After supper he took the cup.
Again he gave you thanks, and gave it to his disciples, saying,
   "Drink this, all of you: this is my blood of the new covenant,
      which is shed for you and for many for the forgiveness of sins.
      Do this, as often as you drink it, in remembrance of me."

Great is the mystery of faith.
Christ has died; Christ is risen; Christ will come again.

God of healing and grace,
   bless those who are in exile and see no way to reach home.
Be close to all who have no house to live in,
   no garden to plant, no food to eat,
      no respite from sickness, prejudice, oppression, or danger.
By the power of your Holy Spirit abide with those whose time is short,
   that they may know that if they die with Christ,
      they will also live with him;
         that if they endure, they will also reign with him;
            until that day when he returns in glory
               with judgment enfolded in mercy and truth embraced by grace,
               ever one God, Trinity of holiness and love. **Amen.**

October 16–22, Year A

The Lord be with you. **And also with you.**
Lift up your hearts. **We lift them to the Lord.**
Let us give thanks to the Lord our God. **It is right to give our thanks and praise.**

We praise and thank you, God of Abraham and Moses,
   because you have made your creation out of nothing,
     you have come among us in liberation and covenant,
       and in your Son's dying and rising
         you have opened up your life to share your holiness with us.
In your tender mercy
   you have broken upon us the dawn from on high
    and shown us your glory in the face of Jesus Christ.
You cover us with your loving hand
   that we may dare to stand in your presence,
    and you tell us your name that we may see into your heart.
And so we come before you
   with angels and archangels and all the company of heaven,
    to sing the hymn of your unending praise.

Holy, holy, holy Lord, God of power and might.
Heaven and earth are full of your glory.
Hosanna in the highest.
Blessed is he who comes in the name of the Lord.
Hosanna in the highest.

Merciful God, you have given us the law
   as the covenant between your ways and ours,
    and in Jesus you have renewed that covenant
     by giving us the fulfillment of that law.
In this meal you show us
   how much you long for us to be your companions
    and how constant is your presence among us.

Send down your Holy Spirit upon us now,
   that we might become the body of Christ that you give us to eat.
Give us your very self in these gifts of bread and wine
   and make them for us the body and blood of your Son Jesus Christ;
who, at supper with his disciples, took bread, gave you thanks,
   broke the bread, and gave it to them, saying,
      "Take, eat: this is my body which is given for you;
         do this in remembrance of me."
After supper he took the cup.
Again he gave you thanks, and gave it to his disciples, saying,
   "Drink this, all of you: this is my blood of the new covenant,
      which is shed for you and for many for the forgiveness of sins.
   Do this, as often as you drink it, in remembrance of me."

Great is the mystery of faith.
Christ has died; Christ is risen; Christ will come again.

God of inescapable love,
   you call upon us to give to you the things that are yours.
As we realize with joy that all things are yours,
   turn every action of our lives into ways of worshiping you.
Unite us with the communion of your saints,
   past, present, and eternal, turning all into alleluia,
      turning justice into kindness and trust,
         turning fear into hope, hunger into fulfillment,
            isolation into companionship, and suffering into love,
               until the day comes when we and all your people
                  see you face to face,
                     ever one God, Father, Son, and Holy Spirit. **Amen.**

October 16–22, Year B

The Lord be with you. **And also with you.**
Lift up your hearts. **We lift them to the Lord.**
Let us give thanks to the Lord our God. **It is right to give our thanks and praise.**

Thanks and praise belong to you, Lord God, now and forever,
  because when you laid the foundation of the earth
    the morning stars sang together
      and all the heavenly beings shouted for joy.
You called your chosen people
  to be a priestly kingdom and a holy nation,
    and to Jesus you said, "You are my Son, today I have begotten you."
Although he was your Son,
  he learned obedience through what he suffered on the cross;
    and having been made perfect,
      he became through the resurrection
        the source of eternal salvation for all who obey him.
And so with all the company of heaven we sing your song of glory.

Holy, holy, holy Lord, God of power and might.
Heaven and earth are full of your glory.
Hosanna in the highest.
Blessed is he who comes in the name of the Lord.
Hosanna in the highest.

Humble God, in Christ you were great among us by being our servant,
  and you were first among us by becoming slave of all.
You invite us to your table and serve us as your guests.
We rejoice to be here
  because in Jesus you gave us your life as a ransom for many.
Send your Holy Spirit upon us as we sit at your right and left hand,
  sharing the cup that you drink.
By that same Spirit, sanctify these gifts of bread and wine,

that they may be for us the body and blood of our Lord Jesus Christ;
who, at supper with his disciples, took bread, gave you thanks,
   broke the bread, and gave it to them, saying,
      "Take, eat: this is my body which is given for you;
         do this in remembrance of me."
After supper he took the cup.
Again he gave you thanks, and gave it to his disciples, saying,
   "Drink this, all of you: this is my blood of the new covenant,
      which is shed for you and for many for the forgiveness of sins.
   Do this, as often as you drink it, in remembrance of me."

Great is the mystery of faith.
Christ has died; Christ is risen; Christ will come again.

Our God and King, in the power of your Holy Spirit
   visit all who live under tyranny today.
Lift up the hearts of your children
   who languish with loud cries and tears.
Deal gently with the ignorant and the wayward,
   since in Christ you took on the mantle of our weakness.
Inspire your church to become the high priest of all creation,
   and make your people perfect through obedience.
Hasten the day when heaven comes to earth,
   and the world is full of your glory,
      ever one God, gracious Father, servant Son, gentle Spirit,
         Trinity of mercy and love. **Amen.**

October 16–22, Year C

The Lord be with you. **And also with you.**
Lift up your hearts. **We lift them to the Lord.**
Let us give thanks to the Lord our God. **It is right to give thanks and praise.**

It is our privilege and our joy to give you thanks and praise,
   Lord God, because you created all things
     in order to dwell in covenant love with your people.
When that covenant was broken,
   you promised to make a new covenant
     with the house of Israel and the house of Judah,
       in which you would put your law within them
         and write it on their hearts;
           you would be their God, and they would be your people.
They would all know you, from the least of them to the greatest;
   for you would forgive their iniquity
     and remember their sin no more.
In the body and blood of Jesus you made that new covenant,
   and in his death and resurrection
     we are bound to you and you to us for evermore.
And so we join with all the company of heaven
   in the song of your everlasting glory.

Holy, holy, holy Lord, God of power and might.
Heaven and earth are full of your glory.
Hosanna in the highest.
Blessed is he who comes in the name of the Lord.
Hosanna in the highest.

Abiding God, you shape us through this holy meal
   to be your companions, to befriend one another,
     and to be reconciled with the whole earth.
Send your Spirit on your church,

that your people may endure suffering,
　　and that, being encouraged, they may proclaim your truth
　　　and learn to live in your good patience.
Sanctify these gifts of bread and wine that they may be for us
　　the body and blood of our Lord Jesus Christ;
who, at supper with his disciples, took bread, gave you thanks,
　　broke the bread, and gave it to them, saying,
　　　"Take, eat: this is my body which is given for you;
　　　　do this in remembrance of me."
After supper he took the cup.
Again he gave you thanks, and gave it to his disciples, saying,
　　"Drink this, all of you: this is my blood of the new covenant,
　　　which is shed for you and for many for the forgiveness of sins.
　　Do this, as often as you drink it, in remembrance of me."

Great is the mystery of faith.
Christ has died; Christ is risen; Christ will come again.

God of justice, your children call upon you
　　like a widow pleading her cause.
As you constantly knock on the door of our hearts,
　　inviting us to embrace your ways,
　　　so we seek to wear you out
　　　　with our longing for you to grant justice
　　　　　to your children who cry to you day and night.
Give hope to any who are close to losing heart.
Bring consolation to all who can hardly continue another day.
Uphold those who have nowhere to turn.
Hasten the day when every tear turns to joy and all sorrow to dancing,
　　when you are all in all, one God, Trinity of peace and love. **Amen.**

October 23–29, Year A

The Lord be with you. **And also with you.**
Lift up your hearts. **We lift them to the Lord.**
Let us give thanks to the Lord our God. **It is right to give our thanks and praise.**

Joyful, joyful we adore you, God of glory, Lord of love.
You wrote your law not only onto stone tablets
   but into the very life of your holy people.
Through Moses you summoned your people
   to love you with all their heart,
     all their soul, and all their might.
When your Son, walking in the way of the law and the prophets,
   came to live among us,
     loving you with all his heart and soul and mind and strength,
       he showed us how to love our neighbors as ourselves.
When his neighbors did not love him,
   and raised him up in shame on the cross,
     you raised him in the glory of the resurrection.
You, O Lord our God, are holy, and you are one.
And so we remember and celebrate your covenant
   with angels and archangels and all the company of heaven
     as we join the unending hymn.

Holy, holy, holy Lord, God of power and might.
Heaven and earth are full of your glory.
Hosanna in the highest.
Blessed is he who comes in the name of the Lord.
Hosanna in the highest.

Abiding God, you are our dwelling place in every generation.
You sent your spirit of wisdom to rest upon Joshua,
   and blessed him through the hands of Moses
     to continue the story of your mighty works.

You sent Jesus as the new Joshua,
   our savior and the pioneer of our hope.
As we remember our Lord's saving mercies,
   send down your Holy Spirit
      to continue in and through us your story of salvation,
         and sanctify this bread and cup
            to be for us the body and blood of our Lord Jesus Christ;
who, at supper with his disciples, took bread, gave you thanks,
   broke the bread, and gave it to them, saying,
      "Take, eat: this is my body which is given for you;
         do this in remembrance of me."
After supper he took the cup.
Again he gave you thanks, and gave it to his disciples, saying,
      "Drink this, all of you: this is my blood of the new covenant,
         which is shed for you and for many for the forgiveness of sins.
      Do this, as often as you drink it, in remembrance of me."

Great is the mystery of faith.
Christ has died; Christ is risen; Christ will come again.

Embracing God, you invite us to love you by loving our neighbors.
Open wide every heart to the way of your commandments.
Make your church a living body of your law,
   written into one shared life.
Fill your children with the zeal of the prophets.
Show your people how to love their neighbors
   not only in word but in action.
Pour your transforming Spirit
   upon any whose most difficult struggle is learning to love themselves.
Reveal yourself in the face of friend and stranger,
   until that day when your world shall see you face to face;
      when, by the fullness of your grace,
         we come to share in your lasting glory,
            ever-loving God, Father, Son, and Holy Spirit. **Amen.**

October 23–29, Year B

The Lord be with you. **And also with you.**
Lift up your hearts. **We lift them to the Lord.**
Let us give thanks to the Lord our God. **It is right to give our thanks and praise.**

We lift our hearts to you in praise and thanksgiving,
   God of mercy and grace,
     because you called all things into being in creation,
       and in covenant you made Israel your chosen people.
You brought your people out of the pit of slavery
   and the wilderness of exile.
In Jesus you placed your very life in the midst of ours,
   taking the worst of us upon his crucified body
     and redeeming us through the joy of resurrection.
He is the great high priest, holy, blameless, exalted above the heavens,
   and made perfect forever, saving all who approach you through him.
And so we rejoice to thank you,
   joining angels and archangels and the company of heaven
     in songs of everlasting praise.

Holy, holy, holy Lord, God of power and might.
Heaven and earth are full of your glory.
Hosanna in the highest.
Blessed is he who comes in the name of the Lord.
Hosanna in the highest.

Healing God, you call us to cast aside the cloak of our poverty
   that we may follow you in faith and hope.
Open our eyes to see your glory.
Speak your word of transformation and truth.
Send your Spirit upon your church
   that in this holy meal
     we may be turned from despair to joy and from doubt to wonder.

By that same Spirit, sanctify this bread and this cup,
    that they may be for us the body and blood of our Lord Jesus Christ;
who, at supper with his disciples, took bread, gave you thanks,
    broke the bread, and gave it to them, saying,
        "Take, eat: this is my body which is given for you;
            do this in remembrance of me."
After supper he took the cup.
Again he gave you thanks, and gave it to his disciples, saying,
    "Drink this, all of you: this is my blood of the new covenant,
        which is shed for you and for many for the forgiveness of sins.
        Do this, as often as you drink it, in remembrance of me."

Great is the mystery of faith.
Christ has died; Christ is risen; Christ will come again.

Generous God, make your church holy
    that it may bear your aching world to you,
        and may reveal your longing heart to the world.
Give your people, like Bartimaeus, a spring in their step,
    that they may be eager in seeking you,
        clear in asking you, and ready in following you.
When your children yearn for healing
    yet search in vain for tangible signs,
        bring them the comfort of your presence,
            the encouragement of your word,
                and the power of your Spirit.
To all who have known loss, or suffering, or disaster,
    bring a double portion of your abundant love,
        that every eye may see, and every tongue may tell
            how great is your almighty hand
                that draws all things to completion in you,
                    one God, Father, Son, and Holy Spirit. **Amen.**

October 23–29, Year C

The Lord be with you. **And also with you.**
Lift up your hearts. **We lift them to the Lord.**
Let us give thanks to the Lord our God. **It is right to give our thanks and praise.**

We lift our hearts in thanks and praise, God of truth,
  because you have dealt wondrously with us,
    pouring down the abundant rain
      of forgiveness, reconciliation, and healing.
Constantly you meet your people in their shame
  and restore to them the years the swarming locusts have eaten.
You rescued the children of Abraham from slavery
  and made a covenant with them to be your people;
    you called Judah home from exile;
      and when your people were still bereft,
        you sent your Son to be the fullness of your grace among us.
From the shame of the cross and the abandonment of the tomb
  you raised him to glorious life,
    and sent your Holy Spirit that the young might prophesy
      and the old might learn to dream again.
And so we join with all heaven in the everlasting song of praise.

Holy, holy, holy Lord, God of power and might.
Heaven and earth are full of your glory.
Hosanna in the highest.
Blessed is he who comes in the name of the Lord.
Hosanna in the highest.

We gather expectantly in your midst, God of grace,
  because you promise
    that your people will eat in plenty and be satisfied.
Send your Spirit on your church
  that all who call upon your name may be saved.

Breathe your Holy Spirit on this bread and this cup,
    that they may be for us the body and blood of our Lord Jesus Christ;
who, at supper with his disciples, took bread, gave you thanks,
    broke the bread, and gave it to them, saying,
        "Take, eat: this is my body which is given for you;
            do this in remembrance of me."
After supper he took the cup.
Again he gave you thanks, and gave it to his disciples, saying,
    "Drink this, all of you: this is my blood of the new covenant,
        which is shed for you and for many for the forgiveness of sins.
    Do this, as often as you drink it, in remembrance of me."

Great is the mystery of faith.
Christ has died; Christ is risen; Christ will come again.

We wait humbly on your mercy, God of peace.
Look with favor on all who know
    they have fallen short of your grace and scorned your love
        and yet seek you with hope and with penitent hearts.
Show compassion to your children who cannot say
    they have fought the good fight, or finished the race,
        or kept the faith.
Make your church a place of second beginnings,
    gentle hearts, kind understanding, and a forgiving spirit,
        where all saints know they have a past
            and all sinners discover they have a future.
Raise to new life all whose heads have been bowed down with shame,
    and reserve for them your crown of righteousness;
        until the day when you humble the exalted and exalt the humble,
            and your Spirit enlivens all flesh,
                through Christ our Lord, Father most holy. **Amen.**

All Saints

The Lord be with you. **And also with you.**
Lift up your hearts. **We lift them to the Lord.**
Let us give thanks to the Lord our God. **It is right to give our thanks and praise.**

Creating and redeeming God,
  in Adam, Abraham, and Moses, in Deborah, Esther, and Mary,
    you have chosen not simply to direct the course of events
      but to be in relationship with us and to entrust your children
        with the embodiment and exercise of your will.
In the dying and rising Christ
  you give us not just a savior but an example,
    and in every generation
      you call people to imitate the pattern of his life and death
        and so witness to your glory.
You call us to be not heroes who go it alone
  but saints whose every breath depends on others and on you.
We rejoice that those saints take their place in the company of heaven,
  with whom we join in singing the unending hymn of your joy and praise.

Holy, holy, holy Lord, God of power and might.
Heaven and earth are full of your glory.
Hosanna in the highest.
Blessed is he who comes in the name of the Lord.
Hosanna in the highest.

Transforming God, in this gathering
  you take the fruit of the vine and human hands
    and make them a blessing for your people now and forever.
As our earthly bodies decay and die,
  and resemble your Son's body taken down from the cross,
    send your Spirit and remake us
      in the image of your Son's resurrected body,

that our scars may become signs of your glory
and our hearts may be one with yours.
Sanctify this bread and cup that they may be for us
the body and blood of your Son Jesus Christ;
who, at supper with his disciples, took bread, gave you thanks,
broke the bread, and gave it to them, saying,
"Take, eat: this is my body which is given for you;
do this in remembrance of me."
After supper he took the cup.
Again he gave you thanks, and gave it to his disciples, saying,
"Drink this, all of you: this is my blood of the new covenant,
which is shed for you and for many for the forgiveness of sins.
Do this, as often as you drink it, in remembrance of me."

Great is the mystery of faith.
Christ has died; Christ is risen; Christ will come again.

Resurrecting God, bless those who mourn, that they may be comforted.
Bless the poor in spirit, that they may inherit the kingdom of heaven.
Bless the pure in heart, that they may see you.
Visit those who face death amid persecution and violence,
that they may know the gladness and rejoicing of your kingdom.
Be close to any who end their days in agony and isolation,
that they may enter the joy of their reward.
Where your children feel all is lost, meet them in their fear,
touch them in their loneliness, and raise them by your mercy,
so that on the last day, when you bring a new heaven and a new earth,
they may discover you as an infinite circle
whose center is everywhere and whose circumference is nowhere,
and be changed from glory into glory, with and by you,
one God, Father, Son, and Holy Spirit. **Amen.**

November 6–12, Year A

The Lord be with you. **And also with you.**
Lift up your hearts. **We lift them to the Lord.**
Let us give thanks to the Lord our God. **It is right to give our thanks and praise.**

God of time and eternity, you set out the glory of your heavens
   and show us reflections of that glory
     in the tiniest details of the atoms of life.
When we find a thousand ways
   to pervert and turn away from your grace,
     you transform our rejection into your providence.
You dwelt among your people
   in the cloud and pillar of fire, in the tabernacle and temple;
     and finally you dwelt among us in your Son Jesus.
In his death you defeat death,
   and in his resurrection you offer us life with you forever,
     where we shall dwell with you,
       with angels and archangels and all the company of heaven,
         singing the hymn of your unending praise.

Holy, holy, holy Lord, God of power and might.
Heaven and earth are full of your glory.
Hosanna in the highest.
Blessed is he who comes in the name of the Lord.
Hosanna in the highest.

God of deliverance, in the cross of Jesus
   we see what it costs you to dwell among us,
     and in this broken bread and poured wine
       we see your costly love among us today.
Send down your Holy Spirit,
   that your people may be sanctified by your grace,
     and these gifts of bread and wine may be for us

the body and blood of your Son Jesus Christ;
who, at supper with his disciples, took bread, gave you thanks,
  broke the bread, and gave it to them, saying,
    "Take, eat: this is my body which is given for you;
      do this in remembrance of me."
After supper he took the cup.
Again he gave you thanks, and gave it to his disciples, saying,
  "Drink this, all of you: this is my blood of the new covenant,
    which is shed for you and for many for the forgiveness of sins.
  Do this, as often as you drink it, in remembrance of me."

Great is the mystery of faith.
Christ has died; Christ is risen; Christ will come again.

God of everlasting fidelity,
  you have promised us that in marriage
    we may glimpse the relationship of your Son and your church.
Renew the love and ministry of those who are married
  that they may witness to your bond with us,
    until the day comes when the new Jerusalem descends
      as a bride prepared for her husband
        and all creation meets its fulfillment
          in the marriage of heaven and earth,
            where every tear is dried and all the oppressed are vindicated,
          all prisons are opened, and the fear of death is no more,
            and we see you face to face and dwell in your presence,
              ever one God, Father, Son, and Holy Spirit. **Amen.**

November 6–12, Year B

The Lord be with you. **And also with you.**
Lift up your hearts. **We lift them to the Lord.**
Let us give thanks to the Lord our God. **It is right to give our thanks and praise.**

God of judgment and mercy,
   we rejoice to give you thanks and praise,
     for like the widow who put into the temple treasury
       two copper coins, which were all she had,
         you give to us your very heart
           in the flesh and blood of your Son Jesus Christ.
For he is our great high priest who once for all
   removed sin by the sacrifice of himself.
He entered into heaven and appeared in your presence on our behalf.
Having been offered once to bear the sins of many,
   he will appear a second time
     to save those who are eagerly waiting for him.
And so with all the company of heaven we gladly sing the praise of your glory.

Holy, holy, holy Lord, God of power and might.
Heaven and earth are full of your glory.
Hosanna in the highest.
Blessed is he who comes in the name of the Lord.
Hosanna in the highest.

Generous God, as creator you give to us out of your abundance,
   but as redeemer you take on our poverty.
Since the foundation of the world
   you have longed to bring us to share in the banquet of your kingdom.
Send upon your people the comfort of your Holy Spirit
   that we may be clothed with power from on high.
Through your Spirit's grace, bless this bread and this cup,
   that they may be for us the body and blood of our Lord Jesus Christ;

who, at supper with his disciples, took bread, gave you thanks,
  broke the bread, and gave it to them, saying,
    "Take, eat: this is my body which is given for you;
      do this in remembrance of me."
After supper he took the cup.
Again he gave you thanks, and gave it to his disciples, saying,
  "Drink this, all of you: this is my blood of the new covenant,
    which is shed for you and for many for the forgiveness of sins.
  Do this, as often as you drink it, in remembrance of me."

Great is the mystery of faith.
Christ has died; Christ is risen; Christ will come again.

Redeeming Lord, you made the orphan, the widow, and the stranger
  a trusted place of encounter with your grace.
In Ruth you brought to Canaan
  one who was an orphan, a widow, and a stranger,
    and from her faithfulness and imagination
      you brought forth the line of David, whose son was your Messiah.
Visit today in the power of your Spirit
  those who are alone, bereaved, powerless, and lost,
    and make them bearers of your hope and carriers of your redemption,
      that as your people continue to meet you
        in the hungry and the homeless,
          the least of these
            may be a source of renewal for your church and world;
              until the day when every knee shall bow
                and every tongue confess your Son as savior,
                  ever one God, Trinity of grace. **Amen.**

November 6–12, Year C

The Lord be with you. **And also with you.**
Lift up your hearts. **We lift them to the Lord.**
Let us give thanks to the Lord our God. **It is right to give our thanks and praise.**

God of time and eternity, the living and the dead,
  we thank and praise you
    because in you the future is always bigger than the past,
      the splendor of your coming glory always greater than the former.
You made a promise with your people when you led them out of Egypt;
  you held fast to that trust through waywardness and exile,
    and in Jesus you fulfilled and embodied that covenant in flesh and blood.
In him you love us,
  and through grace you give us eternal comfort and constant hope.
And so we gladly thank you,
  with angels and archangels and all the company of heaven,
    praising you in everlasting joy.

Holy, holy, holy Lord, God of power and might.
Heaven and earth are full of your glory.
Hosanna in the highest.
Blessed is he who comes in the name of the Lord.
Hosanna in the highest.

God of wisdom and grace,
  you chose us as the firstfruits of salvation through sanctification.
Through the power of your Holy Spirit,
  make us a people who walk with your Son on the way of the cross
    and share with him in the glory of resurrection.
By that same Spirit, make this bread and cup be for us
  the body and blood of your Son Jesus Christ;
who, at supper with his disciples, took bread, gave you thanks,
  broke the bread, and gave it to them, saying,

"Take, eat: this is my body which is given for you;
   do this in remembrance of me."
After supper he took the cup.
Again he gave you thanks, and gave it to his disciples, saying,
   "Drink this, all of you: this is my blood of the new covenant,
      which is shed for you and for many for the forgiveness of sins.
   Do this, as often as you drink it, in remembrance of me."

Great is the mystery of faith.
Christ has died; Christ is risen; Christ will come again.

God of Abraham, Isaac, and Jacob,
   you have given us marriage as an earthly sign of your heavenly will
      to be inseparable from us forever.
Bless any who find their marriage a source of grief instead of joy,
   sadness rather than comfort, or pain instead of hope.
Be close to all who find themselves alone
   without the life-partner they feel called to meet
   or without the one they fondly remember.
Heal those for whom home is or has been a place of fear and distress.
Make your church a community that fosters children of the resurrection,
   strengthened in every work and word;
      until the heavens and earth are shaken,
         the nations are drawn to you,
            and you fill all creation with the splendor of your majesty,
               God the one in three, Father, Son, and Holy Spirit. **Amen.**

November 13–19, Year A

The Lord be with you. **And also with you.**
Lift up your hearts. **We lift them to the Lord.**
Let us give thanks to the Lord our God. **It is right to give our thanks and praise.**

We praise and thank you, abounding God,
   because you demand so much from us
      and at the same time give us everything you expect of us.
In the glory of creation and the grace of liberation
   you set the contours of our journey with you.
By crafting the covenant and by renewing your people in exile
   you showed us the manner and purpose of your ever-flowing love.
In Jesus you gave us your most precious talent.
Though we buried him through our ignorance and sin,
   you raised him to multiply your church
      and spread abroad your kingdom.
And so we give you thanks
   with saints and angels and the company of heaven,
      joining their unending hymn.

Holy, holy, holy Lord, God of power and might.
Heaven and earth are full of your glory.
Hosanna in the highest.
Blessed is he who comes in the name of the Lord.
Hosanna in the highest.

Encouraging God, your Son Jesus died for us
   so that we might live together with you.
He went through the deep night of betrayal, anguish in Gethsemane,
   trial by his own people, and scourging by his oppressors,
      that we might live in endless day.
Send your Holy Spirit that your people may be turned
   from the fear of your wrath to the anticipation of your glory.

By that same Spirit of salvation and hope,
   sanctify these gifts of bread and wine
      that in your kingdom of grace they may be for us
         the body and blood of your Son Jesus Christ;
who, at supper with his disciples, took bread, gave you thanks,
   broke the bread, and gave it to them, saying,
      "Take, eat: this is my body which is given for you;
         do this in remembrance of me."
After supper he took the cup.
Again he gave you thanks, and gave it to his disciples, saying,
   "Drink this, all of you: this is my blood of the new covenant,
      which is shed for you and for many for the forgiveness of sins.
   Do this, as often as you drink it, in remembrance of me."

Great is the mystery of faith.
Christ has died; Christ is risen; Christ will come again.

Generous God,
   when your church is entrusted with a little, make it faithful,
      and when your people are sent forth to take care of much,
         make them wise and true and kind.
As you invested your whole heart in the uncertain market of our love,
   show your children where to take risks, when to enter the unknown,
      and how to trade with your bounty.
Prepare the hearts of the flourishing and the fragile
   for the day of your revelation,
      that when all secrets are made known and all desires laid bare,
         your understanding and forgiving grace may see
            the virtue behind our clumsiness and the goodness amid our folly.
Fill every heart with the sure and certain hope
   that we shall enter into the fullness of your joy,
      when your whole creation is justified by faith and sanctified by love,
         and you are all in all, ever one God, Father, Son, and Holy Spirit. **Amen.**

November 13–20, Year B

The Lord be with you. **And also with you.**
Lift up your hearts. **We lift them to the Lord.**
Let us give thanks to the Lord our God. **It is right to give our thanks and praise.**

Faithful and abiding God, we give you thanks and praise,
   for from the foundation of the world
      you sought to bring us into covenant relationship with you.
You created us to enjoy you and one another,
   you called Abraham to lead a family in your ways,
      and through Moses you liberated your people
         to be your companions forever.
After those days you promised
   to put your laws in our hearts and write them in our minds,
      and to remember our sins no more.
In Jesus our great high priest
   you opened a new and living way into your presence
      to share eternal communion with you.
And so with saints and angels and all the company of heaven
   we sing the praise of your unending glory.

Holy, holy, holy Lord, God of power and might.
Heaven and earth are full of your glory.
Hosanna in the highest.
Blessed is he who comes in the name of the Lord.
Hosanna in the highest.

Inviting God, you bring us to your table,
   meeting true hearts that yearn to come before you
      with full assurance of faith.
Give us a double portion of your Spirit
   that we may glow with the radiance of your glory.
Through the power of that same Holy Spirit,

bless this bread and this cup, that they may be for us
   the body and blood of our Lord Jesus Christ;
who, at supper with his disciples, took bread, gave you thanks,
   broke the bread, and gave it to them, saying,
      "Take, eat: this is my body which is given for you;
         do this in remembrance of me."
After supper he took the cup.
Again he gave you thanks, and gave it to his disciples, saying,
   "Drink this, all of you: this is my blood of the new covenant,
      which is shed for you and for many for the forgiveness of sins.
   Do this, as often as you drink it, in remembrance of me."

Great is the mystery of faith.
Christ has died; Christ is risen; Christ will come again.

Completing and perfecting God,
   in your Son's cross you took on the grief and failure of the world,
      and in his resurrection you dismantled the power of sin and death.
Look with mercy on all your people whose longings are unmet.
When your children plead for the chance
   to be creative, productive, or nurturing,
      give them gentleness, fulfillment, and purpose.
When your people yearn to bring joy into the life of others,
   comfort to the afflicted, or trust to the wounded,
      give them courage, wisdom, and patience.
When your kingdom seems far off,
   strengthen your church to wait with faith and hope and love,
      until the day when you are all in all,
         one God, Father, Son, and Holy Spirit. **Amen.**

November 13–19, Year C

The Lord be with you. **And also with you.**
Lift up your hearts. **We lift them to the Lord.**
Let us give thanks to the Lord our God. **It is right to give our thanks and praise.**

We lift our hearts to you in praise and thanksgiving, faithful God,
   because in your generosity you created all things in overflowing plenty,
      in love you called the children of Abraham to be your companions,
         in covenant goodness you sent prophets to restore their life,
            and in grace you sent your Son
               to redeem the past and embody our future in you.
In his crucifixion we see the worst that we can do,
   yet in his resurrection we behold your will and your power
      to make sin and death the threshold of everlasting life in you.
And so we gladly thank you, with saints and angels,
   singing the praise of your glory.

Holy, holy, holy Lord, God of power and might.
Heaven and earth are full of your glory.
Hosanna in the highest.
Blessed is he who comes in the name of the Lord.
Hosanna in the highest.

God of destiny and coming joy,
   you have prepared for those who love you
      such things as pass our understanding.
As wheat and grapes reach their fulfillment in bread and wine,
   so we your children await the day
      when you will turn us from faltering followers into faithful friends.
Bless your church in the power of your Spirit
   that it may be made ready to meet you in glory.
Send your Holy Spirit on this bread and this cup,
   that they may be for us the body and blood of our Lord Jesus Christ;

who, at supper with his disciples, took bread, gave you thanks,
  broke the bread, and gave it to them, saying,
    "Take, eat: this is my body which is given for you;
      do this in remembrance of me."
After supper he took the cup.
Again he gave you thanks, and gave it to his disciples, saying,
  "Drink this, all of you: this is my blood of the new covenant,
    which is shed for you and for many for the forgiveness of sins.
  Do this, as often as you drink it, in remembrance of me."

Great is the mystery of faith.
Christ has died; Christ is risen; Christ will come again.

God of hope, in you the future is always bigger than the past.
Visit your children when the sound of their weeping is heard in your cities;
  comfort your people when an infant lives but a few days;
    transfigure the lives of any who labor in vain,
      or bear children for calamity.
Strengthen those who build houses and plant vineyards,
  and inspire all who strive to restore communities after conflict or disaster.
Give endurance to those who are hated and betrayed,
  until the time when you create new heavens and a new earth,
    and the former things shall pass away,
      and you make Jerusalem a joy, and its people a delight,
        and your whole creation is once again a blessing,
          one God, Father, Son, and Holy Spirit, now and forever. **Amen.**

Christ the King, Year A

The Lord be with you. **And also with you.**
Lift up your hearts. **We lift them to the Lord.**
Let us give thanks to the Lord our God. **It is right to give our thanks and praise.**

It is our duty and our joy to thank and praise you,
   God of heaven and earth;
      for you are our shepherd, who called Abraham by name,
         gathered a people under Moses, fed your flock in the wilderness,
            and led them out of Egypt and Babylon
               to take refuge in your sheepfold.
In the fullness of time you sent Jesus to be our shepherd king,
   leading us beside still waters,
      delivering us from the valley of the shadow of death,
         and restoring our souls.
And so with all your gathered flock,
   with sheep that are not of this fold,
      and with saints and angels surrounding your glorious throne,
         we praise your name and join the unending hymn.

Holy, holy, holy Lord, God of power and might.
Heaven and earth are full of your glory.
Hosanna in the highest.
Blessed is he who comes in the name of the Lord.
Hosanna in the highest.

Abundant God, you bestow upon your people
   the riches of your glorious inheritance
      and the immeasurable greatness of your power.
You send upon your disciples the Spirit of wisdom and revelation.
Send now that same Spirit to breathe upon your church
   and make it resound with your praise.
Sanctify this bread and cup, that they may be for us

the body and blood of your Son, Jesus Christ our Lord;
who, at supper with his disciples, took bread, gave you thanks,
    broke the bread, and gave it to them, saying,
        "Take, eat: this is my body which is given for you;
            do this in remembrance of me."
After supper he took the cup.
Again he gave you thanks, and gave it to his disciples, saying,
    "Drink this, all of you: this is my blood of the new covenant,
        which is shed for you and for many for the forgiveness of sins.
    Do this, as often as you drink it, in remembrance of me."

Great is the mystery of faith.
Christ has died; Christ is risen; Christ will come again.

God of glory, you sent Jesus to be our prophet, priest, and king,
    and you show us his face
        in the face of those on whom the world turns its back.
As the tempted Christ was hungry in the wilderness,
    make yourself known to all who search for food.
As the crucified Christ was thirsty hanging on the tree,
    reveal your love among those who lack clean water.
As the infant Christ was a stranger in Egypt,
    manifest your presence through any who are pilgrims from afar.
As the newborn Christ was naked in the manger,
    live in all who experience shame and exposure.
As Christ in his passion was sick to the heart in Gethsemane,
    declare your grace among those who suffer in body, mind, or spirit.
And as Christ under judgment was a prisoner under Pontius Pilate,
    be with all who are incarcerated by folly, injustice, or fear.
Renew your church by making it resemble Jesus,
    our crucified king, our savior, Lord, and friend,
        with you and the Holy Spirit, one God, forever. **Amen.**

Christ the King, Year B

The Lord be with you. **And also with you.**
Lift up your hearts. **We lift them to the Lord.**
Let us give thanks to the Lord our God. **It is right to give our thanks and praise.**

Glory and dominion be to you, Lord God,
   for your Word was alive in creation,
     is present in the power of the Spirit,
       and will come in glory on the last day.
You made with the house of David an everlasting covenant,
   and your goodness is like the sun on a cloudless morning,
     gleaming from the rain on a grassy land.
You sent Jesus Christ, the faithful witness,
   the firstborn of the dead, and ruler of the kings of the earth.
He freed us from our sins by his blood
   and made us to be a kingdom of priests serving you forever.
And so with all the company of heaven, we rejoice to sing your praise.

Holy, holy, holy Lord, God of power and might.
Heaven and earth are full of your glory.
Hosanna in the highest.
Blessed is he who comes in the name of the Lord.
Hosanna in the highest.

God of truth, your Son came to testify to you
   and lead us into all righteousness.
You have prepared for us such things as pass our understanding.
Send your Holy Spirit upon your people
   that your word may be on our lips.
Sanctify this bread and this cup, that they may be for us
   the body and blood of your Son Jesus Christ;
who, at supper with his disciples, took bread, gave you thanks,
   broke the bread, and gave it to them, saying,

"Take, eat: this is my body which is given for you;
  do this in remembrance of me."
After supper he took the cup.
Again he gave you thanks, and gave it to his disciples, saying,
  "Drink this, all of you: this is my blood of the new covenant,
    which is shed for you and for many for the forgiveness of sins.
  Do this, as often as you drink it, in remembrance of me."

Great is the mystery of faith.
Christ has died; Christ is risen; Christ will come again.

God of all beginnings and endings,
  your Son declared his kingdom was not of this world.
Bless the governance of every earthly kingdom,
  that it may be ruled justly, in spirit and in truth.
Visit your children who live in fear, dwell under oppression,
  experience cruelty, or suffer discrimination.
Turn struggle into hope, hope into freedom,
  freedom into justice, and justice into love.
Bring to those who have never known you,
  or have forgotten or rejected you,
    the light of your grace and the thirst for your mercy;
      until your Son comes with the clouds, and all eyes will see him,
        and every tribe and tongue will lift your name on high,
          ever one God, Father, Son, and Holy Spirit. **Amen.**

Christt the King, Year C

The Lord be with you. **And also with you.**
Lift up your hearts. **We lift them to the Lord.**
Let us give thanks to the Lord our God. **It is right to give our thanks and praise.**

Blessed are you, Lord God,
  for you have looked favorably on your people and redeemed them.
You raised up a mighty savior for us
  in the house of your servant David,
    as you spoke through the mouth of your holy prophets from of old.
You have shown the mercy promised to our ancestors,
  and have remembered your holy covenant,
    the oath that you swore to our ancestor Abraham,
      to grant that we, being rescued from the hands of our enemies,
        might serve you without fear,
          in holiness and righteousness before you all our days,
            and finally coming to dwell with you,
              with angels and archangels and all the company of heaven,
                singing the hymn of your unending praise.

Holy, holy, holy Lord, God of power and might.
Heaven and earth are full of your glory.
Hosanna in the highest.
Blessed is he who comes in the name of the Lord.
Hosanna in the highest.

God most high, you sent Jesus as a prophet and a promise;
  for he went before you to prepare your ways,
    to give knowledge of salvation to your people
      by the forgiveness of their sins.
You show us the cost and glory of your salvation
  in the breaking and pouring and sharing of bread and wine.
Send down your Holy Spirit,

that your people may be sanctified by your grace,
and these gifts of bread and wine may be for us
the body and blood of your Son Jesus Christ;
who, at supper with his disciples, took bread, gave you thanks,
broke the bread, and gave it to them, saying,
"Take, eat: this is my body which is given for you;
do this in remembrance of me."
After supper he took the cup.
Again he gave you thanks, and gave it to his disciples, saying,
"Drink this, all of you: this is my blood of the new covenant,
which is shed for you and for many for the forgiveness of sins.
Do this, as often as you drink it, in remembrance of me."

Great is the mystery of faith.
Christ has died; Christ is risen; Christ will come again.

By your tender mercy, Lord God,
the dawn from on high will break upon us,
to give light to those who sit in darkness
and in the shadow of death,
and to guide our feet into the way of peace.
Inscribe in us that tender mercy,
that we may be people of tenderness and mercy.
Clothe us and all your creation in the kingship of Christ,
that we may all know your power in weakness,
your rule through grace, and your triumph through sacrifice,
until all bow before your throne and worship in your glory,
ever one God, Father, Son, and Holy Spirit. **Amen.**

8. Special Occasions

General Use

The Lord be with you. **And also with you.**
Lift up your hearts. **We lift them to the Lord.**
Let us give thanks to the Lord our God. **It is right to give our thanks and praise.**

Covenanting God, you declared your wonders in the heavens
  but made known your character in calling a people.
You shaped your people's life
  through Elijah, Jeremiah, and the prophets.
Then in Jesus you made yourself fully known to us,
  and in his death and resurrection
    you healed the past through forgiveness
      and released the future through the gift of life eternal.
In the power of the Spirit you called into being your church,
  never closer to you than when we gather at this table
    as we long to gather at your heavenly banquet,
      with angels and archangels and all the company of heaven,
        singing the hymn of your unending praise.

Holy, holy, holy Lord, God of power and might.
Heaven and earth are full of your glory.
Hosanna in the highest.
Blessed is he who comes in the name of the Lord.
Hosanna in the highest.

Revealing God, you came among us in the flesh and blood of Jesus,
  and you come among us now
    in the materials of daily sustenance and joyful celebration.
Send down your Holy Spirit,
  that these gifts of friend and neighbor may become your church,
    and these offerings of bread and wine may be for us
      the body and blood of your Son Jesus Christ;
who, at supper with his disciples, took bread, gave you thanks,

broke the bread, and gave it to them, saying,
  "Take, eat: this is my body which is given for you;
    do this in remembrance of me."
After supper he took the cup.
Again he gave you thanks, and gave it to his disciples, saying,
  "Drink this, all of you: this is my blood of the new covenant,
    which is shed for you and for many for the forgiveness of sins.
  Do this, as often as you drink it, in remembrance of me."

Great is the mystery of faith.
Christ has died; Christ is risen; Christ will come again.

Embodied God, you met us in the body and blood of your Son Jesus,
  and you meet us now in the body and blood we see on this altar.
Show us your face and the face of one another
  in the body and blood of your church,
    that we, your people, may be taken by you,
      blessed through you, broken for you,
        and given for the life of your world.
Through this sacrament of thanks and praise,
  inscribe your church into the life of your Trinity,
    that we may have the creativity of the Father,
      the passion of the Son, and the empowerment of your Spirit.
Bring us to your presence on the last day,
  and hasten that time when every tear is dried from every eye,
    all secrets are transformed to your glory,
      all oppression is healed by your grace,
        and you are all in all. **Amen.**

Martin Luther King Jr. Day

The Lord be with you. **And also with you.**
Lift up your hearts. **We lift them to the Lord.**
Let us give thanks to the Lord our God. **It is right to give our thanks and praise.**

Reconciling God, you draw together heaven and earth,
   and in the death and resurrection of Jesus
      you break down the dividing wall of hostility.
Your Holy Spirit draws all people to yourself,
   in one race and nation,
      and heals the cancer of prejudice and fear
         within the hearts of children on your way.
You judge us not by the color of our skin
   but by the content of our character,
      and you turn the truthful story of our past
         into a hopeful story for our future in you.
And so you draw us into the company of your angels
   around your eternal throne, singing their hymn of unending praise.

Holy, holy, holy Lord, God of power and might.
Heaven and earth are full of your glory.
Hosanna in the highest.
Blessed is he who comes in the name of the Lord.
Hosanna in the highest.

God the three-in-one,
   as we bring our diverse gifts to the altar of your sacrifice,
      transform them into your food that never runs out.
Sanctify us by your grace,
   that we may enjoy the unity of your Spirit in the bonds of peace,
      and that this bread of the field and wine of the hillside
         may be for us the body and blood of your Son Jesus Christ;
who, at supper with his disciples, took bread, gave you thanks,

broke the bread, and gave it to them, saying,
"Take, eat: this is my body which is given for you;
do this in remembrance of me."
After supper he took the cup.
Again he gave you thanks, and gave it to his disciples, saying,
"Drink this, all of you: this is my blood of the new covenant,
which is shed for you and for many for the forgiveness of sins.
Do this, as often as you drink it, in remembrance of me."

Great is the mystery of faith.
Christ has died; Christ is risen; Christ will come again.

God of justice and mercy, bless your whole creation.
Be close to all who know their need of you.
Succor those living in the midst of death,
and dying in the midst of life.
Flood this earth with your kingdom,
that justice may roll down like a river,
and righteousness like a never-failing stream,
until we see you face to face
and recognize our diverse faces in the face of your Son,
through whom, and with whom, and in whom,
in the unity of the Holy Spirit,
all honor and glory are yours, now and forever. **Amen.**

Ordination/Ministry

The Lord be with you. **And also with you.**
Lift up your hearts. **We lift them to the Lord.**
Let us give thanks to the Lord our God. **It is right to give our thanks and praise.**

Promising God, at Christmas you gave us your presence,
   at Easter you dismantled sin and death,
     and at Pentecost you empowered us
       to bear your image and spread your grace.
In mission you equip us to go to the four corners of the earth,
   to rediscover what your Spirit is doing
     and meet you in the face of the stranger.
In ministry you share with us the abundance of your love
   in sacrament and in story, in prayer and in teaching,
     in reconciliation and in bringing your world home to you.
And so we gladly thank you, with saints and angels and archangels,
   and all the company of heaven, singing the hymn of your unending praise.

Holy, holy, holy Lord, God of power and might.
Heaven and earth are full of your glory.
Hosanna in the highest.
Blessed is he who comes in the name of the Lord.
Hosanna in the highest.

Fulfilling God, in Jesus' dying and rising
   you show us the extent of mission and the cost of ministry.
Send your Holy Spirit,
   that your people may be filled with love, joy, and peace,
     and that these gifts of bread and wine
       may be for us the body and blood of your Son Jesus Christ;
who, at supper with his disciples, took bread, gave you thanks,
   broke the bread, and gave it to them, saying,
     "Take, eat: this is my body which is given for you;

do this in remembrance of me."
After supper he took the cup.
Again he gave you thanks, and gave it to his disciples, saying,
    "Drink this, all of you: this is my blood of the new covenant,
        which is shed for you and for many for the forgiveness of sins.
    Do this, as often as you drink it, in remembrance of me."

Great is the mystery of faith.
Christ has died; Christ is risen; Christ will come again.

Revealing God, as you take bread and wine
    and make them the bearers of your Son's risen life,
        take our flesh and blood and make us channels of your peace.
Transform your church that it may resemble
    the generosity, joy, and abundance of your Trinity.
Raise up those whose gifts
    have been suppressed, neglected, ignored, or rejected.
Renew your people through humble service and prophetic witness,
    that your name may be known
        in the face of injustice, poverty, and tyranny.
Show your glory through agents of healing and learning,
    and shower your people with your love,
        until the day comes when every eye beholds you,
            full of grace and truth, ever one God, world without end. **Amen.**

Mother's Day

The Lord be with you. **And also with you.**
Lift up your hearts. **We lift them to the Lord.**
Let us give thanks to the Lord our God. **It is right to give our thanks and praise.**

Cradling God, we thank and praise you
  because like a mother you brought all things into being.
Through trial and truth-telling, touch and tenderness
  you nurtured a people
    and led them in the ways of justice and of peace.
When the time came for you to dwell among us in flesh and blood,
  your Holy Spirit called a woman to be the God-bearer,
    that in her we may behold
      that our bodies could bring forth your glory.
And so we join with angels and archangels
  and all the household of heaven to sing the song of your eternal joy.

Holy, holy, holy Lord, God of power and might.
Heaven and earth are full of your glory.
Hosanna in the highest.
Blessed is he who comes in the name of the Lord.
Hosanna in the highest.

Redeeming God, you called a woman to be closest to your Son
  at the moment of his nativity, at the place of his crucifixion,
    and in the wonder of his resurrection.
Like a mother hen gathering her chicks
  you draw the weary, the lost, and the betrayed
    to the abundant table of your kingdom.
Send your Holy Spirit on your church
  that it may radiate gladness at its destiny with you.
By that same Spirit, sanctify this bread and this cup,
  that they may be for us the body and blood of our Lord Jesus Christ;

who, at supper with his disciples, took bread, gave you thanks,
  broke the bread, and gave it to them, saying,
    "Take, eat: this is my body which is given for you;
      do this in remembrance of me."
After supper he took the cup.
Again he gave you thanks, and gave it to his disciples, saying,
  "Drink this, all of you: this is my blood of the new covenant,
    which is shed for you and for many for the forgiveness of sins.
  Do this, as often as you drink it, in remembrance of me."

Great is the mystery of faith.
Christ has died; Christ is risen; Christ will come again.

Yearning God, bless every mother
  who gives and does not count the cost,
    who toils and does not seek for rest,
      who labors and does not ask for any reward,
        save that of knowing that she does your will.
Visit and heal the sadness of those
  whose calling to be a mother has not been fulfilled.
Transfigure the distress of any whose experience of raising a child
  has meant a sword has pierced their own heart.
Come close to all who find they cannot look upon a parent
  with either gratitude or grace.
Hasten the day when the holy city descends
  like a bride prepared for you,
    when all desires are known and from you no secrets are hid,
      ever-living, ever-giving God, Trinity of mercy and love. **Amen.**

For All Creation

The Lord be with you. **And also with you.**
Lift up your hearts. **We lift them to the Lord.**
Let us give thanks to the Lord our God. **It is right to give our thanks and praise.**

Hearts and minds and souls and voices
   we lift in thanks and praise to you,
      Lord God of heaven and earth.
You made the earth as a playground for us to enjoy your glory,
   and yet we consistently turn your abundance into our scarcity,
      your elegance into our meanness,
         and your simplicity into our corruption.
In Noah you drew all the goodness of your creation into one ark,
   and in Moses you placed the law of love into the ark of your covenant.
In Christ you turned the wood of manger and cross
   into the ark of your salvation.
And so we rejoice to thank you, singing, with all the company of heaven,
   the hymn of your unending praise.

Holy, holy, holy Lord, God of power and might.
Heaven and earth are full of your glory.
Hosanna in the highest.
Blessed is he who comes in the name of the Lord.
Hosanna in the highest.

God our rock, to trust in you is to build a house on solid ground
   that will never shift through wind and rain.
You make and renew your church through your word of life.
Send your Holy Spirit upon your people,
   that all who eat and drink in your name
      may behold you face to face and taste and see that you are good.
By that same Spirit come down upon these gifts of bread and wine,
   that they may be for us the body and blood

of your Son, Jesus Christ our Lord;
who, at supper with his disciples, took bread, gave you thanks,
   broke the bread, and gave it to them, saying,
      "Take, eat: this is my body which is given for you;
         do this in remembrance of me."
After supper he took the cup.
Again he gave you thanks, and gave it to his disciples, saying,
   "Drink this, all of you: this is my blood of the new covenant,
      which is shed for you and for many for the forgiveness of sins.
   Do this, as often as you drink it, in remembrance of me."

Great is the mystery of faith.
Christ has died; Christ is risen; Christ will come again.

Renewing God, after half a year of flood
   you brought the ark of hope to solid ground
      and gave your creation new birth.
Heal your stricken world today,
   that the groaning of the soil, the skies, and the seas
      may foretell the greater glory you have prepared
         for your time of eternal covenant grace.
As you justify your children by faith,
   uphold all who face injustice and neglect and cruelty.
Hasten that day when your new heaven and new earth
   will engulf the distress and disappointment
      and destruction of your people,
         and you will be all in all, everlasting God,
            Father, Son, and Holy Spirit. **Amen.**

Marriage

The Lord be with you. **And also with you.**
Lift up your hearts. **We lift them to the Lord.**
Let us give thanks to the Lord our God. **It is right to give our thanks and praise.**

Ever-renewing God, you laid out the earth and the stars,
  you called a people,
    you came among us in the flesh of Christ,
      you sent your Spirit,
        and you will one day draw us into the perfection of your glory,
          that we may share your life as your companions forever.
You give us the gift of marriage
  to discover what it means to abide with you
    as the church abides with your Son.
In marriage we discover how to create with you,
  be redeemed by your Son's death and resurrection,
    and be transformed by the power of your Spirit.
And so we sing the praise of your glory,
  with thankful hearts sharing the constant song
    of the angels at your throne on high.

Holy, holy, holy Lord, God of power and might.
Heaven and earth are full of your glory.
Hosanna in the highest.
Blessed is he who comes in the name of the Lord.
Hosanna in the highest.

Tender God, in Jesus you fully shared our humanity
  as you expressed and embodied your full divinity.
Through the covenant of marriage
  you meet us in our fragile humanity
    and restore us through the grace of your divinity.
Send your Holy Spirit on your people,

that desire may turn to forbearing faithfulness,
  need become humble gentleness,
    and good intentions be fulfilled in sacrificial kindness.
By that same Spirit, sanctify this bread and this cup,
  that they may be for us the body and blood of our Lord Jesus Christ;
who, at supper with his disciples, took bread, gave you thanks,
  broke the bread, and gave it to them, saying,
    "Take, eat: this is my body which is given for you;
      do this in remembrance of me."
After supper he took the cup.
Again he gave you thanks, and gave it to his disciples, saying,
  "Drink this, all of you: this is my blood of the new covenant,
    which is shed for you and for many for the forgiveness of sins.
  Do this, as often as you drink it, in remembrance of me."

Great is the mystery of faith.
Christ has died; Christ is risen; Christ will come again.

Generous God, in Christ you show us what it means to love.
Bless your children with patience and kindness.
Dispel envy and pride, self-seeking and anger.
Turn our record of others' wrongs
  into wonder at your forgiving mercy.
Protect us, empower us, inspire us, persevere with us,
  that we may each find our vocation in the mission of your church,
    and your church may discover its purpose
      in witness and service to your world,
        and your world may enter its destiny
          in the glory of your kingdom;
            until the day when prophecies, tongues, and knowledge cease,
              and we see you face to face, and find love in you forever,
                Father, Son, and Holy Spirit. **Amen.**

Remembering War and Commemorating Those Who Have Died in War

The Lord be with you. **And also with you.**
Lift up your hearts. **We lift them to the Lord.**
Let us give thanks to the Lord our God. **It is right to give our thanks and praise.**

God of the living and the dead,
  in Abraham you called a people
    to be a kingdom of priests and a holy nation;
      and yet that people were often at war,
        and suffered and inflicted great loss and grief.
Your prophets proclaimed a day
  when swords would be turned into plowshares.
In the cross of Jesus you took into your own body
  the hatred and cruelty and violence of humankind,
    and responded with sacrificial forgiveness and redeeming resurrection.
You showed us a love than which there is no greater,
  as your Son laid down his life for his friends.
And so we thank and praise you, with all the company of heaven,
  in the eternal song of the angels.

Holy, holy, holy Lord, God of power and might.
Heaven and earth are full of your glory.
Hosanna in the highest.
Blessed is he who comes in the name of the Lord.
Hosanna in the highest.

God of resurrection, in Jesus you suffered the horrors of conflict,
  in betrayal and brutality and injury and agony.
Together with his friends he shared a meal
  that showed us how to remember,
    and so to piece together
      the hopes and dreams and bodies and loves

broken by violence and death.
Send your Holy Spirit on all who remember in sadness,
   that their mourning may be turned to deeper trust in you.
By that same Spirit, sanctify this bread and this cup,
   that they may be for us the body and blood of our Lord Jesus Christ;
who, at supper with his disciples, took bread, gave you thanks,
   broke the bread, and gave it to them, saying,
      "Take, eat: this is my body which is given for you;
         do this in remembrance of me."
After supper he took the cup.
Again he gave you thanks, and gave it to his disciples, saying,
   "Drink this, all of you: this is my blood of the new covenant,
      which is shed for you and for many for the forgiveness of sins.
   Do this, as often as you drink it, in remembrance of me."

Great is the mystery of faith.
Christ has died; Christ is risen; Christ will come again.

Redeeming and reconciling God,
   your love is made manifest when enemies become friends
      and woundedness turns to healing.
Bless all who live with the daily grief
   of losing a precious person in battle.
Strengthen any who carry injuries in body, mind, or spirit.
Make the nations worthy of the blood shed in their name,
   that those who have given much find honor,
      any who are brokenhearted find wholeness in you,
         and all who work for peace are empowered by your Spirit;
            until the day when there is no more war,
               and your gentle paths lead us to togetherness in you,
                  ever one God, Father, Son, and Holy Spirit. **Amen.**

The Bible

The Lord be with you. **And also with you.**
Lift up your hearts. **We lift them to the Lord.**
Let us give thanks to the Lord our God. **It is right to give our thanks and praise.**

Storytelling God,
  you had too much love within your Trinity to keep it to yourself,
    and so you made a universe in which to bring forth the earth,
      and an earth in which to raise up a people,
        and a people in which to come among us in your Son,
          that we may know your purpose
            never to be except to be with us in him forever.
Through patriarchs and prophets,
  through women of courage and kings,
    through the redemption of failure
      and the transformation of faithlessness
        you embodied your relentless will to abide with us.
In the death and resurrection of your Son
  and the sending of your Spirit
    you turned your covenant with your people
      into an invitation to all the world.
And so we thank and praise you, with angels and archangels,
  singing your song of glory.

Holy, holy, holy Lord, God of power and might.
Heaven and earth are full of your glory.
Hosanna in the highest.
Blessed is he who comes in the name of the Lord.
Hosanna in the highest.

Inscribing God, in Jesus your Word was made flesh.
In your scriptures that flesh was made word.
In your church and your kingdom that word is made flesh again.

By the power of your Holy Spirit
  bring your scriptural promises to fulfillment
    in your people gathered in your name today.
By that same Spirit, sanctify this bread and this cup,
  that they may be for us the body and blood of our Lord Jesus Christ;
who, at supper with his disciples, took bread, gave you thanks,
  broke the bread, and gave it to them, saying,
    "Take, eat: this is my body which is given for you;
      do this in remembrance of me."
After supper he took the cup.
Again he gave you thanks, and gave it to his disciples, saying,
  "Drink this, all of you: this is my blood of the new covenant,
    which is shed for you and for many for the forgiveness of sins.
  Do this, as often as you drink it, in remembrance of me."

Great is the mystery of faith.
Christ has died; Christ is risen; Christ will come again.

Inspiring God, you give us your scriptures
  for teaching, for reproof, for correction,
    for training in righteousness,
      and for building us up in service to you and your world.
Open your children's hearts
  each time your church opens your Word of life.
Send your Spirit upon evangelists, teachers, preachers, and healers,
  that the wind and fire of Pentecost
    may thrill and transform your people today.
Make your Son's disciples feel their hearts burning within them
  as you speak with them and they find their story in your story;
    until the day you draw us into your Book of Life,
      and we are gathered between the covers of your glory,
        ever one God, Father, Son, and Holy Spirit. **Amen.**

World Communion Sunday

The Lord be with you. **And also with you.**
Lift up your hearts. **We lift them to the Lord.**
Let us give thanks to the Lord our God. **It is right to give our thanks and praise.**

Blessed be your name throughout the earth, Lord God,
   for you have created wonders and, from the beginning,
     have drawn every living thing into communion with you.
In the bounty of your creation you fashioned land and sea,
   sun and stars, plants and animals,
     that we might know the constancy of your love for us.
In covenant life you drew a people to yourself,
   to give and receive love in your name.
In the fullness of time you drew near to us in your Son,
   to bind us to you in the promise of everlasting life.
In every time and place you offer us brothers and sisters
   with whom to live your ways of forgiveness and grace.
In every age you surround us with a great company of saints
   that we might be bound to one another in this world that you so love.
And so with the company of earth and heaven
   we praise your name and join the unending hymn.

Holy, holy, holy Lord, God of power and might.
Heaven and earth are full of your glory.
Hosanna in the highest.
Blessed is he who comes in the name of the Lord.
Hosanna in the highest.

God of holy unity, you are perfectly three and perfectly one:
   from many, make your people one in you.
Sanctify your church around the world
   and transform our fractures into fruitfulness.
Send your Holy Spirit upon this bread and this cup,

that they may be for us the body and blood of our Lord Jesus Christ;
who, at supper with his disciples, took bread, gave you thanks,
    broke the bread, and gave it to them, saying,
        "Take, eat: this is my body which is given for you;
            do this in remembrance of me."
After supper he took the cup.
Again he gave you thanks, and gave it to his disciples, saying,
    "Drink this, all of you: this is my blood of the new covenant,
        which is shed for you and for many for the forgiveness of sins.
    Do this, as often as you drink it, in remembrance of me."

Great is the mystery of faith.
Christ has died; Christ is risen; Christ will come again.

God the one Father of us all, you gather us
    in one faith, one hope, and one baptism.
Draw near to your children
    when their lives are overshadowed by what divides.
Where wars have not yet ceased, come quickly.
Where hostility tears apart brothers and sisters,
    open your path of peace.
Where the relationship between your people and your creation falters,
    renew our awe in the wonders you have made.
Where your church's diversity fails to reflect
    the glorious kaleidoscope of your kingdom,
        lead us to greater love and wider mercy
            than we have ever before imagined.
Hasten the day when we who share Christ's body
    will join with him in perfect and holy communion,
        in the everlasting embrace of the Holy Spirit,
            as you draw all things to yourself, now and forever. **Amen.**